Practice and Belief

Studies in Society

A series edited by Ronald Wild which sets out to cover the major topics in Australasian sociology. The books will not be 'readers', but original works — some will cover new ground and present original research, some will provide an overview and synthesis of source materials and existing research. All will be important reading for students of sociology.

Titles include:

Studies in Society: 15
Series editor: R. A. Wild

Practice and Belief

Studies in the sociology of Australian religion

Edited by ALAN W. BLACK
Senior Lecturer in Sociology, University of New England

PETER E. GLASNER
Principal Lecturer in Sociology, Polytechnic of North London

Sydney
George Allen & Unwin
London   Boston

First published in 1983 by
George Allen & Unwin Australia Pty Ltd
8 Napier Street, North Sydney, NSW 2060 Australia

George Allen & Unwin (Publishers) Ltd
Park Lane, Hemel Hempstead, Herts HP2 4TE, England

Allen & Unwin Inc.
9 Winchester Terrace, Winchester, Mass 01890 USA

National Library of Australia
Cataloguing-in-Publication entry:
Practice and belief.
  Bibliography.
  Includes index.
  ISBN 0 86861 357 6.
  ISBN 0 86861 365 7 (pbk.).
  1. Australia — Religious life and customs.
  I. Black, Alan W. (Alan William), 1937– .
  II. Glasner, Peter E. (Peter Egan). (Series:
  Studies in society (Sydney, N.S.W.); 15).
306'. 6'0994

Library of Congress Catalog Card Number: 82-46022

Set in 10 on 11 pt Times by Syarikat Seng Teik Sdn Bhd,
Kuala Lumpur, Malaysia

Printed in Singapore by Singapore National Printers (Pte) Ltd.

Contents

Tables

Contributors

Alan W. Black
Senior Lecturer in Sociology, University of New England

Norman W.H. Blaikie
Head, Department of Social Science, Royal Melbourne Institute of Technology

Gary D. Bouma
Senior Lecturer in Sociology, Monash University

Kenneth Dempsey
Senior Lecturer in Sociology, La Trobe University

Edwin Dowdy
Reader in Sociology, University of Queensland

Peter E. Glasner
Principal Lecturer in Sociology, Polytechnic of North London

Frank W. Lewins
Lecturer in Sociology, The Faculties, Australian National University

Ralph G. Locke
Director of Field Research, Experiential Learning Laboratory, Duke University

Gillian Lupton
Lecturer in Sociology, University of Queensland

Leslie N. O'Brien
Lecturer in Sociology, School of Social Sciences, Flinders University of South Australia

Preface

The first comprehensive study of the sociology of religion in Australia was written by Mol (1971). Based primarily on survey data gathered in 1966 together with material from other sources, Mol's work has provided both a backdrop and a stimulus to further studies. The present volume brings together some of the results of this more recent research. As such, it does not pretend to cover all aspects of the sociology of religion in Australia. Nor does it deal with traditional Aboriginal religion, which has already been the subject of many anthropological studies. It does, however, give some indication of the variety of recent sociological analyses of religion in this country.

The introductory chapter provides a brief overview of the place of religion in Australian society since white settlement and opens up issues to be considered later in the book. Next Gary Bouma examines some trends in Australian religiosity since 1966. With data from the Census, Morgan-Gallup Polls and denominational statistics, he analyses changes in patterns of religious identification, membership and practice. This is followed by a paper based on the methods of observation and interview used in classical community studies. Here Ken Dempsey sensitively explores the form and place of religion in a particular Australian country town.

Then, on the basis of a survey of parish clergy in the major Protestant denominations in Victoria, Norman Blaikie analyses different styles of ministry and shows how these relate to different conceptions of the relationship between the church and the world. Edwin Dowdy and Gillian Lupton address a somewhat similar issue by comparing and contrasting the perceptions held by clergy, theological students, involved laity, the general public, and persons who have left the ministry. Their samples include both Catholics and Protestants. Frank Lewins looks at the relationship between the Roman Catholic Church and migrants, especially those from non-English-speaking countries. Using documentary analysis, interview and observational data, he argues that culture divides more than religion unites and he considers the impact of this on the functioning of the church. Alan Black gives a critical review of various approaches to the sociology of ecumenism, going on to examine the extent to which they throw light on events surrounding the formation of the Uniting Church in Australia.

Four chapters deal with some forms of religious or quasi-religious practice and belief which differ in style or content from the forms of religiosity institutionalised in the mainline churches. Ralph Locke provides a wealth of ethnographic evidence in his analysis of the interplay of charisma, consciousness and social order in a Spiritualist cult in Western Australia. Leslie O'Brien reports on a study of the Hare Krishna movement, paying particular attention to the reasons why participants have adopted an alternative lifestyle and belief system, the ways in which they achieve resocialisation, and the problems they encounter in their relationship with the wider society. Alan Black examines the aims, membership, activities, achievements and problems of a form of organised irreligion, the New South Wales Humanist Society, comparing and contrasting it with conventional religious organisations. Peter Glasner discusses the concept of folk religion in the Australian context. In what was originally the Inaugural Address to the Australian Association for the Study of Religions, he argues that such folk religion might be expressed in a variety of forms ranging from cults and communes to Anzac rituals and football crowds.

In the concluding chapter, we draw together some of the major issues raised in earlier chapters and look towards the future.

Acknowledgements

This collection originated from a suggestion by Dr Norman Habel, the foundation President of the Australian Association for the Study of Religions, which has contributed much to the greater understanding of all aspects of religion in Australia. The Association is thanked for permission to reprint the Inaugural Address as Chapter 11.

The publication would never have materialised, however, were it not for the patience and understanding of the contributors during its elephantine gestation period. Nor would it have been possible without the help and support of the sociology departments, and especially the typists, in the Australian National University, the University of New England, and the Polytechnic of North London.

Alan W. Black
Peter E. Glasner

1 Introduction

Alan W. Black

What part has religion played in the formation and functioning of Australian society? Whereas there was a specifically religious impulse in the founding of some of the early British colonies in America, this was not so in the case of Australia. At the outset, white settlement in New South Wales was little more than an extension of Britain's prison system. Although Governor Phillip was instructed that he should 'by all proper methods enforce a due observance of religion and good order among the inhabitants of the new settlement' and 'take such steps for the due celebration of publick worship as circumstances will permit' (*Historical Records of Australia*, I, i: 14), most of the convicts were antagonistic or apathetic towards the established forms of religion in Britain at that time, and these attitudes tended to persist in Australia. The convicts generally resented having to attend religious services and regarded the officially appointed chaplains with contempt, seeing them as allies of a regime which they despised (Grocott, 1980). In other words, religion was perceived both by the colonial authorities and by the convicts as a form of social control.

In later years, as the number of free settlers increased, so too did the number of those who had a more positive attitude towards some form of religious practice and belief. The particular religions which they espoused were typically one form or other of Anglo-Celtic Christianity: most frequently Anglicanism or, to a lesser extent, Methodism in the case of the English, Presbyterianism in the case of the Scottish, and Catholicism in the case of the Irish. Whatever other functions it served, their religion provided a nostalgic link with the 'old country' (Bollen, 1973: 54; Campion, 1982: 47). This is one indication of a common feature of much Australian religion: its essentially derivative character. Unlike America, Australia has not been the birthplace of new religious movements such as Mormonism, Seventh Day Adventism, Christian Science and Jehovah's Witnesses. For the most part, its white population has imported its religious traditions from overseas, and this has been reflected not only in doctrine, but also in such matters as church polity, architecture and forms of worship.

One of the questions which arose during the nineteenth century was whether the churches in Australia would have the same relationship to the state and to each other as they had in Britain. In the early years of the colony, the Church of England was officially regarded as the established church in much the same sense as it was in England (Border, 1962). Consequently the state extended much greater assistance to the Anglican Church than to other denominations for the erection of churches, the payment of clergy and the establishment of schools. By the 1830s, however, clergy and lay members of other denominations were present in sufficient numbers to consider that they should be afforded similar state recognition and assistance. Governor Bourke was sensitive to this opinion. At the same time he was critical of the adequacy of the education provided in most of the church schools. He therefore proposed one measure relating to churches and another relating to schools. After receiving approval from the British government, he presented these proposals to the Legislative Council in 1836.[1]

The first proposal led to the passing of what was generally known as the Church Act in New South Wales. This Act applied also to the Port Phillip district [Victoria], and similar Acts were passed in Van Diemen's Land [Tasmania] in 1837 and in Western Australia in 1840 (cf. Austin, 1963: 36, 45). The Church Act stipulated that if at least £300 was raised by voluntary effort for the purpose of erecting a church or chapel and, if necessary, a minister's residence, the state would provide a equal amount up to a limit of £1000; the state would also pay stipends of up to £200 per annum for duly appointed clergy, the amount of the stipend being determined by the number of adult residents who registered a desire to attend the church or chapel at which the particular clergyman officiated. As such state aid was not limited to the Church of England, the Act was heralded as an expression of the principle of religious equality. Bourke stated that it was his hope that 'in laying the foundations of the Christian Religion in this young and rising Colony by equal encouragement held out to its Professors in their several Churches, the people of these different persuasions will be united together in one bond of peace, and taught to look up to the Government as their common protector and friend, and that thus there will be secured to the State good subjects and to Society good men' (*Historical Records of Australia*, I, xvii: 229–30).

Certainly the Act secured a more equitable distribution of aid than had previously been the case, though it was still not always in direct proportion to the size of the various denominations, as a higher percentage of Catholics than of Protestants belonged to lower social strata; Catholics were therefore less able to afford the initial contributions required to secure aid for the erection of buildings. Moreover, some of the smaller denominations such as the Baptists and Congregationalists received little, if any, aid, either because their numbers and their financial resources in any particular locality did not reach the qualifying threshold or because they were opposed to the principle of such aid. There was also controversy as to whether Jews were entitled to aid. And some Anglicans, especially clergy, objected to what they considered to be the subsidisation of error as well as truth. Thus, while it enabled some of the major denominations such as Anglicans, Catholics, Presbyterians and Methodists to consolidate their position in the colony, the Church Act also promoted strong denominational rivalries and developed what Turner (1972) has termed 'Sinews of Sectarian Warfare' — scarcely the 'bond of peace' which Bourke had desired.

These denominational rivalries also hindered the introduction of the other measure which Bourke proposed, namely a school system similar to that which had been introduced into Ireland in 1831. There the state-supported schools were expected to provide a basic education for all, such education including the reading of approved extracts from Scripture, but no specifically denominational instruction by the ordinary teacher; instead, clergy of the various denominations would attend the school at specified times to teach the children of their own denomination. Despite legislative approval for an initial allocation of £3000 to commence the proposed system in New South Wales, the system was vehemently opposed by Protestant leaders as being 'subversive to the fundamental principle of Protestantism' (*Historical Records of Australia*, I, xviii: 472) on the grounds that it did not allow free use of the whole of the Authorised Version of the Scriptures (see Austin, 1963: 50). Moreover, some of the most influential Protestants such as Bishop Broughton were intent on maintaining the existing denominational schools and, in some cases, establishing new ones; they were not keen on paying for a system which they believed would benefit mainly the children of Irish Catholic convicts. Such sectarian and ethnocentric feeling was sufficiently strong to prevent the implementation of Bourke's school plan; subsidies to denominational schools continued (Barrett, 1966; Austin, 1963 and 1972).

The denominational schools were nevertheless still unable to provide education of sufficient quantity and quality to satisfy all. Consequently, by about the middle of the nineteenth century, 'national' or public schools had also been established in each of the colonies. Even so, in all colonies except South Australia, state aid continued for some time to be given to at least some denominational schools. This, then, was the period of the 'dual system' which varied in form from one colony to another. Concurrently with these developments, the attitudes of various denominations were also changing. From a position of support for the introduction of the Irish system into Australia, the Roman Catholic Church moved to a position of opposition. This change was prompted in part by growing dissatisfaction with the operation of that system in Ireland itself, in part by a realisation that there were insufficient Catholic clergy in Australia to make the system work effectively from their point of view, and in part by a toughening of the Vatican's attitude to any form of education conducted outside the full control of the church. So most of the Catholic clergy now wanted state aid for their own school system (Barrett, 1966: 101-3; Austin, 1972: 201-30; Austin, 1963: 41, 80-3, 187). Non-Anglican Protestant opinion, on the other hand, tended to move away from advocacy of denominational schools to support for a public school system, as long as provision was made for Christian observances and religious instruction at some stage during the school week. Thus J. D. Lang, a prominent Presbyterian clergyman who initially opposed the Irish system, later come to favour it. Many other Presbyterians, Methodists, Baptists and Congregationalists came to a similar point of view (Austin, 1963: 53-7, 146-51; 1972: 118-20). This change in Protestant attitudes was brought about partly by a realisation that denominational schooling was unduly divisive and inefficient in a society with such a scattered population, partly by a belief that there was much which Christians held in common and which could be taught in the public schools, and partly by a conviction that such teaching could be supplemented by specific denominational instruction given by clergy visiting the schools or within their own churches and Sunday schools (Austin, 1963: 41-2; Austin, 1972: 118-23; Bollen, 1973: 37-9).

Anglican opinion was slower to change. Some of the hierarchy continued to advocate denominational schooling, although by the 1840s they were prepared to tolerate a dual system which would enable them to maintain their own schools. But lay opinion, and that of some clergy, moved steadily closer to that of other Protestants (Cable, 1952; Austin, 1972: 120-3). Furthermore, within the community at large, especially in Victoria, there was a small but growing body of opinion which favoured a system of public education in which there was no place for religion at all. Faced with such conflicting attitudes, various compromise arrangements were tried in the different colonies during the 1850s and 1860s (Austin, 1972: 112-72).

In this same period, there was also debate about whether the state should continue to give aid for the building of churches and the stipends of clergymen. The sheer cost of such aid, a growing belief on the part of some churchmen that true religion was most likely to flourish when it embraced the principle of voluntarism, and a recognition that in practice the distribution of aid scarcely did justice to the increasing diversity of religious beliefs within the colonies — considerations such as these eventually led to the termination of state aid for these purposes in each of the colonies. Just as the Church Act of 1836 implied that the Church of England would no longer be the established church in New South Wales, the Grants to Public Worship Prohibition Act of 1862 indicated that the four denominations which had hitherto received virtually the whole of the aid under the Church Act would no longer be accorded this privilege. In other words, both these Acts were attempts to apply the principles of justice and equality in the particular circumstances of the time (Turner, 1972).[2]

In due course, much the same logic was applied to the issue of state aid for education. As a result of Acts passed in the period from 1872 to 1895, systems of what was called 'free, compulsory and secular' education were established in all the colonies, and state aid for denominational schools was abolished. These Acts were products, varying in mix, of the forces of liberalism, religious voluntarism, agnosticism and anti-sectarianism (Austin, 1972; Dow, 1964; Gregory, 1973; Phillips, 1981). It would be wrong to assume that the term 'secular' necessarily implied the elimination of religion from public schools. Thus, in both the New South Wales and Western Australian legislation, 'secular instruction' was specifically defined as including 'general religious teaching as distinct from dogmatical or polemical theology'; furthermore, provision was made for the children of any religious persuasion to be instructed periodically by the clergyman or other religious teacher of such persuasion. Parents nevertheless had the right to withdraw their children from any form of religious education. In the Education Acts of the other colonies, 'secular' was left undefined. In Tasmania, provision was made for denominational instruction in segregated groups, much the same as in New South Wales. In Queensland, there was a clause permitting the use of public school buildings for religious instruction when secular instruction was not being given. Although 'sectarian or denominational religious teaching' was forbidden in public schools in South Australia, voluntary attendance at Bible reading at the commencement of the school day was expressly permitted. In Victoria, there was no specific mention of religious education in the Education Act of 1872, but the way was left open for local Boards of Advice to arrange for religious education after the children were dismissed from school; here and there, cautious steps in this direction were taken.[3]

It is clear that although the relationship between church and state had been significantly modified by these developments, it was not wholly broken. Indeed much of the effort of the churches during the closing decades of the nineteenth century and on into the twentieth century was aimed at maintaining, and hopefully extending, their influence in Australian society. This concern underlay their programmes of evangelism, their religious education activities in schools and Sunday schools, their efforts at securing public recognition of God, and their campaigns on various social issues (Phillips, 1981).

They had mixed success. They might have been more successful if they had agreed among themselves. But on some issues the division between Catholics and Protestants was so sharp that it was impossible to satisfy both. The Catholic Church refused to capitulate on the question of education and redoubled its efforts to maintain its own schools. Anglican bishops generally refused to regard their Roman Catholic counterparts as equals, and certainly not as deserving greater precedence than them on public occasions. The Catholic hierarchy, on the other hand, resisted any behaviour which might be construed as implying Anglican pre-eminence or Protestant religious legitimacy. Consequently, on some occasions when the churches' place in the community might have been formally acknowledged, it was at best given muted recognition, for fear of sectarian rivalry. Even on issues where Protestant and Catholic opinion was fairly similar, Catholics were generally urged by their church to set up their own organisations rather than participating in inter-church councils and the like.

Spurred on by denominational rivalry, aided by a buoyant economy and by rapid population growth, the churches increased greatly in size between 1870 and 1890. The number of churches, clergy, members and Sunday school pupils doubled during this period (Bollen, 1973: 40). This did not mean that in terms of church attendance they were outstripping population growth. It did mean, however, that they experienced some of the outward marks of success.

The sharp economic downturn and the social unrest of the 1890s dealt a severe blow to the optimism of the churches. Bollen (1972) has argued that in response to this new situation some of the Protestant churches developed a genuine concern for social justice, rather than simply for personal piety and moral reform; but that, after a brief flowering between 1894 and 1900, this mild radicalism withered because the emerging Labor Party was seen as an instrument of Catholic influence, whereas the Liberal Party embraced other long-standing Protestant concerns — those of restricting the availability of liquor and reducing gambling.

Broome (1980) and Phillips (1981) maintain that Bollen has overestimated the Protestant interest in social reconstruction in the 1890s. The former writers hold that a deep concern for social justice was felt by only a small minority of Protestants at that time, the majority being more interested in securing conformity to middle-class moral standards. At all events, Protestant strictures against liquor, gambling and Sunday entertainment alienated the working classes still further from these churches. Though critical of drunkenness, profligacy and failure to attend mass, the Catholic Church was less inclined to 'wowserism' on these issues. It was more concerned with the dangers of Protestant–Catholic marriages and of liberalised divorce laws, matters which were lower down, though not absent from, the Protestant agenda.

Another issue in which the churches sought to exercise an influence was that of the federation of the colonies to form the Commonwealth of Australia. Both Catholic and Protestant churchmen were actively involved in this campaign. Ely (1976) argued that the churches' interest in this issue was largely prompted by the social and economic crises of the 1890s, crises which reinforced their conviction that religion was important for social well-being. Phillips (1981) traces this concern back to at least the 1880s, seeing it as part of the churches' efforts to stem the rising tide of secularism. The major churches looked to federation as an opportunity to secure public recognition of the Deity. While it would be wrong to regard the churchmen's concern as being motivated simply by a desire to bolster their own status in society, it is difficult to escape the conclusion that this was a contributing factor in some cases (Ely, 1976: 6, 38–9; Phillips, 1981: 260–1).

In response to pressure from various churchmen, it was finally agreed that the preamble to the Commonwealth Constitution should include the words 'humbly relying on the blessing of Almighty God'. At the same time, in response to representations made by Seventh Day Adventists and others who wished to ensure that there was no encroachment by the Commonwealth on religious liberty, Section 116 of the Constitution read

> The Commonwealth shall not make any law for establishing any religion, or for imposing any religious observance, or for prohibiting the free exercise of any religion, and no religious test shall be required as a qualification for any office or public trust under the Commonwealth.

Although the first phrase of Section 116 was closely modelled on the

First Amendment of the United States' Constitution, these words have been given a somewhat different interpretation in the two countries. In America, where the First Amendment has been the basis of much litigation, especially in relation to education, the Supreme Court has generally taken the Constitution as prohibiting any form of direct government assistance to any religion (Webb, 1960: 113-4). In Australia, where this section of the Constitution has been the subject of relatively little litigation, the High Court has taken it as forbidding the Commonwealth from making any law which would confer on a particular religion or religious body the position of a state or national religion or church. In other words, what is forbidden in Section 116 of the Australian Constitution is establishment of religion in the sense in which the Anglican Church is established in England, rather than in the wider sense given to this term in America. This was made clear in 1981 when the Full Bench of the High Court ruled, by a majority of six to one, that the provision by the Commonwealth of funds for education in denominational schools was not unconstitutional. A further difference between Australia and America is that whereas the First Amendment to the United States' Constitution applies with equal force to each of the states, Section 116 of the Australian Constitution applies only to actions of the Commonwealth (Webb, 1960: 113). On the other hand, all donations to recognised religious bodies are deductible from personal income for taxation purposes in America, whereas this is not so in Australia. Such tax deductibility could be regarded as a form of indirect financial assistance to religious organisations. In both countries, buildings used exclusively for worship or for certain other church purposes are generally exempt from local government rates or property taxes. This, too, is a form of indirect subsidy.

In much the same way as many churchmen saw the movement towards federation as an opportunity to assert the importance of religion in national life, many saw World War I as another such opportunity. As McKernan (1980: 1) concluded after a careful study, with few exceptions 'clergymen from all denominations... welcomed war as Australia's testing time, her baptism of fire, because it would have a regenerating effect on Australian society weaning the people from materialism and a love of pleasure, encouraging them, instead, to reflect on eternal truths'. Notwithstanding the achievement of some reductions in hotel trading hours and some restrictions on horse racing and thus on gambling, these churchmen were soon to be disappointed. The war did not, as they had hoped, lead to any permanent increase in regular church attendance, nor was the standing of the churches in Australian society bolstered.

Although most Protestant church leaders claimed that conscription was justified on moral grounds, proposals for conscription failed on two occasions to secure majority support in national referenda. Catholic opinion on this matter went through a process of change. In 1915 most Catholic leaders were in favour of conscription or, at the very least, neutral on the issue. They regarded the question as a predominantly political matter rather than as a moral one. As time went on, various factors contributed to a hardening of Catholic opinion against conscription. Just as Protestant leaders used the war as an opportunity to press home some of their long-standing demands for moral reform, various Catholic leaders continued to assert their deep-felt demands for educational justice (O'Farrell, 1977: 305-6). The latter issue was seen by non-Catholics as an unnecessary, even unpatriotic, distraction during wartime. Antipathies between Protestants and Catholics were aggravated by reports of the Easter 1916 rebellion in Ireland on the one hand and of its brutal suppression by the British on the other. In the end, attitudes to conscription were shaped by a complex interplay of religious, ethnic, class and political party divisions (McKernan, 1980; Broome, 1980: 165). The result was a period of sectarian strife which continued strongly until about 1925.

Despite, or perhaps because of, this sectarian episode, the period from 1919 to 1939 saw various attempts at promoting Christian unity. Some of these, such as the formation of inter-denominational councils at state level, had a measure of success. Others, such as attempts at church union, failed. In truth, there was division both within and between the major denominations on many social and theological issues. In the major Protestant denominations there were differences between those who adhered to a fairly literalist view of the Bible and those who adopted a more liberal perspective. In an effort to promote church growth, the former tended to favour the use of itinerant evangelists in special evangelistic efforts, whereas the latter were more inclined to try to win support by application of the 'social gospel' and by showing the relevance of Christian faith to everyday life. Though the churches continued to pursue the vision of a Christian Australia, they were by no means unanimous as to what this meant in terms of such issues as prohibition, gambling, Sunday observance, divorce and birth-control. Nor did they have much success in increasing the level of church-going or in securing significant social reforms during this period (Hansen, 1978).

This should not be taken to mean that there was general antagonism towards the churches. Most members of the community maintained at least a nominal denominational allegiance and they considered it appropriate that rites of passage should be conducted in church at birth, marriage and death. Even if they were not regular church attenders, they considered themselves Christians and they were generally content with their existing level of religiosity. As Hansen (1978: 412–3) said of the 1920s and 1930s:

> In general, the community seems to have had a relatively clear concep-
> tion of the Churches' role in society: people expected them to enun-
> ciate Christian principles, provide moral guidance, preach informative
> and uplifting messages, exert a stabilising influence in times of stress,
> and where possible, provide temporal assistance to those in need. So
> long as the Churches did these things they were deemed worthy of
> respect and their services remained in demand... But when the Chur-
> ches departed from the role expected of them, some people gave
> evidence of disquiet. Controversy was likely to ensue if churchmen
> ventured beyond generalities in their economic and political pro-
> nouncements, took sides in industrial disputes, attacked other religious
> organisations, or waged sectarian warfare on the members of other
> communions. In [this] period churchmen were anxious to promote
> peace, and most tried to avoid initiating any such controversy.

The economic depression of the 1930s and the perceived threat of Communism led to the formation of a lay movement of Catholic intellectuals and workers with the aim of building a new social order based on Catholic social teaching. This Catholic Action movement, which took a variety of organisational forms, developed quietly in strength during the 1940s and early 1950s. In 1954, Dr H.V. Evatt, federal parliamentary leader of the Australian Labor Party (ALP), publicly accused a small group of Labor members with being 'disloyal to the Labor movement and Labor leadership' and so 'deflecting the Labor movement from the pursuit of established Labor objectives and ideals' (quoted in Santamaria, 1961: 88). He claimed that these members were being directed by persons within the Catholic Action movement. This charge led to a revival of religious sectarianism and eventually resulted in a split in the Labor movement, with the formation of the Democratic Labor Party (DLP).

The resurgence of sectarianism was partly neutralised by the fact that Catholics were themselves divided over this issue. The hierarchy in New South Wales, South Australia and Queensland generally favoured a continuation of Catholic participation in the ALP. In Victoria, Tasmania and Western Australia they generally saw the DLP as a more appropriate vehicle for Catholic involvement. To some extent, lay attitudes mirrored those of the hierarchy in each particular state, though in all states a considerable body of Catholic voters maintained their previous allegiance to the ALP. The overall effect, however, was to weaken the alliance between Catholicism and the ALP, a process hastened by the upward social mobility which a significant number of Catholics had experienced (O'Farrell, 1977: 378–403; Henderson, 1982).

By the 1950s the religious composition of the Australian community was beginning to change, largely as a result of government-sponsored immigration, especially from southern Europe, and of a higher birth-rate among Catholics than Protestants. Between 1947 and 1971 the Catholic proportion of the population rose from 20.7 per cent to 27.0 per cent. In twenty years the number of Catholics doubled. This created great difficulties for the Catholic school system, difficulties intensified by rising educational expectations in the community at large and by the Catholic teaching orders' inability to obtain sufficient recruits to keep pace with population growth. Though various state governments had given indirect assistance to denominational schools for a number of years, it was not until 1963 that the Menzies Liberal and Country Party government offered direct federal assistance to non-government schools throughout Australia. In subsequent years such aid was increased and was supplemented with aid given by state governments. This reversal of the policy which had applied since the late nineteenth century was brought about by a combination of factors: demographic trends, economic circumstances, political expediency, pressure group activities, and a decline in sectarianism (Hogan, 1978).

Hogan (1978: 259) has argued that the Catholic campaign for state aid was the 'last hurrah for "Catholic" politics' in Australia; that the thaw in relationships between Catholics and Protestants since the Second Vatican Council has resulted in the absorption of 'Catholic' politics into the broader field of 'Christian' politics. He sees the Australian Festival of Light as evidence of this. This organisation aims to 'alert and inform Australians of the dangers of moral pollution' and to 'register the support of people of goodwill for Christian moral standards in such a way that national leadership is influenced' (quoted in Hickman, 1977: 249). In particular, it opposes secular humanism, abortion, relaxation of censorship, and decriminalisation of homosexuality. Though the Festival of Light has attracted the support of socially conservative Christians, both Catholic and Protestant, it would be wrong to assume that it necessarily represents the only, or even the main, focus of social concern within the major denominations. For a broader view of the churches' current concern with social issues, reference should also be made to the publications of bodies such as the Australian Council of Churches, the Catholic Commission for Justice and Peace, and the Anglican and Uniting Church Commissions on Social Responsibility.

This chapter has traced the movement in Australia from a

relatively close alliance between church and state, in the form of Anglican establishment, to increasing pluralism and a much weaker relationship between church and state. By way of summary, it can be said that in many respects religion in Australia occupies a position intermediate to that which it occupies in Britain on the one hand and the United States of America on the other. In terms of denominational variety and especially the relative numerical strength of different denominations, America has the greatest degree of religious pluralism, Australia comes next, then Britain. Likewise, although in each of these countries Christianity claims at least the nominal allegiance of the majority of the population, the rate of church-going in Australia is lower than in the USA and higher than in Britain. Martin (1978: 35) suggests that in Western societies there is a direct connection between religious pluralism and rates of participation, though he recognises that there are some exceptions to this, especially where a monopoly religion is a vehicle for the expression of cultural identity in the face of external threat (e.g. Catholicism in Poland). What, then, are the current trends in religious identification and participation in Australia? This is the question addressed in the next chapter.

National trends might or might not apply in a particular locality, depending upon how far that locality is subject to much the same influences as the rest of the society. Despite the economic importance of its rural and extractive industries, Australia is a highly urbanised society. Seventy per cent of its population lives in metropolitan regions or cities of 100 000 or more. It is in the largest urban areas that the bulk of the population growth has taken place since World War II. By contrast, rural areas and small country towns have tended to decline in population. Chapter 3 analyses the place of religion in one such town.

At various times in Australia's history, clergymen have served as 'moral policemen', magistrates, educators, evangelists, pastors, priests, campaigners for moral reform, dispensers of aid to the needy, legitimisers or critics of government action, and so on. As the relationship between church and state has altered, so to some extent have the roles performed by clergy. Chapter 4 looks at different styles of ministry adopted by Protestant clergy, and at the ways in which these relate to other characteristics such as age, education, degree of satisfaction with the ministry, and so on. Underlying these findings are different views of the relationship between the church and the world.

Chapter 5 examines the extent to which the clergy's views of the church and of their own role correspond with the views held by involved laity and other members of the general public. It argues that any discrepancies between such views are likely to have implications for organisational effectiveness and organisational change.

As has already been noted, the different religious traditions in Australia have in part been an expression of ethnicity. Greeley (1972) observed a similar phenomenon in America. Throughout much of its history the Roman Catholic Church in both these countries reflected a strong Irish influence. During the past 50 years this influence has gradually diminished, especially as an increasing proportion of Catholic priests in Australia and America have been both born and trained outside Ireland. But with migrant waves from other countries into Australia since World War II, the link between religion and ethnicity has again been highlighted. Chapter 6 examines some of the impact of this upon the Catholic Church.

It is clear that over the years there has been a degree of rivalry among the various religious denominations in Australia and that at times this has erupted into open conflict. Underlying such conflict have been not only theological and ethnic factors but also differences in social class and in political alignment. Although moves for interdenominational union failed in early decades of this century, they had some success in the formation of the Uniting Church in Australia in 1977. To what extent was this event an expression of a growing cultural unity in Australian society? What other factors were at work in this development and in the efforts of some to prevent it? Chapter 7 is devoted to questions such as these.

Both this introduction and most of the chapters concentrate on aspects of religion institutionalised in the mainline denominations. This is in keeping with the stated religious affiliations of the great majority of Australians. It must nevertheless be noted that recent immigration and other forms of cultural diffusion have brought about increasing religious diversity in Australia and that even persons who claim an affiliation with one of the mainstream churches may embrace beliefs and practices which are different from those officially adopted within these denominations.

One case of a different religious form is that of Spiritualism. Although not widely practised in Australia, Spiritualism is of a particular interest as an example of a religious cult. The term 'cult' is used here without pejorative connotations. A key characteristic of religious cults is that of 'epistemological individualism' (Wallis, 1976: 14); that is, the cult has no firm locus of final authority beyond the individual member. Cults tend to be eclectic in belief, usually concentrating on some form of mystical, ecstatic or esoteric experience. Chapter 8 makes an analysis of practice and belief within a Spiritualist group in Perth.

Another small but more highly visible religious movement in

Australia is that of the Hare Krishna people. Like most forms of religion here, this comes from overseas; but, unlike most, its basic elements are more Eastern than Western. As part of the counter-culture which emerged in Western societies in the 1960s, the Hare Krishna movement has had an uneasy relationship with the dominant institutional order. In sociological terminology, it has many of the characteristics of a sect. Once again, this term is meant to be non-pejorative. Sects are typically characterised by 'epistemological authoritarianism' (Wallis, 1976: 17); that is, the sect rigidly defines what is acceptable belief and behaviour, usually claiming that it is the *one* true fellowship of believers. Who are the Hare Krishna people, how does the movement operate, and what have been the responses to it? Chapter 9 answers these questions.

Recent Censuses have revealed a growing number of persons who state that they have no religion. Over one-tenth of the Australian population now falls into this category. Though some of these people are militantly anti-religious, most simply feel that they have no need for religion. In recent years there has been conflict between bodies such as the Festival of Light and various humanist or secular organisations. Chapter 10 examines the New South Wales Humanist Society as a form of organised irreligion, looking *inter alia* at points of similarity and difference between it and the churches.

In Chapter 11 there is a discussion of some of the theoretical and methodological issues involved in the study of folk religion in Australia. Using a fairly broad definition of religion, it examines a variety of phenomena, some of which are distinctively Australian, and others of which are also found elsewhere.

The final chapter draws some general conclusions about the sociology of religion in Australia.

Notes

1 On the background and outcome of these proposals, see Barrett, 1966; Turner, 1972.
2 For details on the other colonies, see Barrett, 1966: 52–6; Gregory, 1973: 68–123; Austin, 1972: 105–6.
3 For an outline of later developments in the various states, see Black, 1975.

2 Australian religiosity: Some trends since 1966

Gary D. Bouma

The history of participation in and membership of the major religious denominations[1] in Australia until 1966 has been adequately mapped by Mol (1971). As revealed both in Census figures and denominational statistics, the pattern to 1966 was one of fairly continuous growth in the absolute size of each of these denominations. There was, however, some variation in the relative size of particular denominations, especially as a result of differential birth-rates and immigration after World War II. The question to be addressed in this chapter is, what have been the main trends in religious identification, membership and participation since Mol's review?

Problems in assessing trends in churches

It is very difficult to assess the varying fortunes of churches. There are no systematically kept data which are directly comparable across the several religious groups. 'Membership' means different things in different groups. Some groups keep no records at all. Others are meticulous. Hence, it is nearly impossible to compare churches accurately. It is possible, however, to identify some trends. While a comparison between groups at one point in time may have problems, a comparison of the way in which group A has been faring compared with how group B has been faring can certainly be made so long as there is some consistency of measurement over time in each group. This effort can be frustrated by incidences of church merger or by changes made in the record-keeping procedures of a group. The formation of the Uniting Church in Australia has complicated the analysis of trends for Methodists, Presbyterians and Congregationalists because it was not a total merger of the previous denominations, and the maintenance of records was extremely difficult for several years. Thus, the task of assessing trends in mainline religion is not easy.

What data are there to help assess these trends? First, there are the Census data. These reflect only identification, rather than membership, participation, or practice. The second kind of data available are supplied by national Morgan-Gallup Polls. These data are also useful in assessing trends in identification as well as providing evidence on church attendance. The third form of data is denominational statistics. While each of these forms of data has it' drawbacks, taken together they help to provide a general picture.

Religious identification of Australians since 1966

Every five years Australians are asked to indicate their religion on a Census form. This measure of religion is used as a basis for allocating certain resources to religious groups — the number of chaplains each gets in the military, the amount of time on the broadcasting media made available to each, and so on. Since it is compiled at five-year intervals, this information is ideal for analysing trends in religious identification, at least for those denominations which are large enough to be separately listed.

Table 2.1 shows that there was continued growth between 1966 and 1971 in the *absolute numbers* of persons identifying with the listed religious denominations, except for Church of Christ, Congregational, Methodist, Presbyterian and Hebrew; these five denominations declined during that period. From 1971 to 1976 *all* listed religious denominations other than Catholic, Orthodox, Jehovah's Witnesses and Muslim declined in absolute numbers. Absolute numbers rose again between 1976 and 1981 for all listed denominations expect Congregational, Methodist and Presbyterian. In short, in terms of absolute numbers, after a long period of growth until 1971, there was in most denominations a decline between 1971 and 1976, and renewed growth between 1976 and 1981. Except for Jehovah's Witnesses, the only listed denominations which continued to grow in absolute numbers throughout the 1970s were those containing substantial numbers of recent immigrants as well as having relatively high birth-rates.

In terms of their proportion of the Australian population (one measure of *relative size*) Anglicans, Methodists and Presbyterians continued to decline from 1966 to 1981. When one takes account of the formation of the Uniting Church in 1977, Congregational, Methodist, Presbyterian and Uniting numbers can be added together in order to compare the situation in 1981 with that in previous Censuses. The absolute and relative figures thus obtained are, for 1966: 2 249 146 (19.4 per cent); 1971: 2 195 759 (17.2 per cent); 1976: 1 936 634 (14.3 per cent); 1981: 1 864 210 (12.8 per cent).

Table 2.1 *Trends in religious identification in Australia: selected Census figures, 1947–81*

	1947		1966		1971		1976		1981	
	Persons	%	Persons	%	Persons	%	Persons	%	Persons	%
Anglican	2 957 032	(39.0)	3 885 018	(33.5)	3 953 204	(31.0)	3 752 222	(27.7)	3 810 469	(26.1)
Baptist	113 527	(1.5)	166 222	(1.4)	175 969	(1.4)	174 151	(1.3)	190 259	(1.3)
Brethren	13 002	(0.2)	15 671	(0.1)	22 963	(0.2)	20 719	(0.2)	21 489	(0.2)
Catholic	1 570 356	(20.7)	3 042 507	(26.2)	3 442 634	(27.0)	3 482 847	(25.7)	3 786 505	(26.0)
Church of Christ	71 771	(1.0)	103 260	(0.9)	97 423	(0.8)	86 850	(0.6)	89 424	(0.6)
Congregational	63 243	(0.8)	76 622	(0.7)	68 159	(0.5)	53 444	(0.4)	23 017	(0.2)
Jehovah's Witnesses	NA		NA		35 752		41 359		51 815	(0.4)
Latter Day Saints	3 499		NA		NA		NA		32 444	(0.2)
Lutheran	66 891	(0.9)	179 833	(1.6)	196 847	(1.5)	191 548	(1.4)	199 760	(1.4)
Methodist	871 425	(11.5)	1 126 960	(9.7)	1 099 019	(8.6)	983 240	(7.3)	490 767	(3.4)
Orthodox	17 012	(0.2)	255 500	(2.2)	338 632	(2.7)	372 234	(2.8)	421 281	(3.0)
Pentecostal	NA		NA		NA		38 393	(0.3)	72 148	(0.5)
Presbyterian	743 540	(9.8)	1 045 564	(9.0)	1 028 581	(8.1)	899 950	(6.6)	637 818	(4.4)
Salvation Army	37 572	(0.5)	56 685	(0.5)	65 831	(0.5)	63 336	(0.5)	71 570	(0.5)
Seventh Day Adventist	17 550	(0.2)	38 052	(0.3)	41 617	(0.3)	41 471	(0.3)	47 474	(0.3)
Uniting	—		—		—		—		712 609	(4.9)
Protestant, undefined	73 270	(1.0)	105 374	(0.9)	243 202	(1.9)	206 160	(1.5)	220 679	(1.5)
Other Christian	53 246	(0.7)	133 144	(1.1)	180 546	(1.4)	236 928	(1.7)	253 770	(1.7)
Total Christian	6 672 936	(88.0)	10 230 412	(88.2)	10 990 379	(86.2)	10 644 851	(78.6)	11 133 298	(76.4)
Buddhist	411		NA		NA		NA		35 073	(0.2)
Hebrew	32 019	(0.4)	63 275	(0.5)	62 208	(0.5)	53 441	(0.4)	62 126	(0.4)
Muslim	NA		NA		22 311	(0.2)	45 205	(0.3)	76 792	(0.5)
Other non-Christian	4 132	(0.1)	13 647	(0.1)	14 404	(0.1)	30 422	(0.2)	23 577	(0.2)
Total non-Christian	36 562	(0.5)	76 922	(0.7)	98 923	(0.8)	129 069	(1.0)	197 568	(1.4)
Inadequately described	18 708	(0.2)	36 550	(0.3)	29 413	(0.2)	51 271	(0.4)	73 551	(0.5)
No religion	26 328	(0.3)	96 140	(0.8)	855 676	(6.7)	1 130 300	(8.3)	1 576 718	(10.8)
Not stated	824 824	(10.9)	1 159 474	(10.0)	781 247	(6.1)	1 592 959	(11.8)	1 595 195	(10.9)

Thus, Anglicans and the 'mainline non-conformist' denominations make up a steadily decreasing proportion of the Australian population.

By contrast, the Roman Catholic Church and most of the smaller listed denominations, such as Baptist, Brethren, Jehovah's Witnesses, Orthodox, Salvation Army, Seventh Day Adventist and Hebrew, have managed to maintain or slightly increase their precentage of the population since 1976. Though still relatively small in numbers, Pentecostalists and Muslims have substantially increased their proportion of the population in recent years.

There has also been a substantial growth of those indicating no religious identification. For purposes of analysis, some writers have combined those who indicate 'no religion' with those who fail to answer this particular question. As it has not been compulsory in recent Censuses to answer this question, and as some persons regard information about their religion as of no concern to the government, it seems preferable, as in Table 2.1, to separate those who indicate 'no religion' from those who do not respond. The trends suggest that having some religious label is declining in importance among Australians. Whether this amounts to a falling away from religion or an increase in honesty is unclear. Some data relevant to this issue will be presented in the section on church membership.

The 1981 Census figures require a further comment. Although since the formation of the Uniting Church there is no longer a Methodist Church of Australasia, 3.4 per cent of the population continue to identify themselves as Methodist. Similarly, a larger proportion of Australians identify themselves as Presbyterian or Congregational than would be expected from the size of the continuing Presbyterian Church or the number of continuing Congregational churches. These data illustrate the importance of the distinction between religious identification on the one hand and religious membership or practice on the other. It is likely that some members, even practising members, of the Uniting Church still identify themselves as Presbyterian, Methodist or Congregational. In addition, those who were nominally Presbyterian, Methodist or Congregational but not actively involved in the life of these churches may have had little reason to change this identification merely because of a change of name in the formal organisation of their sector of Christianity.

Three conclusions can be drawn from these data. First, the vast majority of Australians claim some religious identity when asked to do so. Secondly, the proportion who do so has declined somewhat, indicating that having religious identity is less important than it once was. Thirdly, religious identification must be distinguished both analytically and empirically from religious membership and practice.

We now turn to an examination of trends in these latter aspects of religiosity.

Australian church membership, 1966–81

Would that all denominations kept statistics like the Lutherans! They are careful, methodical and reliable. By contrast, some Anglican dioceses, Sydney for example, keep no statistics on membership, while others, like Melbourne, keep them but no longer tally the results. Trends are ascertainable for the Lutheran Church in Australia, the Anglican Diocese of Melbourne and the Uniting Church in Australia.[2]

The Lutheran Church evidenced growth to 1971, then a decline to 1976 and growth to 1981. This pattern is shown in the numbers of baptised members (1967: 111 216; 1971: 115 706; 1976: 112 132; and 1981: 115 069) and confirmed members (1967: 70 015; 1971: 76 310; 1976: 75 871; and 1981: 79 297). This pattern is found not only in the national statistics but also in each of the states. The Lutheran growth rate between 1976 and 1981 of 0.5 per cent per annum in baptised membership and 0.9 per cent per annum in confirmed membership was, however, less than the 1.5 per cent per annum rate of growth for the Australian population as a whole.

Data available from the Anglican Diocese of Melbourne indicate that the number of estimated communicants rose to 96 263 in 1971, declined to 89 849 in 1976 and then rose to 96 113 in 1981. While, according to the 1981 Census, the population of Melbourne had grown at a rate of 0.6 per cent per year since 1976, the growth in the number of Anglican communicants was at the rate of 1.4 per cent per year during this period.

Whereas both Australian Lutherans and Melbourne Anglicans show a pattern of numerical decline from 1971 to 1976 and increase from 1976 to 1981 in membership, the Uniting Church shows a different pattern. The first data on membership were made available for the year 1978. At the national level the Uniting Church reported about 2500 fewer confirmed members in 1981 than in 1978 (225 732 vs 228 196 respectively). Only the Synod of Queensland showed significant growth (2100). The Synod of Victoria lost 3100 confirmed members. The pattern here is one of continued decline in membership, though some of this loss may be due to a tidying-up of church rolls since union.

The difference between identification and active membership has already been noted. The proportion of active members among those identifying with a group is a variable which has not been systematically examined before. Table 2.2 presents data for the Anglican Diocese of Melbourne. Although, according to Census figures, the proportion of Melbournians who identify themselves as Anglican has declined from 37.2 per cent in 1951 to 19.5 per cent in 1981, the proportion of those calling themselves Anglicans who actually show up on church rolls has gone from a low of 9.2 per cent in 1956 to 14.8 per cent in 1956 to 14.8 per cent in 1976 and 16.9 per cent in 1981 (see Table 2.2). These data indicate that the incidence of nominalism is declining among Melbourne Anglicans.

Table 2.2 *Estimated communicants in the Diocese of Melbourne of those Melbournians indicating an Anglican preference in the Census 1951-76* (%)

1951	1956	1961	1966	1971	1976	1981
10.9	9.2	12.5	13.7	14.2	14.8	16.9

The pattern for Lutherans is somewhat different. Confirmed members of the Lutheran Church made up the following proportions of persons identified as Lutherans in the Census: 1966 (38.9 per cent); 1971 (38.8 per cent); 1976 (39.6 per cent) and 1981 (39.7 per cent). A higher percentage of those who identify themselves as Lutherans are active members than is the case for Anglicans. Put differently, a lower percentage of Lutherans than of Anglicans are nominals.

Thus there is evidence for an increase in church membership in some denominations. The lack of data on more groups limits the generalisability of this conclusion. However, evidence of growth has been found among urban Anglicans and Australian Lutherans. This suggests that it is not just the new religious movements or the smaller Christian groups that are growing. The evidence on religious observance in Australia may shed some light on this.

Trends in religious observance in Australia

There are two measures of religious observance which are available on a comparative basis through time: church attendance and sacramental observance.

Church attendance

Since 1950, Australians have been asked to answer the question: 'How long has it been since you last went to church, apart from weddings, funerals and similar occasions?' Table 2.3 displays the

Table 2.3 *Trends in Australian church attendance, according to Morgan-Gallup Polls 1950–81* (%)

	1950	1960	1970	1972	1976	1980	1981
Last at church:							
Within a week	23	30	25	21	20	19	22
Week to a month	13	15	11	10	9	8	9
Month to a year	11	22	24	21	20	20	21
Rarely/never	53	33	40	48	51	53	48

answers to this question obtained over the years by the Morgan-Gallup Poll.[3]

As can be seen from Table 2.3, Australian church attendance as measured by responses to Morgan-Gallup Polls has varied somewhat. The high was in 1960 (the year after the largest Billy Graham crusade in Australia) and the low was in 1980, with a recovery in 1981. The variation in Australian church attendance from 1861–1901 was roughly the same (Mol, 1971: 11). Indeed, attendance varying around the 25 per cent mark has been the rule for Australia since about 1860. A look at historical trends reveals a pattern of remarkable stability in the percentage attending and in the outcries of religious leaders that it is so low due to the usual reasons — laziness, hedonism, and the competition of other activities.

Table 2.4 *Australians of several denominations who claim to have attended church in the last week, according to Morgan-Gallup Polls 1970–81* (%)

	Anglican	Roman Catholic	Methodist	Presbyterian	Other Christian
1970	10.6	50.8	20.6	19.5	35.8
1976	8.6	42.1	16.4	11.1	28.0
1981	11.9	37.4	5.4	7.7	39.3

In the past, there have been significant denominational differences in the rate of church-going (Mol, 1971: 9–19). Table 2.4 provides evidence on recent trends in weekly attendance for those identifying with selected denominations. Whilst there has been rather minor variation in the rate of participation for the population as a whole, there have been significant shifts within various denominations. Anglican percentages have declined and recovered. From a relatively high level, Roman Catholic figures show a steady decline. Methodist and Presbyterian data show decline, but the 1981 percentage of those identifying with the Uniting Church who claimed to have attended church in the last week was 33.9 per cent. If those identifying with the Presbyterian, Methodist and Uniting churches are combined, the following pattern emerges for this sector of Christians: weekly attendance was claimed by 20.1 per cent in 1970, 13.6 per cent in 1976 and 15.5 per cent in 1981. Taken as a whole, this group of mainline 'non-conformist' denominations shows a pattern of variation similar to that of Anglicans. Much the same pattern of variation applies to the 'Other Christian' category, though the overall rate of weekly attendance is noticeably higher here.

The basic point on attendance is that roughly one-quarter of Australians claimed to have gone to church in the last seven days before they were interviewed. This figure, while subject to variation, in particular a recent high in 1960, has been the common figure for Australia since 1860. Pictures of golden eras of church attendance in the past refer more to 1960 than to days of long ago. There appears to be a slight return from a low point in 1976 in church attendance as well as in religious membership. However, there are differences among denominations in church attendance trends since 1966. These differences must be taken seriously in any assessment of the overall religious picture of Australia. In terms of denominational composition, the nearly one-quarter of Australians who claimed to have gone to church in the past week in 1981 are different from the one-quarter who made such a claim in 1970. They are now less likely than before to be Catholic, more likely than before to belong to a small religious group.

Sacramental participation
While there are no Morgan-Gallup Poll data on sacramental participation, some churches keep reasonably accurate records of these things. I have had access to both Lutheran and Anglican data.

Anglican data show that in the Diocese of Melbourne annual acts of communion have followed the pattern observed above: a decline from 992 884 in 1966 to 953 390 in 1976 and a subsequent rise to 1 226 867 in 1981. At first this was taken as evidence of a change in religious practice. To check this, a rate of acts of communion was calculated by dividing the total number of acts of communion by the estimated number of communicants in the Diocese. This revealed that the rate of communion in the Diocese of Melbourne has varied slightly around 9.5 acts of communion per year per estimated communicant. Thus as the number of communicants has risen so has the number of acts of communion. The fact that the trends in these figures reflect each other is an indication of their reliability. The number of acts of communion is a quite reliable figure as the procedures for counting and recording these are fairly regularised and not difficult. This is further confirmed by the fact that the number of acts of communion on Christmas Day follows the same trend, down from 1971 to 1976 and up in 1981 to a figure above 1971 levels.

The Lutheran Church has seen a spectacular rise in acts of communion. Acts of communion have risen from 274 662 in 1967 to 591 833 in 1980. The rate of communion has risen from 3.9 acts per confirmed member to 7.5 acts per confirmed member. In this case the change reflects a change in churchmanship more than growth in membership. In 1967 there were 6405 services of communion offered to the people, in 1980 there were 12 266. The change in the average attendance at communion services from 42.9 in 1967 to 48.2 in 1980 reflects the increase in the number of confirmed members. Thus the dramatic rise in acts of communion among Lutherans appears to be largely due to membership acceptance of a liturgical innovation, namely an increase in the number of times communion is made available.

Thus the records for sacramental participation of the Lutheran and Anglican churches show different patterns. Anglican figures declined from 1971 to 1976 and then increased to 1981 in both membership and sacramental participation. Lutherans showed the same membership trend but a dramatic increase in sacramental participation, the latter resulting largely from a change in churchmanship. Again the importance of the denominational context within which change is occurring can be seen.

Summary and conclusions

From an examination of Census results, poll data and denominational statistics, four main conclusions emerge.

First, most Australians still claim to be religious and identify with one of the mainstream Christian denominations. As has been the case for most of the time since 1860, about one-quarter of Australians (22 per cent in 1981) claim to have attended church in the last week. On the other hand, about half the population rarely or never attends church.

Secondly, although the vast majority of Australians indicate a religious identification, there has been an increase in the proportion of Australians who say they have no religion. About 11 per cent of the population now falls into this category.

Thirdly, some religious groups are increasing in active membership, and sometimes at a faster rate than for general population growth. With respect to church membership and participation there appears to have been a fairly general decline from 1971 to 1976 and some recovery to 1981. The fact that this pattern appears in several kinds of data suggests that it is reasonably reliable. It is not possible to declare that there has been a major return to religion. Similarly, it is impossible to say that decline is the order of the day. The notion that the churches are withering away is simply not supported by the data (cf. Bouma, 1982).

Fourthly, there are denominational differences in the trends relating to religious identification, membership and participation. Those who identify themselves as Anglicans have been steadily declining in terms of their proportion of the total population, but since 1976 the proportion of them who have attended church within the last week has been increasing. Roman Catholics, on the other hand, have continued to increase in their proportion of the total population but to decline in their frequency of church attendance; nevertheless, their rate of weekly attendance is still markedly higher than for the major Protestant denominations, with the possible exception of the Uniting Church. Although confirmed membership of the Uniting Church has declined slightly since its formation, church attendance rates are much higher among those who designate themselves Uniting than among those who continue to identify themselves as Presbyterian or Methodist. Some religious groups with relatively small numbers in Australia, such as Muslims and various Pentecostal groups, have been increasing their share of the religious market in recent years. Most of the other smaller religious groups listed in Census reports have at least maintained their relative size since 1976. Persons who identify with one of the smaller Christian groups generally attend church more frequently than do those who identify with one of the larger Protestant denominations.

Notes

1 Throughout this chapter, 'denomination' is used as a generic term for an identifiable religious grouping, rather than to refer to a specific type of religious collectivity.
2 All denominational data are taken from their official annual publications or reports. I wish to thank the Rev. Vernon Kleinig for making the Lutheran data available, Ethel Easton for compiling the Uniting Church data, the Rev. John Davis, the Venerable S.C. Moss, the Rt Rev. David Shand and the Rt Rev. James Grant for their invaluable assistance in compiling and interpreting the Anglican data. Finally, a note of gratitude to Craig Bouma who laboriously tallied the Anglican figures.
3 Data in Tables 2.3 and 2.4 are drawn from Morgan-Gallup Poll, Finding 860, October 1981, and Morgan-Gallup Poll reports in 1970 (no. 215), 1976 (no. 123) and 1981 (no. 403).

3   Country town religion[1]

Kenneth Dempsey

Theologians and churchmen alike are commonly heard saying that the church's mission is to bring abundant life. They offer quite varying interpretations of what this means but among the things frequently mentioned are freeing people from guilt and fear; helping them realise their own worth and develop their potential to the full; helping them celebrate the gift of life itself; supporting them and helping them support others during the crises of life; breaking down the divisions of age, sex, class, education and ethnicity among them; and enhancing their capacity to love others including those they would otherwise ignore or reject. Achieving such goals entails challenging people to surrender fiercely held prejudices and positions of advantage; it means asking them to risk rejection and invite criticism, to give what might be perceived as inordinate amounts of their time, their emotional resources, and their money to individuals and causes they might otherwise neglect. It also means encouraging them to confront and help overcome social injustice and chronic deprivation in their own community and beyond.

The following appraisal of church life in one country community is based on the premise that the church's task is to bring such abundant life to its supporters and, through them, to the community at large. This appraisal shows that there are a number of obstacles to the church's carrying out such a programme. These include the inherent difficulty of challenging as well as comforting laymen; the indispensability of lay support to the church's survival as an institution;[2] the church's alliance with the more privileged sections of the community; fundamental differences among clergy concerning the direction the church should go; and disagreement between clergy and laity on the part each should play in the church's programme. It also shows that one of the greatest obstacles to the church's realising its goal is its desire to have it both ways: that is, to follow Christ's example of self-sacrifice and, at the same time, materially prosper and enjoy the good opinion of the community at large.

Method and setting

The community which is the focal point of this paper is situated in a mixed farming district in Western Victoria. I have called it Smalltown. The township proper has a population of approximately 2800 persons and it draws its lifeblood from an agricultural hinterland whose 1200 inhabitants obtain many of their goods and services in the town and join with townspeople in educational, recreational, service and religious activities.

Fieldwork trips were made to Smalltown in 1973, 1974, 1975, 1976 and 1982. These encompassed many aspects of community life and enabled us to look at the ways in which such things as age and status divisions affected religious activities. At the same time these trips gave us an understanding of the interests and priorities of community members, of the place of religion in their daily lives and of the place of the churches in the life of the community.[3]

For several decades, Smalltown has experienced the problem of numerous other small rural communities: diminution in the number and variety of its economic activities, accompanied by a declining population. The combined population of the town and district is today less than half its size at the beginning of the century. There are fewer jobs than in earlier years and only limited opportunity for skilled employment. So, in order to 'better themselves' the majority of its offspring, including many of the more able young people, are moving to the city. This pattern creates a great deal of anxiety among the residual population including church leaders and, in fact, caused a number of them to commission the research from which this paper emanates.

During the period of most intensive fieldwork (1973, 1974 and 1975) Smalltown possessed six churches. In descending order of size (based on active membership) these were: Roman Catholic, Church of England, Presbyterian, Methodist, Church of Christ, and the Salvation Army. In 1977 the Presbyterian and Methodist congregations joined to form the local branch of the Uniting Church. In 1982 with, on average, 80 to 90 adults and children attending its Sunday services it had the largest active membership of any of the Protestant churches. On average 50 to 60 people were attending the Anglican Church. The local Church of Christ and Salvation Army corps were much smaller, usually less than a dozen people attending a service of worship at either church. The Roman Catholic Church, which had 400–450 people attending mass on any particular Sunday, was by far the biggest worship centre in Smalltown.

The primary focus of this study is on the major Protestant churches: the Anglican and the Uniting. The Roman Catholic Church receives less attention because of my much more limited exposure to the denomination's activities and the reluctance of the parish priest to participate in the study.

Smalltown inequality

In any Western society, towns are not homogeneous structures; they always have a status and power hierarchy which reflects the diversity of economic interests that characterise the total society. Occupation is one of the most important factors in the allocation of status in the Smalltown community. On the basis of the amount of status accorded to household heads I have divided the people of Smalltown into three strata: upper, middle and working. The upper stratum is composed of well-to-do farmers and graziers, the more prosperous businessmen, bank managers, leading local-government officers and traditional professionals; the middle stratum includes farmers with smaller holdings, smaller businessmen, school teachers and a variety of clerical workers; the working stratum comprises skilled, semi-skilled and unskilled employee manual workers, and service workers.

Most of those who run the town and its organisations and who are the most vocal in local affairs are drawn from the upper stratum. They constitute the town's establishment. The values and goals of the establishment include political conservatism, support for the existing system of the inequitable distribution of goods and services, and the maintenance of Smalltown as a pleasant and attractive place to live. Establishment people, then, are committed to the status quo.

The interests of the establishment tend to end at the town boundaries. Activities are supported which focus on community needs, rather than those of outside groups. For example, the local Council refused permission to the Ministers' Fraternal to conduct a doorknock campaign for Austcare. Establishment members are also eager to convey the image of Smalltown as a happy, harmonious family. As one leading figure (a prominent church leader) said to me, 'We like to think the poorer members of our town accept the rightness of the way the cake is carved up and are content with their lot.'

As the last statement implies, the community is in fact a pleasanter place for some to live than for others. According to Professor Henderson's criteria a significant proportion of Smalltown people (probably as high as 15 per cent) are on or below the poverty line. Working stratum families, in particular, need to supplement the income of the household head through the wife's working. However, there is only limited opportunity for work in Smalltown and that work is usually of a manual and often boring kind.

The experience of social, economic and psychological deprivation is real enough in Smalltown; I am stressing its occurrence in the present context because the lives of the more disadvantaged members of the community are largely untouched by the major Protestant churches.

In principle, the organisations of Smalltown are open to all members of the community, irrespective of their social status. In practice, however, the leadership and ordinary membership of a majority of non-recreational organisations come mainly from members of the first two strata. Members of the upper stratum are especially prominent in the more prestigious and influential organisations. Whether the prevailing situation is indicative of the lack of interest of lower stratum members, or of their informal exclusion, is difficult to determine. Whatever the reason, it is symptomatic of the dominance of the business, farming and professional strata in town affairs. It is also symptomatic of the failure of the town's more prestigious organisations to integrate people of all strata.

Institutional religion in Smalltown also fails to integrate the social strata. The middle and upper strata form the bulk of the active membership of the Anglican Church and the Presbyterian component of the Uniting Church. The middle stratum is disproportionately represented in the Methodist component. The Church of Christ is a mixture of working and middle strata and the Salvation Army draws its support exclusively from the working stratum. Only in the Roman Catholic Church are all three strata proportionately represented.

Religious practices and beliefs

Over 90 per cent of Smalltown people describe themselves as Christians and claim that they belong to a particular church. In practice, most of them ignore their church most of the time: less than 20 per cent of them are in church on any given Sunday. Of these, over two-thirds are Catholics, a denomination which constitutes only one-fifth of Smalltown's population.

Protestants claim they stay away from church because they believe it is irrelevant to their lives. 'I fail to get anything from church services', was the kind of thing repeatedly said during interviews. In descending order of importance the other reasons given for staying away from church were: lack of time, health problems, lack of faith, the hypocrisy of the church and its members, disagreement with views held by the clergy, and the church's preoccupation with money.

It is extremely unusual to find any Smalltown church supporter speaking with great enthusiasm about attending worship. Only a handful — usually elderly widows living by themselves — mentioned it as the activity they most looked forward to each week. Lukewarmness was more prevalent among Protestants than Catholics. The typical Protestant attends church less frequently than his or her Catholic counterpart. As one Protestant clergyman observed, 'Attendance at worship is just one of a number of possibilities for Sunday morning.'

The clergy and their congregations

With the exception of the Catholic priest, Smalltown's clergymen were profoundly disappointed with both the individual and collective response of their people to their claim to be Christians. In the mid 1970s the Anglican minister of the time said that the Christian faith was a matter of fundamental significance in the lives of only 10 per cent of his members, whilst the Uniting Church minister said it was of marginal significance or of no significance at all in the lives of two-thirds of his members. In 1982, two ministers said that church people, like the people of the town generally, were apathetic and self-satisfied, and a third said that his congregation sold itself short, that very few members showed the potential for developing the type of corporate life he believed was an intrinsic part of the Christian gospel. Only the Roman Catholic priest was prepared to say that the Christian faith was of fundamental significance in the lives of most of his parishioners. This judgement was made in the context of equating attendance at mass and financial support for the church with Christian commitment.

Although the Protestant clergymen did not make such an equation and although the financial needs of their causes were not of the magnitude of those of the Catholic Church (the priest had to find funds for day schooling for the Catholic children of the district) they were, nevertheless, eager for laymen to support their church. I also found most clergymen very anxious to convey the impression that under their leadership their church was proving successful in these terms. So, for example, they usually exaggerated the size of their congregations and volunteered explanations as to why the congregation was considerably smaller than what they claimed it usually was on the particular Sunday that I attended church. Frequently, they were defensive about the disappearance of a particular organisation or the fall in support for another and were ready to blame these changes on the apathy of the people and, in one instance, on the godlessness of the town.[4]

The minister who was probably the least defensive about the church's numerical and organisational decline was an Anglican priest, Father Michael, who came to Smalltown in the late 1970s. This man believes the church has placed too much emphasis on tangible success and that it has masked an essential aspect of the gospel through the development of a plethora of special interest groups. For Father Michael the gathering of Christians on a Sunday is by far the most important event in the life of the church but, from his perspective, it is the gathering rather than the worship of God that is primary. As he put it:

> We are created to live our lives not to worship God. We have to make sure that when we come together we celebrate each other. If other things flow from this, well and good, but if they don't it is a clear sign that we have not got to first base. It is the gathering and reconciliation of people of diverse backgrounds that matters.

Consequently, he has proven lukewarm about the organisations that existed when he came to Smalltown and has opposed the introduction of any new ones. Such groups, he believes, shift the emphasis from the congregation as a whole and siphon off energies that should be given to breaking down the barriers between young and old, male and female, prosperous and poor, and to building up a community of people who care for others in very specific ways.

In articles in the local newspapers, in his sermons, in changes he has made to the worship and through his lack of enthusiasm for several church organisations, he has made clear his dissatisfaction with the character of church life in this community. Predictably, his actions have generated a good deal of resentment, certainly among Anglicans, especially as his very popular predecessor, Father Thomas, had emphasised the centrality of traditional liturgical forms and worked hard to make a success of church groups. The gulf in outlook between at least some members of the congregation and Father Michael was clearly shown during an incident that occurred at a Sunday service of worship. When, on coming into church, he found everybody was sitting far apart, he said to the congregation, 'I cannot stand coming into church and pretending to worship when we are functioning as a collection of individuals.' He appealed to them to move closer together, but no-one moved. A number of worshippers subsequently let him know that they were going to worship the way they chose. Nevertheless, Father Michael believes that some members of the congregation took the point and recognised that they were not functioning as a community. This last assessment was possibly right — certainly the Sunday services of worship were less formal and a greater sense of community prevailed than is usually the case in Protestant churches. For example, members of the congregation enthusiastically, and unselfconsciously, made the Greeting of the Peace with several other worshippers.[5] Also, some of them, at the invitation of the priest, called out the names of people they wanted the congregation to pray for. This happened at a normal Sunday morning worship.

The Uniting Church minister, the Reverend Bill Watson, who like Father Michael had, in 1982, been working in Smalltown for several years, has also found that many of his plans for change have been effectively resisted by local laymen and that his ability to press for change has been impeded by the church's need of lay support and his own economic and social dependence on laymen. He has not shared Father Michael's misgivings about the place of special interest groups in the life of the church; in fact, he has made them a primary focus of his ministry. But at the same time he has put across ideas from the pulpit that are at variance with those of some of the leading members of the congregation. He has tried to make significant changes to the worship and, like Father Michael, attempted to involve his laymen more actively in Sunday worship. They have at best been lukewarm about his efforts at reform and usually highly critical.

Mr Watson rejects the idea that he was ordained to serve as a pastor, arguing that pastoral work is the responsibility of the elders of the congregation. In their turn, laymen have rejected this point of view and have been critical of Mr Watson's practice of usually restricting his visiting to 'shut ins', the seriously ill and the bereaved. The difference between the minister and the people on this issue would have probably led to serious conflict but for three things. First, laymen are aware that Mr Watson's approach to pastoral work is becoming more common among ministers of the Uniting Church. Secondly, they have appreciated the efforts he and his wife have put in to making a success of church organisations, especially the Sunday school and several women's groups. Thirdly, many of them do not care enough to put up a fight. For a growing proportion of church goers their church affiliation is of marginal significance in their lives.

So, as Bill Watson said, 'A minister can do what he likes provided he works at it. They want you to run the show, to be the one who comes up with the ideas. They want you to do it all for them.' Yet this does not necessarily mean that he can get his people to do things they have not done before. Mr Watson pointed out that the apathy of the local people was the biggest problem he faced as a minister. In the face of this apathy and his need for the congregation's financial and numerical support, it is not surprising that his enthusiasm for change has been blunted and, like most Smalltown clergy of the last decade, he has come around to accepting the laymen on their own terms.

The clergy and the community

If, during the 1970s and the early 1980s, Smalltown's clergy made few demands on their congregation, they made even fewer on the community in general. Rarely were non-churchgoers called upon to become active supporters. Even the Salvation Army officers, who are instructed by their organisation to give first place to evangelism, did not conduct street-corner meetings in Smalltown nor did they use the opportunity provided by their weekly rounds of the hotels of the district to confront men with their need for salvation. In 1982 the incumbent Salvation Army officer said that the local corps was too small to provide sufficient people for an effective street meeting and that, whilst the Army said his first responsibility was to evangelise, he believed it was to be a pastor.

The Church of Christ, which also sees itself primarily as an evangelical church, has not, in any regular way, called upon community members to place their faith in Jesus Christ as their Saviour and Lord. The leading layman of this church said that there were too few active members to carry out an effective programme of evangelism; he himself had given up visiting potential supporters because it had failed to produce any new recruits. He stated that 'What really holds us back is the fact that we do not have a minister living in the town. There hasn't been one here for over forty years. The people really want a minister to visit.' He then went on to say, 'You know I write a regular column for the newspaper. This is the way we witness to the community.'

The reluctance of even those who believe in traditional evangelism to attempt to evangelise in a context where they are well-known and where members of the community have traditionally demonstrated their resistence to old-fashioned evangelism is understandable. The Catholic priest and the ministers of the mainstream Protestant churches did not have to cope with such problems because they do not perceive themselves as older style evangelists. These men have elected to use less direct methods for bringing their ministry to bear on the community. During the 1970s these included the organisation and participation in processions of witness and in carols-by-candlelight services.

Several ministers have played sport, served on various local committees and written promotional material for town events. Probably the most active in town affairs has been Bill Watson, the Uniting Church minister, who at one time or another has been a President of Rotary, President of the High School Council, Secretary of a Junior Football Club, Scout Leader, bowler, and a regular driver of the community bus. This man's predecessor, who was only marginally less active in community affairs, explained his involvement in this way: 'I see the Church as having some relevance for everybody and my community activity is a point of contact with the non-churchgoer: through me the Church touches the life of everybody.'

During the last decade, the ministers of the Anglican and Uniting churches have also regularly written columns for the local paper in which they have offered a 'Christian perspective' on various national events, and on the day-to-day problems individuals experience in their private lives. With few exceptions, what the clergy have said has been cast in fairly general terms and has usually been compatible with middle-class or establishment sentiments. Through their writing, as well as their participation in community affairs, the clergy have expressed their interest in all community members. They have also implied their pastoral oversight of churchgoer and non-churchgoer alike, attempting by word and deed to gently persuade community members of the relevance of Christianity to their personal lives, and of the benefits of aligning themselves with the church.

The minister who has most frequently written columns for the local newspaper which have been at variance with establishment values has been Father Michael. His journalism and his outspokenness in other public contexts have led to many seeing him as a radical, a socialist and 'something of a stirrer' in a politically conservative town that believes religion has nothing to do with politics. On one occasion he attracted a lot of criticism for saying that the Prime Minister, Malcolm Fraser, was not good for Australia. Father Michael has resisted becoming involved in community organisations such as Rotary, the Lions Club, or youth and sporting activities. He has chosen instead to express his personal interest in members of the community at large by regularly visiting hospitalised people of all denominations and sick or bereaved members of the community who had no active church affiliation, and by giving marriage counselling or counselling on other personal problems to anyone who sought it. The pastoral work this minister has performed in the community has largely erased the suspicion or estrangement sparked off by his challenge to many establishment values in the first years of his ministry.

Yet what has been missing from this man's ministry as well as that of the other recent Smalltown clergymen has been a direct challenge to local social injustice. Even if the clergy have seen such a challenge as falling within the ambit of Christian responsibility — and not all have — the feeling has prevailed that there were insufficient inequities to warrant a direct confrontation or that a ministry would be placed in jeopardy if a man adopted a course of action which is totally out of phase with the convictions of a majority of church and community leaders. For example, Father Michael said, 'I will sacrifice principle for the sake of maintaining good relationships and to avoid a serious disruption to church life. Anyhow the congregation doesn't belong to me and it rightly resists my efforts to impose my programmes on it.'

Laymen's expectations of the church and its clergy

On the basis of research spanning almost a decade, it can be said that most of those who are actively associated with the church — irrespective of denomination — are seeking comfort, support and the meeting of personal needs rather than seeking to change their lives in accordance with the more radical demands of Christ's teachings. In essence they are looking to the church to buttress lives, the direction of which is set by societal or class values. So, for example, when a child is brought for baptism this is often to acknowledge the child's membership of his natural family and signify his arrival in the community rather than his entry to the Kingdom of God.

The changes that laymen are looking for in their clergymen are consistent with the notion that the church is to be a source of comfort rather than challenge. For example, in 1982, laymen wanted both the Anglican and Uniting ministers to stop challenging them over such issues as wealth, landrights for Aborigines, and so on. In one survey of church attenders, 50 per cent of respondents said that they would like more home visits from their minister. Many people were concerned about the absence of adolescents from the Protestant churches. Most of the concerned said that the young people would return if the minister or priest showed he was genuinely interested in them and if interesting activities were initiated in the church for them. None of our informants argued that young people or, for that matter, people of any age, would be more attracted to Christianity if it made more demands on them. The emphasis was on the clergy and the church accommodating themselves to those who were absenting themselves from church life.

Consistent with the conception of Christianity as a source of comfort rather than of challenge, the great majority of church members do not perceive any need for a radical alteration to the organisational or worship life of Smalltown churches. For example, in a survey conducted in the mid 1970s, only one of a total of 230 respondents stated that their church needed a social action group and only one respondent recognised any need for the introduction of a programme of Christian education. Our enquiries indicated that most leaders and ordinary members alike had little interest in extending their knowledge of the faith or in discussing its practical implications for their daily lives. Hardly any leaders, when questioned, said that in the previous twelve months they had read any literature bearing on their role as church leaders. In recent years, there has not been a permanent adult study group in either the Anglican or Uniting churches. However, a Bible study group has been meeting in each of these churches for five-to-six-week sessions during Lent and sometimes during Advent. When these groups last met they were attended by between fifteen and twenty people.

The relative indifference to what is commonly called 'the spiritual side' of Christianity was also evident in church administration. The Parish Council of the Uniting Church, which takes decisions over financial and organisational aspects of church life, meets regularly whereas the Elders' Council, which is concerned with the pastoral oversight of the members, and which is meant to meet each two months, often does not meet for several months at a time. The Uniting Church in Australia believes that the pastoral oversight of the congregation should be shared by the minister and laypersons elected as elders for this purpose. In Smalltown, a dozen or so families were placed under the pastoral care of each elder. Elders were expected to visit regularly the families in their care. It appears that at the time of writing no elder was doing this although some were visiting three of four individuals or families, but not necessarily those assigned to them.

In the Anglican Church there is no equivalent of the Uniting Church Elders' Council. The Vestry Meeting concerns itself mainly with finance and property matters. One of the Anglican priests resident in the town during our field work, Father Thomas, described himself as a Mediaevalist and said that God's grace was channelled through him rather than through the laymen, so he assumed responsibility for the spiritual oversight of the parish. It seems his laymen were more than happy with this arrangement. As his successor, Father Michael, believes that the congregation should share with the

priest the pastoral oversight of the congregation, he has been encouraging the Vestry to give more of its time to a discussion of the
spiritual life of the church and he has supported an initiative by
several women to carry out some pastoral visitation in the parish.
Nevertheless, the overwhelming majority of Smalltown's church attenders, including the elders of the Uniting Church, believe that the
clergy should do most, if not all, of the church's pastoral work.
Several elders said they had been discouraged from visiting because
most of those they called upon made it clear they would rather see
the minister. I was repeatedly told: 'There is no substitute for a
minister's visit.'

The division between laymen and clergy in Smalltown, then, is a
highly significant one. It is the clergyman who bears final responsibility for the institutional success or failure of the church. So, for
example, if a youth club fails or attendance at worship falls off, it is
usually the minister who is blamed. He is perceived as the man of
God *par excellence*. On his shoulders there falls responsibility for
the sacrificial life which, in theory, is to be lead by all Christians.
Active laymen make far less stringent demands on themselves and
they repeatedly excuse themselves for any lapses on the grounds that
the clergy do not live up to the standards they enunciate from the
pulpit. As one commented, 'He tells us to give more of our money
to the poor but he's gone and bought himself a very nice car thank
you.'

Catholic/Protestant relationships in Smalltown

Because they are anxious to maintain the image of Smalltown as a
happy and harmonious community, establishment members play
down the significance of internal divisions. These include the division between Catholic and Protestant as well as those between rich
and poor, young and old, and so on.

During our fieldwork both Catholic and Protestant establishment
people were quite reluctant to discuss Protestant/Catholic relations.
The following type of comment was often made: 'Sectarianism is
something of the past; Protestants and Catholics now live together
in a spirit of mutual acceptance and co-operation.' We were criticised by both Catholics and Protestants for raising the issue of relationships between them. It was argued that by our investigation of
this subject we were stirring the embers of sectarianism.

It is true that sectarianism is less evident in Smalltown today than
twenty years ago. For example, Catholics and Protestants often
attend one another's functions and mix in town organisations,

especially sporting groups.[6] Many Protestants claim they have at least one good Catholic friend and many Catholics make a similar claim about friendship with Protestants. But it is also true that Protestant/Catholic allegiances have a significant bearing on social life in Smalltown. When pressed, many members of both religious groups will acknowledge that this is so. For example, the majority of Smalltown people marry within their religious group. Some of those who have made mixed marriages speak of the criticism they receive for doing so; their loss of identity with their original religious group, and their failure to be fully accepted by their new one. Approximately 70 per cent of Protestants said their friends and relatives would try to discourage them from becoming Catholics and over 90 per cent of Catholics said their friends and relatives would try to discourage them from 'turning Protestant'.

A good deal of mutual distrust and suspicion still exists between the two groups. Half the Catholics who responded to questions concerning Protestant/Catholic relationships expressed the view that they were misunderstood by Protestants, and they were disappointed by, or resentful of, the failure of Protestants to 'get to understand them better'. Many believed that Protestants 'looked down on them' for taking their religion seriously, for acknowledging the hegemony of the Pope and for worshipping the Virgin Mary. It is clear from our work that many Catholics are eager for acceptance by the Protestant section of Smalltown. Lack of acceptance and lack of friendliness were the major concerns expressed to our fieldworkers. At the same time, Catholics were critical of Protestants for not taking *their* own faith seriously. In comments that were made there was a hint of condemnation over the apparent incongruity of Protestants adopting a superior attitude to Catholics and at the same time being indifferent to the practice of their own religion.

Being the majority group, Protestants were predictably less concerned with their acceptance by Catholics than were Catholics with their acceptance by Protestants. Only one-sixth of those Protestants who responded to our questions on this subject spoke of their disappointment that Catholics were not more accepting of Protestants. Nevertheless, about one-third of the Protestant respondents levelled the accusation of bigotry at Catholics, whom they criticised for taking religion too seriously.

In short, even though the Protestant/Catholic division has declined in significance, it still has a profound bearing on life in Smalltown. A majority of local people — especially the young — would like to see its significance diminish still further. About 50 per cent of both our Catholic and Protestant respondents said they favoured church union across this division. Certainly town leaders, concerned with fostering the image of Smalltown as a harmonious community, would welcome a further decline in sectarianism.

What of the church's future in Smalltown?

The future for institutional Roman Catholicism in Smalltown looks good. About 400–450 Catholics attend worship on any given Sunday, compared with less than 200 Protestants. The age structure of the local Catholic church reflects that of the community. This means that no age group is markedly under- or over-represented. Only 25 per cent of the elderly Catholics, as compared to more than 50 per cent of the elderly Protestants, stated that they were attending church less than in earlier years. Young Catholics are much more involved in the church than are their Protestant peers. There is a strong emphasis in the Catholic sub-community on family worship. The majority of older adolescents whom we interviewed said they 'fitted in well' in the local Catholic church. Although some Catholics have been alienated by their priest's strong stand on mixed marriages and their church's unswerving hostility to abortion and contraception, and although these and many younger Catholics are less willing than their predecessors of earlier years to submit to the church's authority, there are no signs that the local Catholic church is soon to decline as a centre of worship in this town.

By comparison, there were many signs during our several years of fieldwork in Smalltown that the ability of the Protestant churches to attract supporters was declining. In 1982 the total number of Protestant worshippers on any given Sunday was about two-thirds the number in 1973. For those who are anxious to see support for the town's churches maintained, an even more depressing picture emerges from an analysis of the age and sex composition of the Protestant congregations. These are ageing as well as numerically declining congregations. People over the age of 50 comprise one-third of the town's population but more than two-thirds of regular Protestant church attenders. Moreover about 80 per cent of this two-thirds consists of people aged at least 70. By contrast, approximately 40 per cent of the town's population is under 25, but this age group only provides 20 per cent of church attenders and most of these are under twelve years of age.

Altogether only a handful of teenagers attend the town's Protestant churches. Church-initiated special interest groups no longer attract teenagers in significant numbers. The Anglican Girls' Friendly Society and the Anglican Youth Club, each of which in the mid 1970s had an active membership of between fifteen and twenty teenagers, have closed down. Strenuous efforts by the present Uniting Church minister failed to rally any more support for the church's youth group than it was gaining in the mid 1970s. As in the past, between twelve and eighteen teenagers attend, but it now meets fortnightly, whereas previously it met weekly. Because students expressed no interest, the Protestant ministers have discontinued periodic high-school seminars on the Christian faith. High-school students' attitudes in the 1980s were consistent with those displayed during a survey I conducted in 1974. In that year more than two-thirds of the pupils in forms 4, 5 and 6 said that the church was irrelevant to them, and the majority of those who did attend church services or a church youth group said 'they did not fit in well'.

The 26-to-50-year-old age group is also under-represented among Smalltown's Protestant church supporters. Whereas members of this group comprise 26 per cent of the town's population, they supply only 14 per cent of its worshipping population. There are no special interest groups for people of this age in the Anglican Church. In the early 1970s the Uniting Church ran a Couples' Club which attracted between fifteen and twenty people, but this has since disappeared. At the present time the minister's wife leads a women's fellowship with about fifteen members aged in their 20s, 30s or 40s. This woman hoped that through friendships between the women attending this group their husbands might be drawn into the life of the church. This has not happened.

Actually, all age groups other than the 50+ category are under-represented among Protestant churchgoers. One interpretation of this situation is that as people advance in age they have a greater need for religion; a need which is reflected in a disproportionately higher rate of attendance among members of this age cohort; a pattern that ensures a continuing 'if elderly' clientele for the church. In fact our data do not support this point of view. More than half of the sample of people over 65 years of age, or older, stated that they attend church less now than when they were 50 years of age. Some members of the sample had stopped attending altogether.

At the present time, the typical Protestant church supporter is elderly rather than young, female rather than male, and from the middle and upper strata rather than the working-class stratum. She is twice as likely to be lonely as the non-churchgoer, which indicates the churches' willingness to accept those who have profound emotional needs, but also often their inability to satisfy those needs. Such a person is likely to be widowed and old. Our own research indicates that the Protestant receiving the greatest support from religion is the late middle-aged and elderly women of business, farming or professional background who is a long-term resident of the community and is usually active in several of the town's activities and organisations.

Those who believe that church life should appeal to men as equally as women find little comfort in the situation that prevails in Smalltown Protestant churches. Although men comprise roughly half the town's population only about a quarter of Protestant church attenders are men and the great majority of those who do attend are of retirement age or close to retirement age. There is an ironical side to the high rate of absenteeism from worship of Protestant men and it is this: men hold the balance of power in church affairs. For example, in 1982 two-thirds of the members of the Anglican Church Vestry were men, as were two-thirds of the members of the Uniting Church Parish Council. Our enquiries revealed that most of these men accepted responsibility for the administration of church affairs, not out of a strong desire to see the Kingdom of God extended or because they wanted an opportunity for Christian fellowship, but because of the store they placed by family and community life. Many said that Smalltown would not be a proper town if the churches disappeared, just as it would not be a proper town without the schools or the hospital. They therefore perceived it as their responsibility as citizens to ensure that the churches survived. It is far from certain that younger Protestant men will feel the same sense of responsibility in the future; the signs are that they will not. Unlike the present male leaders who have attended worship fairly regularly throughout their lives, the younger Protestant men gave up in their teenage years or earlier.

There are also indications that the present modal group of women church supporters will not be replaced. Younger women of Protestant affiliation do not have the same sense of commitment to supporting their church and are much more committed to the notion of personal fulfilment than of church or community work. Many of them complain that Smalltown provides them with little opportunity for such fulfilment and say that the churches are no more promising in this respect than other community organisations.

The findings I have outlined in this paper tend to present a somewhat pessimistic view of the state of Protestantism in Smalltown. This should not be interpreted as meaning that Protestantism as a form of social identity in this town is in jeopardy nor is it in jeopardy as an ethical or religious orientation. Most Smalltown people view themselves as believers and most Smalltown Protestants are aware of the gulf between themselves and the Catholics of the town. What is clear, however, is that the organisational forms of Protestantism are proving unattractive and even irrelevant to an increasing number of people and unless rapidly altered may become moribund. At the present time the Salvation Army survives only because members of other churches are willing to attend its services and other activities and to support it financially. A spokesman for the Church of Christ said that his church's hope for survival rests on the unlikely event of several Church of Christ families moving to the town sometime in the future. The Anglican and Uniting church-folk do not talk in terms of final demise but many of them are worried about the steady drift from the church. If the trend of recent years persists, it is difficult to see much of a future for these churches.

My gloomy prediction of Protestantism's future in this town is not just a response to the decline in numerical support for the churches, it is much more a response to the paucity of signs, especially collective ones, of the abundant life Christianity promises to bring. Individual acts of caring occur; people make sacrifices for others; but such things are as common among non-churchgoers as churchgoers. Former Methodist and Presbyterian congregations are getting along well in the Uniting Church. However, there are few indications that even those officially commissioned to pastor (i.e. the elders) want to get involved in the problems of the active or nominal adherents of this denomination. The societal divisions that were reflected in the former Methodist and Presbyterian churches — those of age, sex and class — are present in the Uniting Church as they are in the Anglican Church, the Church of Christ and the Salvation Army. Many people who have attended these churches for years continue to attend but there is little enthusiasm about it all and, generally speaking, church members get much more excited about their sporting-club or service-club activities than they do about their church ones. The worldliness of the church still serves as a stumbling block to many nominal members, especially when they are individually canvassed to give their support to an institution which claims to exist for them but which in many cases fails to contact them between fund-raising campaigns.

The gloomy future predicted for Smalltown Protestantism is also a response to the impact lay power and apathy have on the clergy. Over the last decade the clergy have not issued many challenges to their laity. Their failure to do so is not grounds for criticism. Given the power of the laity to sanction the clergy economically and socially, the surprising thing is that they have issued as many as they have. The point is that the resistance of laymen to change and their frequent failure to show much enthusiasm for their faith have often worn the clergy down. After only a limited time in Smalltown, they usually begin to speak in more muted tones and to doubt the usefulness of ministering there or, for that matter, in other small rural communities. For a time they may comfort themselves with the thought that their ministry is part of a continuing and much wider ministry and that, therefore, the fate of the promise that Christianity brings abundant life does not rest exclusively with them. However, in the end, they usually choose to leave Smalltown sooner rather than later.

Notes

1 I am indebted to the following bodies for generous support of the research project from which this paper emanates: The R. E. Ross Trust; the Home Mission Department and the Commission for Strategic Ministries of the Methodist Church; and the Research Committee of the Schools of Social Science and Economics, La Trobe University. My thanks are especially due to Rae Ball for doing much of the interviewing for this paper and for contributing very useful ideas during the writing, Norma Cann for patiently typing and retyping my many drafts, and Brian Giddings, Eleanor Hodges and Jim Minchin for sharpening my theological perspective and for many insights into local church life.

2 For a fuller account of relationships and power in the church, see Dempsey (forthcoming), especially Ch. 9.

3 For this study in particular, data were collected through a random-sample survey of 353 households in Smalltown and the surrounding rural district; a random-sample survey of 182 elderly people; a survey of secondary school pupils; extensive interviews with clergymen and lay leaders; and attendance at worship services and at the meetings of some church organisations. For further information on Smalltown, see Dempsey, 1978, 1981 and 1982.

4 Such preoccupations are quite understandable. In assessing a minister, both the wider church organisation and local people place great store by tangible results. Present incomes, social esteem, a personal sense of well-being and future careers depend to a large extent on the number of 'seats on pews' at Sunday worship, the size of the budget and the strength of various church organisations.

5 This requires worshippers to turn and face one another and as they clasp each other's hands to say 'The peace of God be with you'.

6 Smalltown Protestants are more likely to attend a Catholic function than Catholics a Protestant one. This is presumably because the Catholic Church is opposed to its members entering a Protestant church. However, an increasing number of Catholics are avoiding the hassles this creates for them by ignoring the church's directive and attending Protestant functions.

4 Styles of ministry: Some aspects of the relationship between 'the church' and 'the world'

Norman W. H. Blaikie

One of the most basic problems which all religious groups have to face, members and leaders alike, is what stance to take towards 'the world'. This stance includes the attitudes adopted towards the dominant values of the society in which the group is located, the extent of participation in the life of that society, and the degree to which the group endeavours to influence these values and the behaviour and attitudes of the members of that society. This problem has been most frequently expressed as the problem of the relationship between 'the church' (or 'religion') and 'the world'. The task in this paper will be to examine the solutions to this problem adopted by contemporary Australian clergy and the consequences of these solutions for the relationship between the clergyman and his parishioners.

I shall begin by reviewing relevant sociological literature, followed by an analysis of data from a study of Australian clergy. Before proceeding to do this, however, it is necessary to draw attention to a major difficulty in examining this problem. Concepts such as 'religion', 'the church' and 'the world' are frequently reified by clergy, laity, theologians and even sociologists. This is exemplifed in such statements as 'the church *engages in* dialogue with the world', 'the world *takes over* some of the activities of the church', or 'the church *brings its influence to bear* on the world'. When language is used in this way an impression is created that social institutions have a life of their own apart from the human beings that create and maintain them; social reality is viewed as if it were absolute and the product of forces which are more than human.

> Reification is the apprehension of human phenomena as if they were things, that is, in non-human or possibly suprahuman terms. Another way of saying this is that reification is the apprehension of the products of human activity *as if* they were something else than human products — such as facts of nature, results of cosmic laws, or manifestations of divine will. Reification implies that man is capable of forgetting his own authorship of the human world ... It is ex-

perienced by man as a strange facticity, an *opus alienum* over which he has no control rather than the *opus proprium* of his own productive activity. (Berger and Luckmann, 1966: 82–3)

While reification may be a 'normal' phenomenon of everyday life, even necessary at that level, it mystifies what is actually happening and can be potentially alienating and dehumanising.[1] When sociologists engage in reification, they obscure the fact that it is people who act, not institutions, and that collectivities do not always act in unison nor do their members necessarily share the same views. The literature in this area is plagued with reifications; when such concepts are used in this paper they will be identified with quotation marks indicating that they are being used in an everyday rather than a strict sociological sense.

The problem

Each major world religion has solved the problem of its relationship to 'the world' in a particular way. These solutions are related to the theodicy the groups have developed in order to provide meaning for suffering and evil (Weber, 1963; Berger, 1967) and they range from attempts at political or social transformations of this world to waiting for a solution in some future life or in another world. In addition, each religion has adopted either a mystical attitude of resignation or adjustment, or an ascetic attitude of mastery. Hence, four ideal-typical solutions are possible: two other-worldly types in which activity is directed away from the world, the mystic avoiding involvement as it interferes with the pursuit of salvation, and the ascetic seeking mastery of 'the flesh' to facilitate devotional activity; and two this-worldly types, the inner-worldly mystic seeking both personal welfare through contemplation and avoidance of any commitment to worldly institutions, and the inner-worldly ascetic being obliged to transform the world in terms of ascetic ideals (Weber, 1963). Weber was primarily concerned with the economic consequences of the various religious orientations and argued that the orientation of the inner-worldly ascetic produces a practical rationalism that can have a social impact on 'the world'.

Weber used this four-way classification to structure his comparative analysis of the major world religions. It is unnecessary here to pursue this aspect of his work, but we need to note his use of the distinction with Protestantism and Catholicism. He regarded members of the former, particularly the early Calvinists, as having an inner-worldly ascetic orientation, and members of the latter as having an other-worldly ascetic orientation. While this classification of the divisions within Christianity may have been appropriate in the immediate post-reformation period, we require a more sophisticated schema for handling contemporary Protestantism. Some Protestants may have a predominantly other-worldly orientation, while those who have an inner-worldly orientation may view their involvement in 'the world' in a variety of ways of which Weber's Calvinists exhibit only one possibility.

Troeltsch, a colleague of Weber's, developed a typology of Christian religious groups based essentially on their relationship to the social order: the 'church' accepts the social order and endeavours to dominate it, while the 'sect' is opposed to the social order, renounces the idea of domination, but may endeavour to change the world by changing individuals. Troeltsch argued that both types of religious groups are legitimate outcomes of the two major elements in the Christian gospel — the demand for detachment from anything that disturbs communion with God, and the demand to bring in a new order. The latter requires some compromises with 'the world' in order to have some impact on it but this in turn has produced a continual reaction against compromise. Hence, the history of Christianity can be viewed as a struggle between those who search for compromise and those who are opposed to it (Troeltsch, 1931).

The work of Weber and Troeltsch has inspired a vast literature on the variety of social forms in which Christianity has been expressed. Numerous ethnographies of sectarian movements have been conducted (see, for example, Wilson, 1967), there have been various attempts at producing more elaborate typologies (see, for example, Yinger, 1946 and 1970; Berger, 1954; Martin, 1962; Wilson 1969), and a number of explanations have been offered for the rise and development of these sectarian movements (Niebuhr, 1929; Glock and Stark, 1965). Underlying all this literature has been the problem of how such groups deal with 'the world', an integral part of which is how these groups view the solutions to the 'church-world' issue adopted by other Christian groups.

Niebuhr (1951) has discussed the problem in terms of how individuals rather than groups cope with it. He has expressed this as the tension between Christ and culture, between the demands on an individual as a Christian and the demands on him/her as a member of a society:

> Not only pagans who have rejected Christ but believers who have accepted him find it difficult to combine his claims upon them with those of their societies. Struggle and appeasement, victory and reconciliation appear not only in the open where parties calling themselves Christian and anti-Christian meet; more frequently the debate about Christ and culture is carried on among Christians and in the hidden

depths of the individual conscience, not as the struggle and accommodation of belief with unbelief, but as the wrestling and the reconciliation of faith with faith. The Christ and culture issue was present in Paul's struggle with the Judaizers and the Hellenizers of the gospel, but also in his efforts to translate it into the forms of Greek language and thought. It appears in the early struggles of the church with the empire, with the religions and philosophies of the Mediterranean world, in its rejections and acceptances of prevailing mores, moral principles, metaphysical ideas, and forms of social organisation. The Constantinian settlement, the formulation of the great creeds, the rise of the papacy, the monastic movement, Augustinian Platonism, and Thomistic Aristotelianism, the Reformation and the Renaissance, the Revival and the Enlightenment, liberalism and the Social Gospel — these represent a few of the many chapters in the history of the enduring problem. It appears in many forms as well as in all ages; as the problem of reason and revelation, of religion and science, of natural and divine law, of state and church, of non-resistance and coercion. It has come to view in such specific studies as those of the relations of Protestantism and capitalism, of Pietism and nationalism, of Puritanism and democracy, of Catholicism and Romanism or Anglicanism, of Christianity and progress. (Niebuhr, 1951: 10)

Niebuhr has suggested five typical solutions to this problem. At one extreme there is a stance of opposition (Christ against culture) and at the other extreme there is a stance of agreement between the life and teachings of Christ and what is best in any culture (the Christ of culture). Between these extremes Niebuhr proposed three other solutions: one which attempts to establish a synthesis, a second dualist position in which the tension is accepted, and a third conversionist solution which attempts to transform a perverted human nature.

In his typology of sects, Wilson (1969) has focused on typical responses to 'the world'. *Conversionist* sects regard the world as corrupt because people are corrupt. Such sects show little if any interest in social reform, believing that if people are changed the world will change. The *revolutionary* sects reject both social reform and conversion, preferring to bring about change by force and violence if necessary. The *introversionist* sects reject reform, conversion and revolution, preferring to withdraw from 'the world' in order to achieve personal holiness. The *manipulationist* sects accept the goals of 'the world' but prefer to use different means of achieving them based on their special knowledge. In the case of the *thaumaturgical* sects, normal reality and causation are suspended in order to obtain special compensation for personal losses. The *reformist* or humanitarian sects take the role of social conscience and perform good deeds, a more introverted development than the revolutionary response. Finally, the *utopian* sects establish communal alternatives and hence partially withdraw from 'the world'. This response is more radical than the reformist, less violent than the revolutionary, and socially more constructive than the conversionist responses.

These sectarian responses to 'the world' can be found in more established traditions within Christianity as well as in movements within other religions. Some of them can be found within secular movements.

The problem of what kind of stance to take towards the world has become critical for Roman Catholics in recent years, particularly as the result of the deliberations of Vatican Council II. In an attempt to understand the growing diversity of stances in contemporary American Catholicism Neal (1970 and 1971) has proposed a pre-Vatican and a post-Vatican typology of orientations to 'the world'. The pre-Vatican position is an other-worldly orientation in which religious experience requires a withdrawal from involvement in the world with the prospect of salvation in the after-life. The post-Vatican position is concerned with transforming the world by protesting against injustice and living as pilgrims in the service of one's neighbour (Neal, 1971: 154). With samples of priests, women in contemplative orders and lay men and women, Neal found a high degree of polarisation around these orientations. This was no doubt due to both the newness of the post-Vatican orientation and the intensity with which religious groups in the USA confronted social issues in the late 1960s and 1970s.

Adopting an orientation towards the world is not simply a matter of making a choice between a range of available alternatives; it has to be consistent with a theological position and entails strategies for surviving in a religiously pluralistic situation. It is possible to view religious groups as marketing a commodity to a population of un-coerced consumers. In such a situation religious collectivities have two ideal-typical options — accommodation and defence. They can endeavour to make religion 'relevant' to the moral and therapeutic needs of the consumer in his private life, or they can continue in the 'traditional' way in the hope that the 'old customers' will maintain their 'product loyalty' (Berger, 1967: 144).

> The pluralistic situation presents the religious institutions with two ideal-typical options. They can either accommodate themselves to the situation, play the pluralistic game of religious free enterprise, and come to terms as best they can with the plausibility problem by modifying their product in accordance with consumer demands. Or they can refuse to accommodate themselves, entrench themselves, behind whatever socio-religious structures they can maintain or construct, and continue to profess the old objectivities as much as possible as if

nothing had happened. Obviously there are various intermediate possibilities between these two ideal-typical options, with varying degrees of accommodation and intransigence. Both ideal-typical options have problems on the level of theory as well as on the level of 'social engineering'. (Berger, 1967: 152–3)

The defensive option is best achieved by establishing a sub-society in which opportunities are provided for the conversations necessary to maintain this world-view and protection against pluralistic competition can be provided for its members. The accommodative option usually involves attempts to translate 'traditional' doctrines into terms that are more acceptable to 'the world', that is, to make religion *relevant*. Hence, there is a strong tendency to adopt a this-worldly orientation. Both options encounter practical and theoretical difficulties: for the defensive option it is knowing just how strong are the defences; for the accommodative option it is the built-in lapse of plausibility from within (Berger, 1967 and 1969).

Just why a religious collectivity adopts a particular stance is a complex question. In general, we can view these processes as an on-going dialectic in which collectivities that are faced with the problem of making sense of their existence in a changing situation build or borrow a system of meaning to meet their perceived needs, in particular, to cope with anomic experiences. This system of meaning will then react back on the 'inhabitants', restructuring their needs and subjective experiences.

Hence, a religious collectivity's orientation towards 'the world' can be seen as one of a number of possible strategies for survival in a pluralistic situation. The dilemma is one of maintaining the plausibility of a religious world view in the face of competition from other religious and secular definitions of reality.

Diversity of orientations

Among other things, then, the sociological literature which has focused on this problem of the orientation towards 'the world' has provided a basis for an understanding of the diversity to be found within Christianity, particularly within Protestantism. However, all attempts to categorise this diversity in orientations must be treated with some caution for two basic reasons.

First, in examining contemporary religious groups in Australia, whether as denominations or local congregations, no assumptions should be made about intra-group homogeneity in orientation. Some religious collectivities may be able to maintain a relatively homogeneous orientation if they are small and localised, if the members are socially homogeneous, and if there is a high level of involvement and commitment which makes possible the maintenance of common goals and a common identity. However, where groups are large because of their establishment position in a society or have grown in size through effective proselytising, where they include or have recruited members with diverse social backgrounds, where the involvement of members is generally low, where some subgroups have accommodated to secular values, diversity of orientations can be expected to be present. In addition, where a denomination has undergone schisms for one or more of the above reasons, and has subsequently reunited for reasons other than the fact that the subgroups share similar theologies, theological differences will be perpetuated. In short, what is being suggested here is that the major denominations, as well as most local congregations, will contain subgroups which may more or less share a dominant orientation, thus creating intra-group heterogeneity.

The second qualification concerns the extent to which any group or individual holds a 'pure' orientation towards 'the world'; combinations of these orientations are possible. For example, elements of the reformist response may be held by those whose dominant response is conversionist.[2]

The existence of intra-denominational diversity raises a number of questions. How is it possible for differences in orientation to coexist within a religious collectivity? What are the consequences for the parish clergyman? The first question, among other things, raises the issue of what constitutes a religious group. It would appear that denominations as we know them in Australia must be regarded as multi-groups rather than single groups. The second question will be taken up later.

Orientations of Australian clergy

How do Australian clergy resolve the problem outlined above? In what ways are clergy differentiated in terms of the solution they adopt? What consequence does this have for their dealings with their parishioners?

The data on which the discussion of these questions is based come from a mail questionnaire study which included *all* parish clergy in the major Protestant denominations in the state of Victoria. The questionnaires were distributed over an eight-month period commencing late November 1969, with an overall response rate of 87 per cent. This produced a total of 943 respondents: Anglican, n = 299; Methodist, n = 230; Presbyterian, n = 223; Baptist, n = 96; Church of Christ, n = 71; and Congregational, n = 24. The response rate ranged from 81 per cent for Anglicans to 92 per cent for the Church of Christ (see Blaikie, 1974 and 1979).[3]

The questionnaire covered a wide range of issues including goal and role priorities,[4] area in which ministry is concentrated, views of what constitutes a successful ministry, conflict with significant others over role priorities, frustration associated with expectations for role performance, view of secular world views, and theological position. These have been elaborated and the relationship between them discussed elsewhere (Blaikie, 1974 and 1979). Our particular interest here is with the styles of ministry which clergy adopt and with associated characteristics and consequences.

Styles of ministry
Nine styles of ministry emerged from a detailed examination of a wide range of information covering the first three issues above (goal and role priorities, area of concentration and view of success) together with answers to open-ended questions inviting reasons for role priorities and for area of concentration of ministry. All but four respondents have been able to be identified with one of the styles of ministry. The following descriptions, taken from Blaikie (1979: 147-9), outline the characteristics of each style:

1. *Reaper* or *Fisherman*. There are a number of well-used Biblical images associated with this style of ministry; it includes the idea of bringing in the harvest, of being a fisher of men or of saving souls. The primary aim for those who adopt this style of ministry is to fill the barn or the nets, to increase the size of the flock, or in less figurative terms, to get people to commit themselves to Christ. Nineteen per cent of clergy saw their ministry primarily in these terms.

2. *Teacher*. These clergy are concerned with proclaiming 'the gospel' or 'the word' and with building people up in 'the faith'. They do not see themselves as evangelists but give top priority to the goal of *convert*. They see themselves as teaching both the faithful and the marginal members with the aim of increasing their depth of spiritual understanding. Eighteen per cent have adopted this style.

3. *Enabler*. This style of ministry is centred on a leadership relationship with 'the faithful'. These clergy wish to 'train the disciples', 'feed the workers' or 'enable the servants of God' to 'advance the Kingdom'. In contrast to the 'Reaper', the 'Enabler' trains others to evangelize rather than seeing himself in that role. This style was adopted by 19 per cent of clergy.

   Hence, the first three styles of ministry all have a strong evangelical emphasis but differ in significant ways. More than half the clergy (56 per cent) have adopted one of these styles.

4. *Priest*. A relatively small number of clergy (5 per cent) have

adopted a priestly style of ministry. There are a number of variations around this: being God's representative; mediating between men and God; bringing the needs of man before God; and leading the Christian community in worship. Those who have adopted this style see themselves as being in a unique position and as undertaking a particular set of activities which they alone, as a result of their ordination, are able to perform. In short, they are the priest of the people of God.

5. *Shepherd*. In the next two styles of ministry the role of *pastor* is dominant. The 'Shepherd' is essentially concerned with caring for 'the flock' and the 'lost sheep', but in the case of the latter, not in an evangelical sense. The concept of care is regarded in very broad terms and might best be described as a concern for people's (but mainly members) general well-being. This style was adopted by 18 per cent of clergy.

6. *Team Captain*. In a somewhat similar way to that of 'Enabler', some clergy's interest in pastoral care is in training or strengthening a 'core group' to undertake this work in the parish. This is not to suggest that the clergyman does not engage in pastoral care himself but his style of ministry is essentially to train others to do this, and as well, to train them to have some 'influence'. This latter concept was rarely defined, and appears to include a wide range of possibilities, but it does not include the evangelical concern of the 'Enabler'. Six per cent of clergy regarded themselves as the captain of a small caring team.

7. *Interpreter*. A further 6 per cent of clergy have adopted a style of ministry with a strong prophetic emphasis. Their basic concern is to provide people with, or help people find, some meaning for life. They do this by interpreting 'the word' or 'the will of God' for modern society. There is an element of teaching involved in this style, although with contemporary secular issues rather than religious doctrine. For some, the aim is to produce 'informed Christians'; people with an understanding of, and a concern for, the world around them; people who can cope with their rapidly changing social circumstances.

8. *Catalyst*. This style of ministry shares something in common with the 'Enabler' and the 'Team Captain', but in this case, the emphasis is on the community. These clergy seek to train and encourage their parishioners to engage in social service activities which meet the needs of people in their community, and in social action that is seen to be necessary to have these needs adequately met. Eight per cent have adopted this style.

9. *Activist*. This final style of ministry extends the concerns of the 'Catalyst' but with much more emphasis on bringing about social change. However, in this case the clergyman sees himself as undertaking this activity essentially on his own. His identification with his parish appears to be minimal; his primary concern is for 'the world'. Very few clergy (1 per cent) have actually adopted this approach.

It is clear that clergy relate to 'the world' in quite different ways. While each denomination includes clergy with a variety of styles of ministry, particular styles tend to predominate in particular denominations (see Table 4.1).[5] The 'Reaper' style is over-represented amongst Baptist and Church of Christ clergy, with Methodists well represented. The 'Teacher' and 'Enabler' styles are also over-represented amongst Baptists but these styles of ministry are proportionately represented in all other denominations, with the exception of the 'Teacher' style amongst Methodists. It is only amongst Anglicans that the 'Priest' style is over-represented but the 'Shepherd' style is also over-represented in this denomination and to a lesser extent amongst Methodists. The 'Team Captain' style of ministry is proportionately represented amongst Anglicans and is over-represented amongst Methodists. With some minor variations, the three 'worldly' styles, 'Interpreter', 'Catalyst' and 'Activist', are over-represented amongst Presbyterian, Methodist and Congregational clergy. A striking feature of this analysis is the range of styles to be found in the large denominations and the limited range of styles of Baptist and Church of Christ clergy.

In order to pursue further the view clergy have of the relationship between 'the church' and 'the world' the styles of ministry were compared with the view clergy have of 'the church'. Three major views of 'the church' were identified. The first has been designated as the *rescue ship* view in which 'the world' is seen to be evil, corrupting and precarious, and 'the church' a place of refuge, security and hope; people are to be taken out of, and kept apart from, 'the raging storm and the fiery tempest'. The emphasis is essentially other-worldly. In the polar opposite view, 'the church' is the *leaven in the lump*, the necessary ingredient to make 'the world' a better, more human place. In this case the emphasis is this-worldly. Between these two, 'the church' is seen to be coincident with 'the world' in a relationship of acceptance and harmony. In this case 'the church' is viewed as being *passive* and 'the world' as a wholesome place; it is God's Kingdom in which He is working out His purposes in His own good time. While 'the church' is still a separate institution it performs important functions for society and individuals and adopts an essentially accommodated position. It was necessary to establish a fourth residual, or *mixed*, category to include clergy whose views contained elements of all or some of the other three. Forty per cent of clergy held the *rescue ship* view, 17 per cent the *leaven in the lump* view, 22 per cent the *passive* view, and the remaining 21 per cent were in the *mixed* category. Table 4.1 also reports the relationship between style of ministry and view of 'the church'. The close association clearly confirms the fact that these

Table 4.1 *Style of ministry by denomination, view of 'the church' and view of secular world views* (based on Blaikie, 1979: 150 and 156) (%)

Denomination	Style of ministry									
	Reaper	Teacher	Enabler	Priest	Shepherd	Captain	Interpr.	Catalyst	Activist	Total
Baptist	18	15	13	2	4	5	4	—	—	10
Ch. of Christ	15	9	8	—	6	5	3	1	—	8
Anglican	23	31	28	86	42	33	22	15	11	32
Presbyterian	17	25	24	5	20	20	38	47	22	24
Methodist	26	16	25	5	26	31	31	32	56	24
Congregational	*	4	2	2	2	6	4	4	11	3
Total	100	100	100	100	100	100	101	99	100	100
N	180	172	180	43	173	55	55	72	9	939
										(r = 0.24; C/L = 0.42)
View of 'the church'										
Rescue ship	87	53	50	12	15	11	—	—	—	40
Mixed	9	22	27	16	29	27	19	14	—	21
Passive	3	23	14	60	43	20	36	6	—	22
Leaven in lump	1	2	9	12	13	42	45	80	100	17
										(N = 933; r = 0.66; C/L = 0.71)
View of secular world views										
Anti-secular	61	34	41	31	18	18	9	1	—	32
Pro-secular	13	24	23	38	42	55	65	81	56	35
										(N = 926; r = 0.45; C/L = 0.49)

* % less than 1.

styles of ministry reflect some dominant orientations to 'the world'.

Another aspect of this orientation to 'the world' which is associated with style of ministry is the view held of secular world views, in particular, science and humanism. On the basis of the scores produced by the responses to the five items that form this index,[6] three categories have been established ranging from an anti-secular to a pro-secular position. While not as strong as the relationship just examined, the pattern is consistent with it. (See Table 4.1. To simplify the presentation only the two extreme positions are included.) Clergy who adopt 'conservative' styles of ministry are likely to hold an anti-secular position, while those who adopt one of the 'radical' or 'worldly' styles are likely to hold a pro-secular position.

Characteristics

Given the high degree of consistency between the way clergy view 'the world' and the way they endeavour to conduct their ministry, do clergy who adopt a particular style of ministry share any characteristics which differentiate them from other clergy? It is clear from Table 4.2 that there is a close association between style of ministry and theological position.[7] Clergy who adopt the three most 'conservative' styles are predominantly *evangelical*, while those who adopt the three most 'radical' styles are almost entirely *liberal*. Hence, the way clergy relate to the world through their ministry is highly consistent with their basic beliefs.

A number of studies in the USA have supported the idea that the political views and actions of clergy are closely associated with their theological position, that is, religious and political ideologies tend to be consistent (see particularly Johnson, 1966; Hadden, 1969; Stark *et al.*, 1971; Nelsen *et al.*, 1973; Jeffries and Tygart, 1974; Quinley, 1974).[8] This also appears to be the case for Australian clergy, especially for the various styles of ministry. There is a strong tendency for those clergy who hold the 'Reaper', 'Teacher' and 'Priest' styles to support the Liberal/National Country/Democratic Labor parties and for those who hold the styles from 'Team Captain' to 'Activist' to support the Australian Labor Party (See Table 4.2). Hence, clergy who adopt 'conservative' styles of ministry are also likely to be theologically and politically conservative. Similarly, clergy who adopt a 'radical' style of ministry are also likely to be theologically and politically radical, or at least (small '1') liberal.

There are two other characteristics worth noting. Clergy who adopt one of the 'radical' styles tend to be younger and to have received at least some university education, while those who adopt one of the 'conservative' styles tend to be older and not to have

Table 4.2 *Style of ministry by theological position, political preference, age and extent of university education* (based on Blaikie; 1979: 152 and 156) (%)

	Style of ministry									
	Reaper	Teacher	Enabler	Priest	Shepherd	Captain	Interpr.	Catalyst	Activist	Total
Theological position										
Evangelical	88	65	63	19	22	10	2	5	—	47
Conservative	9	27	28	74	52	35	13	17	—	29
Liberal	3	8	9	7	26	55	85	78	100	24
							(N = 929; r = 0.68; C/L = 0.71)			
Political preference										
Liberal etc.	72	70	54	63	52	26	25	6	22	52
Labor	28	30	46	37	48	74	75	94	78	48
							(N = 848; r = 0.38; C/L = 0.46)			
Age										
40 and over	77	72	67	79	71	64	53	42	11	68
Under 40	23	28	33	21	29	36	47	58	89	32
							(N = 938; r = 0.21; C/L = 0.32)			
University education										
No	71	59	50	60	55	44	20	13	—	52
Yes	29	41	50	40	45	56	80	87	100	48
							(N = 931; r = 0.28; C/L = 0.38)			

been to university.[9] However, these relationships are all weaker than those discussed thus far. Space does not permit the reporting of the analysis of the interrelationship amongst these variables but such an analysis suggests that the clergyman's theological position, however it is acquired, has the strongest and most independent influence on his orientation to 'the world' and hence the style of ministry he adopts (see Blaikie, 1979). This is supported by studies in the USA. For example, Quinley (1974: 69) has argued:

> It appears from our data, as well as from our understanding of Protestantism, that the central component of the ministerial belief system is the clergy's religious commitments — the degree to which they adhere to the modernist or the traditionalist religious beliefs. A Protestant minister's stand on questions of religious authority, salvation, and other-worldliness carries direct implications for his ethical and political beliefs as well. It leads him to develop different ethical and political concerns and to define his clerical role in quite different ways.

Consequences

One of the basic problems with which many clergy have to deal, particularly those who are concerned with doing something about social injustices, is the conflict they encounter as the result of the conservative views of the ministry held by their parishioners and church authorities. Numerous studies in the USA have shown that on a whole range of issues, theological, ethical and political, church members are consistently more conservative than clergy (see for example, Glock and Ringer, 1956; Campbell and Pettigrew, 1959; Glock and Stark, 1965; Glock *et al.*, 1967; Hadden, 1969; and Quinley, 1974). This was particularly evident during the civil rights struggles of the 1950s and 1960s. Hadden (1969: 146) has summarised the position as follows:

> The large majority [of church members] indicate that they believe that concern for others is a good indicator of one's religiousness. Similarly, a large majority assent to the abstract idea that clergy should speak out as the moral conscience of this country. Yet in their attitudes towards the civil rights movement and its leadership, and in their feeling about clergy involvement in civil rights, they seem in larger part to contradict these general beliefs about the role of religion and the clergy in the achievement of a moral and just society. This is a perplexing and troublesome dilemma.

Quinley's work has suggested a similar situation with regard to the Vietnam war in the late 1960s and this seems to have had its parallels in Australia. A study of Protestant beliefs and attitudes in South Australia (Bodycomb, 1978) has documented the fact that

Protestant clergy in Australia are far more liberal in their outlook than their parishioners.[10]

Clergy in the study certainly considered that those groups and individuals who have the greatest opportunity to exercise some control over them, or to exert pressure on them (e.g. 'church authorities', 'conservative/active/average members' and 'wife and family'), all place very low priority on clergy being involved in activities of social reform (see Blaikie, 1974 and 1979). Hence, we would expect that clergy who adopt one of the 'radical' styles of ministry would encounter more difficulties in this regard than those who adopt a 'conservative' style. This turns out to be the case in terms of the measures of 'frustration' and 'conflict'.[11] It is also supported by two other measures which identify potential areas of conflict; the extent to which clergy believe their goal priorities are shared by their parishioners and their theological position is shared by various groups of significant others.[12] (See Table 4.3. The higher the score the greater the level of actual or potential frustration and conflict.) There is little doubt that clergy who adopt the 'Reaper' style of ministry experience the lowest level, and those few who adopt the 'Activist' style experience the highest level of frustration and conflict. However, the level is fairly consistent and moderately low for the styles from 'Teacher' to 'Team Captain'.

It would appear that clergy who provide people with what they want or need, be it salvation, spiritual nurture, the sacraments or pastoral care, have an easier time than clergy whose orientation is towards, and whose style of ministry concentrates on, 'the world'. This is not to suggest that no church members have a this-worldly orientation, only that those few who do are likely to be less active and less influential than the majority of church members who want their 'religious' or personal needs catered for ahead of, or to the exclusion of, them or their clergy being involved in social issues.

Summary and conclusions

Australian Protestant clergy have resolved, in a few basic ways, the problem of what kind of orientation to take towards 'the world' and these are reflected in their views of 'the church' and in the styles of ministry they have adopted. These views and styles are closely related to their theological position and are also reflected in their political preferences, clearly indicating a high level of consistency between religious and political ideologies. There is a strong tendency for younger and better educated clergy to adopt a more 'radical'

Table 4.3 *Style of ministry by frustration, conflict, goals shared and theological orientation shared* (based on Blaikie, 1979: 175 and 178) (mean scores)

| | Style of ministry | | | | | | | | | | | |
	Reaper	Teacher	Enabler	Priest	Shepherd	Captain	Interpr.	Catalyst	Activist	Total	r	C/L
Role frustration	34	40	36	38	42	41	41	49	62	39	0.20	0.38
Preaching conflict	46	56	50	54	60	58	59	66	79	55	0.19	0.31
Goals shared	38	45	44	39	46	48	59	62	83	46	0.20	0.31
Theological orientation shared	35	38	37	40	39	44	53	51	65	40	0.34	0.43
Mean	38	45	42	43	47	48	53	57	72	45		

style of ministry and for the older and less well educated to adopt a 'conservative' style.

The more a clergyman sees his role in this-worldly rather than other-worldly terms the more likely he is to experience difficulties in his dealings with his parishioners; he fails to provide most of them with what they appear to want or need and he endeavours to encourage them to hold attitudes, and engage in actions, which are inconsistent with their beliefs and view of 'the church'. The pressure on the more 'radical' clergy is to conform to the needs, expectations or demands of his parishioners, that is, to orient his activities away from 'the world' and towards 'the church', or at least the local parish. To do so requires him to either compromise his theological position and view of 'the church' and adopt a more 'conservative' style of ministry, or to do the latter but somehow compartmentalise his style from his beliefs and views. There is some evidence to support this latter case in the fact that theological *liberals* are more likely to hold a *rescue ship* view of 'the church' and adopt a 'conservative' style of ministry than theological *evangelicals* are likely to hold a *leaven in the lump* view of 'the church' and adopt a 'radical' style of ministry.

Notes

1 See Berger and Pullberg (1965) and Berger (1967: 90) for a discussion of reification and its consequences.

2 Yinger (1970) included this possibility in his treatment of sectarian orientations when he suggested that there are three typical responses — acceptance, aggression and avoidance — two of which may be held in tension. For example, a conversionist response combines acceptance and aggression, an adventist response combines aggression and avoidance, and a pentecostal sect combines avoidance and acceptance.

3 The data were gathered before the Uniting Church was formed. For an analysis of continuing Presbyterians and Uniting Church clergy see Blaikie (1979: 230–2).

4 Goal priorities were established from the rank ordering of eight goals: *convert* (to get people to accept Christ as Saviour and Lord); *give meaning* (to give purpose and direction to life); *educate* (in Christian doctrines and beliefs); *worship* (provide opportunity for public worship); *care* (provide for the physical and material needs of people); *fellowship* (through social activities); *challenge* (social evils and injustices); *control* (the behaviour and morals of people by ensuring Christian ethics and values are generally accepted). The overall rank order from high to low is as listed here. Similarly, role priorities were established from eight occupational activites: *pastor* (visiting, counselling); *preacher* (delivering sermons, expounding the word of God); *priest* (conducting worship,

administering the sacraments); *educator* (teaching, instructing, leading study groups); *evangelist* (converting others to the faith); *scholar* (reading, studying, writing); *organiser* (organising and supervising the work of the parish); *social reformer* (involved directly in attacking social injustices). Again, the overall rank order of these roles is as listed.

5 Two measures of association have been used, the Pearson coefficient (r) and the contingency coefficient corrected for its upper limit which is dependent on the number of cells in a table (C/L). Some of the measures do not meet all the requirements for 'r' but its use in these cases leads only to a slightly conservative value. This coefficient indicates the extent to which two measures are linearly associated, while 'C/L' reflects any form of association. The values for the latter are generally higher than the former, especially where a relationship is not strictly linear. As the data come from a population no tests of significance are necessary.

6 Responses to five items have been used to form an index of the extent to which clergy were prepared to accept secular world views such as those contained within the natural and social sciences and humanism. They were asked to indicate the extent to which they considered there to be conflict between:

The church and the world;

Biblical scholarship and the scientific method; and,

Christianity and humanism.

Also, the extent to which they believed 'the church' should be prepared to accept scientific explanations for the creation of the universe. The fifth item concerned the degree to which they considered the modern theologican should take notice of other academic disciplines, e.g. philosophy, psychology and sociology. The scoring procedure produced a nine-point index; only the two extreme categories are used here, 'anti-secular' and 'pro-secular'.

7 Clergy were presented with a set of nine theological labels with the opportunity of adding others. They were asked to indicate which one best represented their theological position and which of the others would also be appropriate. The method used follows closely that used by Moberg (1969). These responses have been reduced to five categories, strongly evangelical (30 per cent), moderately evangelical (17 per cent), conservative (29 per cent), liberal (18 per cent) and radical (6 per cent). For the present purposes these have been further reduced to three by combining the first two and the last two — *evangelical, conservative* and *liberal*. Theological position has also been assessed in terms of the acceptance or rejection of six statements representing traditional doctrines: Christ rose bodily; Jesus was born of a virgin; A miracle is a divine intervention; Man is predestined; The creation study is an allegory; and, Adam was an historical figure. The resulting Guttman scale (referred to as 'theological orientation') shows a close association with the above measure of theological position (r = 0.64; C/L = 0.68). It is similar to indices used by Stark *et al.* (1971) and Quinley (1974) in their studies of clergy. See Blaikie (1974 and 1979) for further details and analysis using this scale.

8 For a critique of some aspects of this work see Blaikie (1976).

9 Age and extent of university education are, of course, also associated with theological position, view of secular world views and view of 'the church' in a similar way to style of ministry. Age shows a marginally closer relationship with style of ministry than with the other variables.

10 The question of why church members are conservative has received only limited systematic attention. See Blaikie (1972) for a review and critique of some of the relevant literature.

11 For each of the eight roles clergy were asked to indicate the extent to which they are frustrated in performing these activities by what others expect of them. They were also asked to indicate the extent to which they experienced conflict in their preaching between what they think people *want* to hear and what they believe people *need* to hear. These two measures are referred to as 'role frustration' and 'preaching conflict', respectively. The response categories have been weighted in such a way that each clergyman received a score for each within the possible range of zero to 100. Mean scores for subgroups have also been calculated within the same range (see Table 4.3).

12 After asking clergy to rank the eight goals they were also asked to indicate whether they considered the members of their parish/congregation shared their ordering of the goals. The three response categories — Yes, Not sure or Some do, Some don't, and No — have been weighted to produce a possible range of scores from zero to 100, a low score indicating shared goal priorities and a high score a lack of sharing. Clergy were also asked to indicate the degree to which they considered their theological orientation is shared by clergy in their own denomination, by lay men and women in their parish/congregation, and by lay men and women in their denomination. The responses, with reference to all three groups, have been combined to produce a similar range of scores to those for 'frustration', 'conflict' and 'goals shared'. A low score indicates a high degree of sharing, and vice versa. In both cases, goals shared and theological orientation shared, clergy were not asked whether a low degree of sharing caused them any concern. However, both are potential sources of frustration and conflict and the distribution of scores on them, by style of ministry, is similar to that for 'frustration' and 'conflict' (see Table 4.3).

5   Some aspects of organisational efficacy in Australian churches

Edwin Dowdy and Gillian Lupton

Churches are known to have quite varying aims, such as upholding the exclusive validity of a sacred script and associated tradition, or 'witnessing to the Word of God', or gaining converts. It is also recognised that a particular church and its sub-systems may have aims which are more-or-less incompatible with each other (O'Dea, 1966: 91–4). Another, and probably no less important, difficulty arises when church officials mistakenly assume that their traditional arrangements and techniques remain adequate in a changing world. There must be some implication for effectiveness if, for instance, a substantial part of the population thinks that a church's activities are inappropriate to its image.

We should like to present and interpret some data relevant to Australian churches seen as social organisations. Here we are primarily interested in characteristics which appear to weaken them. Previously we alluded to some professional problems of the clergy, for instance ideological difficulties, uncertain criteria of accountability, and varied quality of performance in the discharge of a wide range of social and individual functions (Dowdy and Lupton, 1976). Here we wish to focus attention on organisational aspects which (a) seem to impair the performance desired by the churches; and (b) seem amenable, at least in part, to possible counter-measures undertaken by the churches themselves.

The information presented stems from research carried out over several years in New South Wales and Queensland, using a variety of samples.[1] To understand the significance of institutionalised religion in Australian society, we considered it important to seek the views of participants and non-participants. Thus we identified five categories and sampled them as follows:

1 *Ordained ministers, priests, pastors*:   the professionals and continuing participants. Of these we sampled 519 in Queensland and 533 in New South Wales. Names were obtained from the most recent denominational lists available, and were sampled randomly after

stratfying the sample by denomination to ensure adequate representation of smaller groups. The denominations represented were Roman Catholic, Anglican, Presbyterian, Methodist, Congregational, Baptist, Church of Christ, Lutheran and Salvation Army. The samples were drawn shortly before the joining of the Presbyterian, Methodist and Congregational groups to form the Uniting Church. In analysis of the data, we have sometimes combined the data from three and referred to them by the later name.

2 *Trainees for the ministry or priesthood*: the future professionals. Our samples of trainees consisted of 165 in Queensland, 162 in New South Wales, and 28 Lutherans from South Australia (analysed with the New South Wales sample). All these students were sampled from college lists.

3 *The involved laity*: the continuing non-professional participants. We sampled 366 of these people in Queensland, but obtaining a representative sample was extraordinarily difficult, as we had to depend on ministers to provide lists of names, and thus had little control over criteria of choice. Consequently we did not replicate this sample in New South Wales.

4 *The general public*: the audience of institutionalised religion, some participants, some apathetic, some totally uninvolved or antagonistic. Of these, a cluster sample of 568 was interviewed, covering New South Wales and non-metropolitan Queensland.

5 *The discontinuants*: the ex-professionals, whether from the ranks of students or ordained clergy. The views of those who had committed themselves to the church and then changed their minds seemed to us particularly fascinating. No attempt was made to sample randomly in this category, but by word of mouth we obtained interviews with 26 former students and 15 former ministers, all resident in or near Brisbane.

From these five categories we hoped to obtain a range of comparative data which should throw some light on the problems of the churches.

In this discussion the term 'church' signifies a recognised denomination such as the Uniting Church or Roman Catholic Church. A church is a system containing processual sub-systems (not static entities) and their interrelationships. Some of these sub-systems comprise the role-sets of ordained officials, of ancillary staff, and of the congregation, training programmes for future officials, enunciatory activities (e.g. preaching, use of radio and television messages), indoctrination programmes for the young, money-raising, and pastoral activities.

The environment of a church includes other organisations, in-

cluding other churches. A church co-operates with and also com-
petes with those other organisations; it grows or wanes in strength.
The ways in which a church may operate, its available strategies, are
largely controlled by the circumstance that churches are primarily
'normative' organisations. This means that control over their own
officials depends primarily upon invoking values, rather than upon
some other technique such as remuneration.

> Normative organizations are organizations in which normative power
> is the major source of control over most lower participants, whose
> orientation to the organization is characterized by high commitment.
> Compliance in normative organizations rests principally on internaliza-
> tion of directives accepted as legitimate. Leadership, rituals, manipula-
> tion of social and prestige symbols, and resocialization are among the
> more important techniques of control used. (Etzioni, 1964: 40)

For the purpose of this discussion we propose to extend Etzioni's
consideration of 'lower participants' in two ways. First, we wish to
include 'higher' participants, for it seems appropriate particularly in
religious organisations to recognise that higher-ranking officials are
likely to be normatively committed at least as much as their subordinates. Secondly, we regard as participants the congregation and
also any members of the population who respond in some positive
way to the church's messages or image. The church must be seen to
be operating in a normative mode, not, for instance, in the mode of
a Mafia organisation. This limitation of available strategies imposes
structural conditions to which we shall return later; first, another
sort of limitation should be noted.

Using normative methods both in intra-church and extra-church
activities, Australian churches are promulgating messages about im-
puted supernatural beings and realms, and striving for attention and
assent within various audiences throughout the land. Each denomination takes the entire continent as its field. This is opposite
to the procedure of some more specialised North American churches
which have been successful in terms of increased membership, assets
and cash flow. They have erected a cocoon of infrastructure around
the flock (e.g. the Mormons, the Christian Reformed Church). In
this type, 'communal', non-official sanctions (e.g. disapproval of
dress or social behaviour) reinforce the 'associational', ritual practices to create a very powerful insulation effect.[2] But in the
historical and social situations of Australian denominations which
we are analysing here, such strategies would be considered inappropriate, and hence are not available.

The churches, then, must work in a normative manner and on
a continental scope, and their tasks are challenging. Church

spokespersons make pronouncements on morality, on alleged life after death, on the supposed operations and wishes of 'the Father, Son, and Holy Spirit', and on numerous other matters which are, to say the least, incongruent with the temper of a secularised age. The propositions and admonitions come in rather abstract language, in order to appeal to the widest possible audience. In so far as the churches have something to say which they feel is unique, as well as most important, this is all as it should be — a normal situation for an abnormal message. That the 'world' is 'materialist' does not necessarily mean that the world wishes to ignore the message, or that the message should be altered in content or made more palatable in form. Perhaps its very difference from the world might make the message interesting. It must also be recognised that any change in that message would be as likely to alienate present adherents as to attract new ones.

However, when we look at the evidence from our research, we find anomalies. For instance, whereas the clergy appear to consider that the message is adequately promulgated by traditional methods such as preaching and evangelism, the general population seems to expect that churches should take a more active part in the solution of social problems, and that the clergy should show sympathy and tolerance rather than godliness. In plain language, in the view of the clergy, what the church is doing and what it should be doing *may be* two different things and in the view of the public what the church is doing and what it should be doing *are* two different things; but what the clergy and the public believes the changes should be, are *also* two different things.

The clergy is 'out of touch' with the population. Demographic and socioeconomic information obtained about them in our research may go part of the way to explaining this. The average age of the ministers was higher than that of the adult population, with implied problems of belief and communication. Also, obviously, almost all were male, while half the population is female. The clergy also tended to have higher socioeconomic backgrounds (father's occupation, their own education level) than the lay public. Thus there are *age, sex* and *status* differences. We noted, however, that regular chuchgoers[3] and involved laity in our samples tended to be over 30, relatively well-educated, and high on the socioeconomic scale, and therefore in these respects more like the ministers than most of the population. It is therefore not surprising to find that this group of people shared views similar to those of the clergy about many church activities and problems.

In fact, as to what the churches are doing at present, there is close correspondence between the perceptions of the clergy and the general population. Both groups agree that formal services of worship, spreading the teachings of Christ, and raising money, are the activities most emphasised by the churches. Table 5.1 gives comparisons of the most highly ranked items for the three largest clergy groups in New South Wales and Queensland, and for the population sample.[4] It will be noticed that for the first three items the correspondence is almost absolute across all categories.

However, when we compare the views of population and clergy on what the church *should* be doing, clear divergence between those two categories becomes apparent. Table 5.2 shows that although there are some denominational differences among the clergy, generally they would up-grade such activities as 'gaining converts', thus suggesting a more evangelistically oriented church. The public, again with minor differences by denomination, age, education and so on, generally put little stress on such activities, but would like to see the churches more active in providing social welfare agencies, providing emotional support to the congregation, and generally taking a more active part in social problems. These three are most strongly emphasised by almost all sections of the public, and particularly those under 25. In contrast, the involved laity sample stress spreading the teachings of Christ, and converting people, followed by providing emotional support: they took a 'partly-socialised minister's' position.

Another view of church activities was obtained from the small sample of discontinuants. There was criticism of church structure (from eleven ex-students and six ex-ministers) to the effect that it is rigid, authoritarian, parochial, unresponsive to change, and out of touch with ministers and laity. Three ex-students and three ex-ministers went so far as to consider the churches unchristian, morally inadequate, unfulfilling, or denying the humanity of man.

In addition, it appears that the discontinuant students perceived the *minister's* activities (rather than those of the church as a whole) to be primarily those of organisation, indoctrination, and administration — oriented to activities of committee work, raising money, religious education, leading public worship, and attending local functions. For them, however, the minister's work *should* be oriented rather to supportive individual contact and spiritual self-development — counselling, pastoral work, providing an example of the Christian way of life, and private prayer.

A rather similar discrepancy is apparent for the discontinuant ministers. They also saw the actual role as one of indoctrination and organisation (public worship, religious education, raising money, and retaining/increasing the congregation) but would have liked it to

Table 5.1 *Ranking of 'actual' church activities by clergy and the public*

'Most emphasised' activity	NSW ministers			Qld ministers			Public
	RC	Ang.	Uniting	RC	Ang.	Uniting	
Providing formal services of worship	1	1	1	1	1	1	1.5
Propagating teachings of Christ	2	2	2	2	3	3	3
Raising money	3	3	3	4	2	2	1.5
Missionary activities	4	6	6	3	4	6	7
Providing emotional support to congregation	5	4	4	8	5	5	6
Providing social welfare agencies	6	5	5	6	6	4	4

Table 5.2 *Ranking of 'ideal' church activities by clergy and the public*

'Most important' activity	NSW ministers			Qld ministers			Public
	RC	Ang.	Uniting	RC	Ang.	Uniting	
Propagating teachings of Christ	1	1	1	1	1	1	4
Providing formal services of worship	2	2	2	2	4	4.5	5
Providing emotional support to congregation	3	3.5	3.5	7	7.5	4.5	3
Missionary activities	4	5	5	3	2	3	8.5
Providing social welfare agencies	5	7	7	5	7.5	8	1.5
Gaining converts	6.5	3.5	3.5	6	3	2	8.5
Attracting new ministers	6.5	6	8	4	5	6	7
Taking an active part in social problems*			6		6		1.5
Raising money							6

* This item is not strictly comparable, as in the Queensland survey the question was 'Taking an active part in social and political problems'.

emphasise those same activities which the discontinuant students preferred.

For those still in the ministry there is a much closer match between perceived actual situation and ideal scenario; usually the same activities were chosen although ranked (with one exception) in different order. Trainees in our sample thought there should be more emphasis on counselling and less on providing an example, but they still accorded greatest importance to those activities, plus private prayer and preaching.

It seems that for ministers the activities which should be most emphasised are providing an example, private prayer, and pastoral work, and this matches roughly with the actual situation as they perceived it. The only major difference is that they would have preferred more emphasis on preaching and much less on leading public worship.

As there are relatively few discontinuants in the sample we cannot place much reliance on figures derived from them, but perhaps they indicate the extent of divergence between what they and the ministers consider the church should be emphasising.

Most of the public seemed to think that the characteristics important for a successful minister are those bearing on interpersonal relationships: specifically, friendliness, approachability, honesty and an interest in people's problems. In contrast, the ministers tended to focus more on religiously oriented characteristics ('love of God', 'faith in God', 'prayerfulness') and only after those, on such items as 'love of people', 'sympathy', 'tolerance' and 'understanding of human nature'. The choices of the *involved laity* sample, however, were almost identical with those of the ministers.

The involved laity and the ministers were asked about the particular satisfactions and dissatisfactions of a minister's work; the latter question was also put to the 'religiously oriented' members of the general public. The ministers were quite clear about their main satisfactions: preaching, counselling, pastoral work and leading public worship were consistently mentioned by all denominations surveyed. The involved laity, however, thought of the question in much vaguer, broader terms naming such things as 'serving God', 'serving the community' and 'saving souls'.

The question of dissatisfactions brought particularly significant answers. The religiously oriented members of the public most frequently replied 'failure to communicate'. However, the involved laity looked at the other side of the question and tended to say 'lack of lay involvement, response and understanding'. This same matter of lack of involvement and so on was one of the two most frequently mentioned by the ministers, a possible indication of the position of those laity involved heavily in the organisation and running of churches: it is perhaps another case of partial socialisation to the minister's role. The other item most frequently mentioned by the ministers was administrative work and the demands it makes on time.

In general, both the clergy and the public disapproved of clergy expressing political opinions in public: there are some denominational differences, but among the public all had a disapproving majority. Majorities of clergy in the Uniting (65 per cent) and Anglican (57 per cent) churches approved, while among the general public a slim majority of all those under 30 did also (52 per cent).

The ministers of most denominations tended to feel quite strongly that 'congregations today are interested in the advice of the minister about everyday affairs'. This suggests another problem in the area of communication mentioned above since a minority of the public supported this statement.

We also asked ministers whether they felt there was need for any change in their church's teachings. Among ordained ministers in the two states there appeared to be considerable uncertainty, since for most denominations percentages agreeing and disagreeing were fairly evenly divided. They were much more positive when asked if they felt a need for change in their church's role in society. In every denomination except the Queensland Lutherans (30 per cent), a majority answered in the affirmative, ranging from 57 per cent of NSW Lutherans to 80 per cent of Congregationalists in both states.

Whereas our evidence suggests that the changes the clergy desire would lead to a more evangelistic, 'other-worldly' church, there is

Table 5.3 *Ranking of 'ideal' church activities by youngest and oldest clergy*

'Most important' church activity	Under 30	Over 50
Propagating the teachings of Christ	1	1.5
Providing formal services of worship	2	1.5
Gaining converts	3.5	3
Providing emotional support to congregation	3.5	5
Missionary activities	5	4
Providing social welfare agencies	6	6.5
Taking an active part in social and political problems	7	6.5
Raising money	8.5	8.5
Attracting new ministers	8.5	8.5

evidence for the existence in northern Europe of a radical group among the clergy, generally but not exclusively associated with younger men, which is more in touch with the attitudes of the population (Siefer, 1973: 104). This provides a rallying point in the church for 'progressive' or activist lay people; and it also provides a point of change and growth in the church. But in Australia what the older clergy think the church should be doing, and what the younger clergy think the church should be doing, are much the same thing. This situation is aptly illustrated by figures which we extracted by age categories for the New South Wales clergy. As shown in Table 5.3, when the first and second preferences for ideal church activities are added, little difference is seen. We further substantiated this finding by examining age differences in two denominations, Roman Catholic and 'future' Uniting Church. Here again differences were minimal.

We made a similar analysis of what the New South Wales ministers thought the most important activities of the *clergy* ideally should be. Both for the total sample and for the Roman Catholic and Uniting churches there was again almost no difference by age, except that the younger clergy tended not to rank 'leading public worship' as highly as their older colleagues. Corroborative evidence is to be found in Paul Hewitt's work on the Roman Catholic priesthood in Queensland (Hewitt, 1978). In a detailed analysis of this denomination, he found only slight differences over a wide range of topics among those under 40 and those of 40 years or more.

In a final attempt to discover any indication of age differences among the clergy regarding ideal activities of the church, we examined evidence previously obtained from Queensland trainees for the

Table 5.4 *Ranking of 'ideal' church activities by Queensland ministers and trainees*

'Most important' church activity	Ministers	Trainees
Propagating the teachings of Christ	1	1
Missionary activities	2	2
Gaining converts	3	3.5
Providing formal services of worship	4	5
Attracting new ministers	5	7
Taking an active part in social and political problems	6	8
Providing emotional support for congregation	7	3.5
Providing social welfare agencies	8	6
Raising money	9	9

ministry, whose median age was in the range 23–25 years. Thus this group could reasonably be taken to represent the next cohort of clergy. Table 5.4 illustrates a close correspondence in the ranking of ideal church activities. Forty per cent of the trainees also expressed a need for change in their church's teachings, which is about the same percentage (44 per cent) as for ordained ministers.

Whatever agreement exists among the clergy, and to whatever extent the churches may be meeting the expectations of the general population, it remains to be established whether satisfaction is similar among all age groups. In fact, we have some evidence to suggest that the attitudes of people under 30 differ in some important respects from those of the rest of the population.

We asked respondents in the general population sample whether they thought on the whole there was a need for the churches to act differently, or whether they thought that the churches should continue as they were. Although there was a fairly high level of agreement that the churches should act differently (54 per cent for the total sample), there were marked differences in this trend by age. By far the highest level of support for change was expressed by those under 30 (67 per cent), while only 39 per cent of those over 50 supported this view.

When those favouring change were asked in an open-ended question what sort of change they envisaged as desirable, the most common answer was that the churches should be more practical, and those under 30 were considerably more likely than older people to make this response. Some idea of what they meant by 'more practical' can be gained from examining the answers of this group to some other questions. For example, those under 30 were the only people in the sample having a majority supporting the expression of political opinions by members of the clergy. The trend is as follows: under 30 52 per cent; 30–49 41 per cent; 50 or more 31 per cent. This youngest age group also felt most strongly that the churches put too much strees on formal services of worship. Even among the religiously oriented, those under 30 were least satisfied with their church's teachings. For example, only 57 per cent of those under 25 were 'very satisfied', as opposed to 87 per cent of those of 50 years or more.

Conclusion

A church is a fairly loosely organised structure, relying on normative compliance of its officials and of the religiously oriented laity. It is not comfortable with highly efficient business methods; it certainly cannot countenance any ruthlessness in operation, or indeed any unseemly rigour in its own internal arrangements. Furthermore, it is constrained to minister to an entire continent with groups of widely differing persuasion, the same bait for any and all fish.

Such a situation is already difficult; success is by no means assured. Any detrimental organisational features will then be a further burden on the church's project. Some such features are apparent from our research. The clergy favour preaching and evangelism, but the public expects more activity in the solution of social problems. Clergymen like to give an example of the Christian way of life; the public prefers a 'good guy' to a godly one. Many women and some men are exasperated, and others amused, at still-existing prohibitions on the ordination of women as clergy. In these and other ways, the organisation seems not effectively to be gearing into its environment. It is 'preaching to the converted', more precisely in our terms, to the 'involved laity', whose attitudes are relatively close to those of the church officials.

In our opinion, one of the most surprising features of churches in Australia is the homogeneity of attitude, amounting perhaps to stagnation, among the various age cohorts of the clergy. Our findings suggest that there is not even a slightly radical younger group which might respond to, or challenge, or encourage, the so-called 'progressive' elements of society. They find little inspiration in the churches. But further, the churches may find within themselves little impetus for change and regeneration.

Notes

1 The research was initiated and partially funded by the Australian Council of Churches.
2 Lenski (1963) first made this useful distinction. See his index for 'associational involvement' and 'communal involvement'.
3 Those who claimed that they attended church more than once a month (28 per cent of the sample) were included in this category. They were, therefore, fairly regular attenders, but not necessarily involved in a range of church activities, as was the case with the involved laity sample.
4 We recognise that some questions may be interpreted differently by various denominational groups. For instance 'gaining converts' may mean a conversion to Christianity or a change from one denomination to another.

6 Wholes and parts: Some aspects of the relationship between the Australian Catholic Church and migrants

Frank W. Lewins

Post-war migrants and their children have added over one million affiliates to the Australian Catholic Church. This represents an increase of over 35 per cent and has helped to raise the Catholic proportion of the Australian population from about 20 per cent to over 25 per cent. This increase raises two problems, one substantive and the other conceptual. First, does the common faith that these migrants share with Australian Catholics influence their settlement in Australia? Secondly, at the conceptual level, what can be said to be 'the church'? It is the policy-making apparatus and bureaucratic machinery set up by the Australian bishops to cope with migrants' problems? Or is it the church in the parish where the migrant lives or worships, characterised by the attitudes and actions of the Australian clergy and laity? In other words, is 'the church' here the 'denomination' or the 'congregation'?

The first problem derives from early works in American historiography, which claimed that the American Catholic Church was a powerful assimilator of immigrant masses and that the church was the main vehicle for the Americanisation of foreigners (see Shaughnessy, 1925; Dunne, 1923). According to Vecoli (1969: 217), these generalisations should be regarded 'at best as tentative hypotheses' because of the neglect of ethnic groups as an element of the research. The fact that Catholic ethnic groups in the United States have not fully assimilated (Greeley, 1972) indicates that these early works *assumed* that a common faith constituted part of the migrant Catholic's assimilation into American life. Moreover, by overlooking group life in an unproblematic, monolithic church, these early works display some similarities to Parsons's (1968) later work on social systems. With their emphasis on the significance of shared beliefs, on the unity of the American Catholic Church and on the goal of homogeneity of American society, they can be regarded as precursors to Parsons's 'social systems', which are characterised by unity, order through shared norms and values, and a continual effort to widen consensus.

Parsons's conception of a social system has not passed without criticisms. It is from these criticisms, especially those relating to his lack of emphasis on the nature of the constitutive parts of social systems, that the second problem mentioned above derives. Lockwood (1956), for instance, argues that Parsons's emphasis on ends is at the expense of more realistic elements of the situation — the means or, as he puts it, the substratum', which is

> the factual disposition of means in the situation of action which structures differential *Lebenschancen* and produces interests of a non-normative kind — that is, interests other than those which actors have in conforming with the normative definition of the situation. (Lockwood, 1956: 136)

This tension between the conformist or shared nature of Parsons's normative system and the diversity of individual interests is also described by Gouldner (1971). Gouldner points to the 'endemic tension between the "ideal" and the "actual" in Parsons' social systems'; he views Parsons's work as detached from the world around it and criticises Parsons's categories for being 'the product of an inward search for the world's oneness and a projection of his vision of that oneness' (Gouldner, 1971: 209 and 169). In his criticism of Parsons, Gouldner throws considerable emphasis on the importance of substructures. He claims that the elements which compose a system can be conceived not only as interdependent, but also as having 'low functional autonomy' with respect to one another. That is, while elements have interchange, or interaction and exchange, with one another, they can also have varying degrees of autonomy in their operations. Whereas Parsons's view of interdependence of the parts stresses primarily the 'whole' or 'oneness', Gouldner's notion of functional autonomy focuses on the parts and stresses that their connectedness is problematic. Again, while Parsons sees the parts as 'real' only in and for the system, Gouldner accepts the possibility that the parts may exist in and for 'themselves'. Gouldner's standpoint, then, emphasises not only the mechanisms that protect the independence and equilibrium of the system as a whole, but also the mechanisms that protect the 'functional autonomy of the parts'. Hence, there are two opposing forces in social systems: the tendency of the parts to protect their own boundaries and to resist integration into the larger system, and the tendency for those parts charged with systems management to strive toward fuller integration, reducing autonomy of the parts and increasing the submission of the parts to the requirements of the whole.

What follows in the remainder of this paper is an examination of the above mentioned problems surrounding the relationship of the Australian Catholic Church to migrants.[1] In addressing these problems, I intend examining issues raised by Lockwood and Gouldner concerning interests and autonomy.

The Australian Catholic Church

In examining the Australian Catholic Church in relation to Catholic migration, it is difficult to find evidence to support a Parsonian social system analysis. Although the Catholic Church is often referred to as a monolithic ('one rock') structure, the responses to migrants, both at the level of the Holy See in Rome and in Australia, suggest the existence of several somewhat independent entities constituting 'the church'. Further, and supportive of Lockwood's and Gouldner's analysis of social systems, these entities of the Catholic Church have had or are experiencing a conflict of policies in terms of migration issues. That is, they are not oriented towards a common 'Catholic' policy regarding migrants, despite the claims from representatives from each entity that there does exist a 'Catholic' approach to migrant pastoral care. Moreover, the accounts of several informed priests and laymen point not only to the plurality of policy-goals or ends concerning migrants but also to a discrepancy between such goals and the means adopted within each entity to achieve them.

This plurality of ends and means, or interests, in 'the church' concerning migrants, which is evident in a comparison of Vatican migration documents, the attitudes and directives of the Australian bishops together with the special agencies established in the major cities to cope with migration matters, and the interaction of migrants with Australian Catholics at the parish level, lead to identification of three structural entities constituting the Australian Catholic Church. These entities I have called 'Rome', 'the Australian hierarchy' and 'the parish'. 'Rome' is included because it is regarded as the *de jure* source of policy and as the final court of appeal on all questions. For the present analysis, 'Rome' is constituted by the Pope and the Sacred Congregations involved with migration questions, either directly or indirectly.[2] As used here, 'the Australian hierarchy' is a broader entity than the term usually denotes, for I include not only the Australian bishops, but also the migration offices, the Catholic press, committees and any other structure at a diocesan level which concerns itself in any way with migration questions. Similarly, 'the parish' is used in a very general manner and not in any exclusive territorial sense, for here I refer to the Australian clergy and laity of a particular parish church who are located in the territory in which the migrant lives or worships.

In analysing 'the Australian Catholic Church' it is necessary to consider each of these structural entities. While it is at the parish or congregational level that the migrant generally confronts Australian Catholics, the role of the Australian bishops and the subordinate structures, such as the Federal Catholic Immigration Committee (FCIC) and the Diocesan Immigration Offices, warrants examination. This is because the bishops on the FCIC have consistently authorised statements on behalf of the Australian bishops concerning migration matters, principally in the form of an annual Immigration Sunday Statement which has appeared every February since the early 1950s. In addition, the secretariat of the FCIC, in conjunction with the Diocesan Immigration Offices, handles the International Catholic Migration Fund which provides interest-free loans to potential migrants. Similarly, the response of Rome needs to be included. This is because Rome is invoked by each of these three entities as the source of Catholic policy concerning migrants, the content of which is the legitimator of all responses to migrants. For instance, the 1969 Roman document 'On the Care of Migrants'[3] is invoked by priests of opposing orientations to migrants to legitimate their respective views as 'Catholic'.

But the difference between the responses of each of these entities is more than a product of the difference of their structure and, hence, intended function *vis-à-vis* the migrant. The actual responses by the Australian bishops (as an aspect of the Australian hierarchy) and the parish priests (as an aspect of the parish) have not only differed from what Rome intended, but have actually been in tension with Rome to the point of revolt. A clear instance of this was the Australian bishops' response to *Exsul Familia*,[4] the first major document issued by Rome on the pastoral care of migrants. Issued in 1952, this document appeared as an Apostolic Constitution, which meant that it was legislative and not merely an exhortation from Rome, as are Letters and Encyclicals. It urged bishops to provide pastoral care for migrants by establishing either national parishes or Missions with the Care of Souls. The former is a legally constituted parish consisting of migrants of a particular nationality with their own national priest, whereas the latter is a quasi-parish where the national priest works in a predetermined area but in conjunction with the local parish priests, with whom he has co-responsibility and hence equal status.

But the Australian bishops refused to implement either of these structures; instead they preferred to keep the territorial parish as the prime structure for the pastoral care of migrants. One canonist has described this refusal as a 'quiet revolt', a refusal 'to discontinue effective pastoral procedures in order to conform to a curial blueprint' (O'Leary, 1971: 129-30).

At this point one can see the difficulty in locating 'the church' response to the migrant, for if the bishops' response and that of the parish priests have been in tension with Rome's position, then what of the significance of the Roman documents (*Exsul Familia* and 'On the Care of Migrants'), especially when they are invoked to justify the 'Catholic' nature of the response at the parish level? On the other hand, if it is granted that it is necessary to examine the migrant/Australian clergy-laity interaction at the parish level, can the response at this level be unreflectively labelled 'Catholic' in the light of the past opposition to Rome's 'Catholic' norms?

These sorts of problems cannot be reconciled in terms of the accounts given by each of these three entities. That is, the public or 'official' response to migrants which is claimed by Rome, the Australian hierarchy and the parish, bears little resemblance to the actual response of each. Such 'unofficial' or informal responses include the revolt against *Exsul Familia*, a response in marked contrast to the 'official' claims of the bishops. For instance, in their Social Justice Statement of 1957, the bishops asserted that they

> in obedience to the directions of the Holy See, contained in the Apostolic Constitution *Exsul Familia*, have spared no effort to provide the hosts of newcomers with every possible facility for practising their religion. (*Advocate*, 29 August 1957)

It is within this realm of informal responses, I would contend, that the explanation of the tension between Rome and the Australian bishops is to be found. Like most complex organisations, these entities of the Catholic Church are more than mere parts of the total organisation. In the light of the authority invested in each, there is, over and above each's separate and independent character, a difference in significant interests: namely, each entity's concern for its own preservation *qua* authority structure. These interests correspond with Lockwood's 'substratum', which describes the realistic elements in 'the church' not provided for in Parsons's approach. In the case of Rome, for instance, its main concern is that it be seen to maintain authority over all Catholics in *its* jurisdiction. Hence, subordinate structures should be seen to be subordinate, so that when tensions arise which challenge this significant interest, the primary aim is to accommodate the tension by altering the situation. This, I would argue, was the form of Rome's response to the 'quiet revolt' of the Australian bishops to *Exsul Familia*. More precisely, Rome's response was the issuing of the second document on migration ('On the Care of Migrants') which superseded many of the norms of *Exsul Familia*.

As Fr O'Leary (1971: 133) notes,

> The norms of *Exsul Familia* were...little more than irritants. They required recourse to Rome on many points and sought to impose patterns of ministry that conflicted with those already successfully in operation in Australia.

So one finds in the later document a legitimation of what was the status quo in Australia before 1969. Specifically, decision-making on migration matters is given over to the local bishop, with a wider range of alternatives made available for the pastoral care of migrants. Again, as O'Leary (1971: 129–30) holds,

> *Exsul Familia* was an exercise in centralisation. *Pastoralis Migratorum* a spur to local initiative... [which] approves as legitimate certain procedures in use in Australia since before 1952 but hardly allowed for in *Exsul Familia... These procedures receive full and explicit approval in the new legislation.*

In short, the later document is 'enabling', not 'legislative' and illustrates Gouldner's notion of 'opposing forces' in social systems. On the one hand, there is the tendency of the Australian bishops to preserve their own 'boundaries' or autonomy. On the other hand, there is Rome's attempt to manage 'the church', and at the same time its own boundaries, by creating overt consensus on migration policy.

But if Rome has been influenced by the Australian bishops[5] in the process of resolving there two 'opposing forces', what of the relationship between the Australian bishops and the parish priests? Again, there is evidence to point to a similar situation where the threat to the bishops' authority is accommodated by their calculated response to the source of tension — the parish priests. This is particularly evident in the hesitancy of the bishops of Melbourne and Sydney to implement Missions with the Care of Souls (see above). In both these archdioceses there has been considerable discussion surrounding this form of pastoral care for migrants.[6] According to the private accounts of the representatives of the committees involved, this hesitancy of the bishops[7] springs from their fear of 'treading on the toes of the parish priests' who, it is held, fear that any form of 'national structure will only lead to 'divisiveness' between Australians and migrants. As one priest close to one of the bishops put it, 'The Cardinal fears that these Missions with the Care of Souls will split the diocese right down the middle'.

The parish priests' fear of divisiveness is bound up with their view of the parish as the primary form of pastoral care for migrants. But this emphasis on the parish does not exist in a vacuum, for it has been noted that 'Australian Catholics are well aware that of necessity a major element in pastoral care of migrants in this country is the existing parish network' (O'Leary, 1971: 137). The 'necessity' here lies in the fact that all parishioners are required to contribute to the establishment and maintenance of churches, presbyteries and parish schools. While the establishment phase is not so relevant now, the current financial situation of many Catholic parish schools is sufficient reason to prevent the siphoning off of available financial resources (see Martin, 1972a: 89 and Price, 1963: 196).

This concern of the parish priests to maintain the parish as an ongoing entity, and of course their authority over all Catholics within the parish, explains what has been seen as 'a policy decision in Catholic circles to play down these [national] diversities and to accelerate as much as possible the complete Australianisation of the immigrants or at least of their children' (O'Leary, 1971: 150-1). The parish priests' influence on the bishops is indicated by the fact that no Missions with the Care of Souls have yet been implemented in Australia.

Now in light of the above discussion of tension management by Rome and the Australian bishops, the obvious question is: What is the nature of tension management by, and influence on, parish priests? From my interviews with parish priests and from a case study of one parish with a high migrant population, I would contend that the parish priest is similarly influenced by his subordinates' attitudes and actions. That is, to maintain authority over the laity in his jurisdiction, and hence, to maintain 'the parish', the parish priest responds politically to the dominant interests of the laity. In those parishes where there is a majority of Australians in terms of participation in parish life, the parish priest reflects the orientation of the Australians towards migrants and their pastoral care. This was particularly obvious in the replies of one overseas-born parish priest who had the care of a parish where a majority of parishioners were of his nationality, but where Australians dominated in terms of church attendance, parish activities and, not least of all, financial support of the parish.[8] When I asked him why he did not have more masses for his migrant parishioners, he replied, 'As parish priest I have to think of everyone . . . one has a responsibility to the whole parish'. But the implied sensitivity to the Australian members was made quite explicit in his answer to my question about the existence of ethnic style in the life of the parish (e.g. processions, music, statues). He said that he could not admit these elements because 'the Australians don't like that sort of thing'.

This political sensitivity was evident even in parishes where no one national group, including Australians, constituted a majority. Some parishes in Melbourne's western suburbs are of this type, with the Australian proportion being no more than around 20 per cent of the total parish population. One parish priest, who spent several years in such a parish, conveyed only a concern for the welfare of the whole parish. His sensitivity to national group interest was one of scrupulous equality, even to the point of publicly declaring the need for 'cultural democracy' in the pastoral care of migrants.

However, the majority of parish priests are of the former type, being in the situation of having to respond to the interests of the Australian majority. But I have also argued that the bishops are influenced by the dominant attitudes of their subordinate parish priests; in particular, the latter's objection to national Catholic centres on the grounds of their capacity to divide existing Australian parishes. The important question to which this leads is: What is the nature of the Catholic laity's attitudes and actions towards migrant Catholics? Given the influence pattern which I have argued for here, that is, bishops to Rome, parish priests to bishops, and Australian laity to parish priests, the nature of the laity's response to migrants will help to resolve the initial problems outlined above.

The dominant attitude of the Catholic laity concerning migrants is that the migrant should 'fit in' with the normal life of the Australian parish. Because of the laity's lack of sympathy for special consideration for migrants, there is little or no reflection on alternative structures for their pastoral care, such as the Mission with the Care of Souls. For most Australian Catholics, a 'good' migrant Catholic is one who actively participates in parish life and accepts responsibility for the financial commitments of the parish. Further, such a migrant eliminates his national differences as quickly as possible, a consequence of the Australian Catholic's antipathy towards any foreign import into parish life and his elevation of the worth of the 'Australian' parish.

These characteristics of the laity are clearly articulated by the few reflective Catholic clergy who are associated with migrants. Three priests in particular, who have had experience as parish priests and as directors of diocesan migration offices, pointed to the 'unrealistic' nature of the Australian Catholic's expectation of cultural homogeneity. One of these priests suggested that this 'exaggerated' pressure upon migrant Catholics to conform is traceable to the British who, as a colonising nation, expected conformity from those colonised. Now, he added, we have a case of British conformism acting back in the form of 'Australianism'. Another of these priests posited an 'integrationist mentality' in describing Australian Catholics and thought that it was related to the Irish influence on

Australian Catholicism. He was particularly critical of the inconsistent demands of Irish clergy in Australia who expected migrants to 'fit in' but who themselves 'have never fitted in'.

This expected conformism was particularly obvious in one incident which occurred in an inner Melbourne parish with a high concentration of Italians. The Australian parishioners decided to give a farewell gift to an assistant priest who had been transferred to another parish. Because this priest was Italian-speaking and had established a considerable amount of goodwill among Italians, the Italian parishioners also decided to give him a farewell present, but on behalf of the Italians. This raised considerable antagonism among the Australians of the parish, which was summed up by the comment of one man who argued: 'Why should they want to double up on this matter? We're all a part of the one parish and therefore we should give him one present.'

Generally, this particular attitude of the laity could be summarised by the account given by one migrant of her experience of the Australian parish. In an article reflecting the value of 'belonging', she was given some prominence in the Melbourne archdiocesan weekly. In addressing more recently arrived migrants, she wrote:

> I know from my own experience that you will never feel at home in Australia as long as you do not belong to the parish where you are living...I know how happy you feel to listen to a sermon in your mother tongue. But all that cannot give you the really good feeling of being at home in Australia. You have this feeling only when you have a gratifying and orderly place in your own parish. (*Advocate*, 5 March 1964)

Related to this corporate view of parish life is the laity's lack of sympathy and reflection on migrant problems. One clear expression of this is the antagonism of Australian Catholics towards the provision of special foreign language masses for migrants. In those parishes with a concentration of any one migrant group, it is frequently claimed by the Australian clergy that migrant masses cannot replace English-language masses. The reason, as one priest put it, is that 'you can't take masses away from the Australians and give them to the migrants'. Consequently, if there are to be migrant masses, then they have to be programmed as 'extra masses'. Where migrant masses have replaced the usual English-language mass, there is bitterness among the Australian parishioners. One priest told me that several Australian families no longer come to his second mass on Sunday mornings since it has been an Italian mass, even though attendance at this mass had been their life-long practice.

But the clearest expression of such lack of sympathy for migrant needs, and the absence of reflection on the nature of their cultural differences, is the bitterness Australian Catholics feel towards migrants who neglect their financial responsibilities to the parish. This complaint applies particularly to Italians, who are regarded as being 'poor givers', especially when it comes to paying parish school fees and giving donations. This sentiment was illustrated by the comment of one Australian parishioner, who complained: 'Why should 70 per cent of the parish [i.e. the Italians] contribute 10 per cent of the income? ... Italians just won't give to the sacrificial giving programme.' When I put this complaint to an Italian parishioner, he explained that Italians resent having a financial commitment defined for them, especially those like the 'planned giving' programme of the parish. He countered the Australians' complaints by adding that 'Italians are generous. They will give hundreds of dollars, and they do. But they don't want to be told what to give.'

It is not surprising, therefore, that there is minimal interaction between Australian and migrant parishioners in parishes with large numbers of migrants (cf. Phillips, 1970). The Australian Catholics' antagonism towards special concessions for migrants explains why participation by Italians, for instance, in parish life in not strong in proportion to their numbers (Raccanello, n.d.) and partly explains why Italians have sunk traditional regional differences and joined forces to form 'Italian' groups within the parish structure, a phenomenon which I have discussed elsewhere (Lewins, 1978).

However, is this response to the Catholic migrant at the parish level characteristic of Australian Catholics as *Catholics*; or is it typical of the wider *Australian* response to migrants? Clearly, it is the latter, for it corresponds with the observations and conclusions of other scholars who have documented the nature or the wider Australian attitudes and behavior toward migrants (e.g. Borrie, 1954: 119; Martin, 1972b; Jupp, 1966: 83–120; Cox, 1974: 5–7).

Returning to the original problems surrounding a common faith and the location of 'the Church', my conceptualisation of the latter in terms of Rome, the Australian hierarchy and the parish is an attempt to deal with the problem of whether one should focus on the 'denomination' or the 'congregation' in a study such as this. The description of 'the church' in terms of these entities uncovers elements, such as each entity's concern for its own authority and self-preservation, which are in tension with the official definition of the situation. These informal but significant interests confirm Gouldner's and Lockwood's critiques of Parsons's social systems and account for the chain of influence 'upwards'. In arguing that Rome's position on migration, as expressed in the shift from *Exsul Familia* to 'On the Care of Migrants' (*Pastoralis Migratorum*), has been influenced by Australian cultural attitudes, I am referring to the dominant direction of influence on migration issues. I am not suggesting that there is simply a one-way path of influence on migration questions, or on any other questions. To view the Australian Catholic Church as a social system, or as having social system characteristics, is to accept also a degree of consensus among the faithful on central values and norms, which exert influence 'downwards'. Nevertheless, it remains that for migration issues the content of policy, norms and values — 'ideology' — is of secondary importance. This is not only because of the significance within each entity of its authority maintenance and self-preservation, but also because of the nature of ideology itself. Norms confronting Catholics, like many other Christian norms, do not tell individuals exactly *how* to act. Norms such as 'accept migrants as brothers!', for example, do not tell Catholics what to do; rather, their vagueness of prescription implies variable behaviour, which can include *no* behaviour. Because of this secondary role of ideology on migration issues, it is more an intervening variable in influencing responses to migrants. In this respect, it acts as a *post factum* legitimation of action (e.g. Rome's position as expressed in 'On the Care of Migrants' (*Pastoralis Migratorum*).

Finally, in terms of the role of a common faith, the chain of influence 'upwards' implies that there is an increasing influence of Australian or local factors the closer one gets to the parish where the laity's responses to migrants are more Australian than Catholic. Since such responses are little different from those in the wider milieu, a common faith is of little significance in influencing relations between Australian and migrant Catholics: culture divides more than religion unites.

Notes

1 The data on which this paper is based were derived from numerous sources. I interviewed and corresponded with about 80 clergy and laity, including both migrants and Australians, in Sydney and Melbourne, and to a lesser extent Brisbane, Adelaide and Perth. In addition, I did a parish case study, spending six months observing in an inner suburban parish with a high concentration of migrants. These sources were supplemented with a survey of the contents of the Catholic press in Sydney, Melbourne and Adelaide, an extensive document analysis of material relating to migration, and an examination of Australian Catholic historiography. For an elaboration of some of the issues dealt with in this paper, see Lewins, 1978.

2 The Sacred Congregation for Bishops, as one of the congregations of the

Roman Curia, is the official congregation responsible for the pastoral care of migrants, whereas the Sacred Congregation for the Oriental Churches is indirectly concerned with migration questions as it is the congregation to which the Eastern rite Catholics are responsible (e.g. Ukrainians, Maronites and Melchites).

3 This is the title of the English translation, Australian Catholic Truth Society Edition, 1970. The original Roman publication consisted of two documents, *Pastoralis Migratorum*, an Apostolic Letter of 15 August 1969, and the 'Instruction of the Pastoral Care of People who Migrate', issued by the Sacred Congregation for Bishops, 22 August 1969.

4 One of the few English translations appears in Tessarolo (1962)

5 This influence is difficult to substantiate. Apart from indirect evidence, such as the views of seemingly informed clergy, there is the fact of Australia being the receiving country for a large number of Catholic migrants. More particularly, Australia has received a large proportion of those migrants assisted through the International Catholic Migration Commission. For instance, in 1967 (two years before *Pastoralis Migratorum*) Australia received almost 4000 such migrants which was 33 per cent of the total ICMC movement that year. See *Migration News*, Supplement, No. 64, 1968.

6 This discussion has centred in the Senate of Priests in Melbourne, while in Sydney it has been within 'The Archbishop of Sydney's Senate of Priests-Pastoral Council Joint Sub-Committee on the Care of Migrants'.

7 I refer here to Cardinal Freeman of Sydney and Cardinal Knox, the predecessor of the present Archbishop of Melbourne.

8 This particular case is no exception, for in parishes where the migrant content is greater than the Australian, the common complaint of Australian clergy and laity is that a minority of the parish contributes most to its support.

7 The sociology of ecumenism: Initial observations on the formation of the Uniting Church in Australia[1]

Alan W. Black

On 22 June 1977 the Uniting Church in Australia came into being as the result of a merger of the whole of the Methodist Church of Australasia, about two-thirds of the Presbyterian Church of Australia and about five-sixths of the churches which belonged to the Congregational Union of Australia. The Methodist Church of Australasia and the Presbyterian Church of Australia had come into being at the turn of the twentieth century through a union of previously separate Methodist and Presbyterian churches respectively. The formation of the Uniting Church was, however, the first trans-denominational merger in this country and one of the relatively few such mergers to have occurred anywhere. The closest parallel is in Canada where the same three denominations merged in 1925 to form the United Church of Canada. There, too, all of the Methodist Church, about two-thirds of the Presbyterian Chuch and nearly all the Congregational churches became part of the United Church; but, as in Australia, there were, prior to union, far less Congregationalists than either Methodists or Presbyterians.

What light can sociology throw on events such as these? In particular, what are the factors which have prompted the rise of the ecumenical movement in the twentieth century and have led to negotiations for church union? Why, on the other hand, have some church members remained aloof from the ecumenical movement and opposed to church union negotiations? One of the earliest recognitions of the influence of social factors both in efforts to achieve church mergers and in opposition to such activities came from within the ecumenical movement itself. In preparation for the 1937 World Conference on Faith and Order, a booklet on *The Non-theological Factors in the Making and Unmaking of Church Union* was published (Commission on the Church's Unity in Life and Worship, 1937). While asserting (page 1) that 'the hope for Christian Unity lies in our faith in the divine unity', this publication identified other factors which have sometimes prompted moves for church union; namely, the demand for a national church, the wish to close ranks in the face of non-Christian forces, and the desire for economy in the use of church resources. It gave somewhat greater attention, however, to social factors which have helped to separate churches or which may act as barriers to church union, such as differences of race, class, language, nationality, politics, ethical judgement, and so on. In early issues of *The Ecumenial Review*, published by the World Council of Churches, there were several articles dealing with similar themes (Jenkins, 1951; Clark, 1951; World Council of Churches, Commission on Faith and Order, 1952; Ellul, 1952; Cragg, 1952; Garrison, 1952; Hromadka, 1952).

A few years later Robert Lee (1960) wrote *The Social Sources of Church Unity*, an analysis of unitive movements in American Protestantism. Lee put forward the thesis that such movements are a by-product of the increasing social homogeneity and cultural unity within society at large. He argued that social factors such as those of race, class, region and ethnicity, which were formerly reflected in denominational differences, have declined in significance as a result of relative economic prosperity, modern mass communications, urbanisation, public education, intermarriage, and similar homogenising influences. In Lee's (1960: 219) view, 'the emergence of a common-core Protestantism reflects the common-core culture of American society. As diverse religious groups of racial or sectarian, ethnic or sectional character come to share or emulate the common-core Protestantism, they participate more fully in the church unity movement.' Lee was writing at a time of relative calm in American society, and prior to the emergence of the acute social conflicts which erupted at the time of the civil rights marches and the Vietnam war of the late 1960s and early 1970s. But these events do not necessarily invalidate his thesis. On the contrary, they could be held to explain why progress towards church union has been less rapid there in recent years (Johnstone, 1975: 264–5). Nevertheless, this paper will endeavour to show that Lee's explanation of ecumenism does not deal with all aspects of that phenomenon.

Berger (1963) took a different, though not unrelated, starting point in his analysis of ecumenism. He saw the key feature in the situation of Christianity in contemporary society as being that of pluralism, by which he meant that no single religious tradition can command the loyalty of the whole, or even the bulk, of the population. In countries such as the USA and Australia, this pluralism has arisen in part as a consequence of the immigration of persons from a variety of religious traditions. There have also been challenges from those who deny the importance of any religion. 'As a result, the religious tradition which previously could be authoritatively imposed, now has to be *marketed*. It must be "sold" to a clientele that is no longer constrained to "buy" (Berger, 1973: 142). Hence Berger has developed his 'market model of ecumenicity'.

In this particular model, religious institutions are seen as marketing agencies, and religious traditions are thought of as consumer commodities. In order to appeal to those in the middle class, from whom the bulk of their members ('customers') are drawn, the mainline churches have developed similar 'products' with marginal differentiation in packaging and presentation. (Here Berger's analysis parallels Lee's.) But unrestrained competition between churches could, from each church's perspective, reach a point where its costs outweighed its benefits; for example, if it become so fierce that it resulted in the alienation of some potential customers from the market altogether, or if it prevented the churches from taking the concerted action which might be required to secure particular political objectives. Moreover, free competition between churches has become increasingly costly as a result of inflation, which has affected both capital and recurrent expenses, such as the costs of new church buildings, of publications, of clergy training, and so on. In this situation, the growth of interdenominational agencies and the occurrence of church mergers were seen by Berger as forms of economic rationalisation. They were examples of the 'well known process of cartelisation, facilitated in the ecclesiastical case by the absence of a Sherman Act' (Berger 1963: 86). As in other cases of cartelisation, they resulted in a reduction in the number of competing units and the organisation of the market by means of agreements among those units which remain. Berger gave as examples of the latter phenomenon the 'comity' arrangements under which various churches have agreed not to compete with one another in new residential areas. He concluded that although the market model does not necessarily give a total explanation of all aspects of ecumenicity, it does highlight some of the most important social-structural aspects (see also Berger, 1973: 139-53).

Whereas Berger (1963: 85) spoke of ecumenicity developing in a 'situation of unequalled ecclesiastical affluence' in the 1950s and 1960s, Wilson (1966: 142) took the view that amalgamations and alliances between churches generally occur when such bodies are in decline. According to Wilson, this decline has been evidenced either in dwindling numerical support or in an attenuation of the churches' distinctive beliefs, or both. He saw ecumenism as arising in part from a desire by the clergy to bolster their declining social status and to recover their lost influence in the face of the increasing secularisation of society. He defined secularisation as 'the process whereby religious thinking, practice and institutions lose social significance' (Wilson, 1966: xiv). His analysis incorporated some elements from the work of Lee and Berger, noting 'the disappearance of ethnic, class and regional differences, with which American religion was closely associated' (Wilson, 1966: 126) and detecting a degree of economic rationalisation in the ecumenical movement (Wilson, 1966: 138-41). But he saw as a dominant feature of ecumenism the tendency within the churches to move towards increasingly centralised control, ritualism and sacerdotalism, with a corresponding depreciation of the Protestant doctrine of the priesthood of all believers. Here he cited evidence from Robert Currie's study of divisions and reunions in British Methodism (originally presented as a D Phil thesis in 1966 and later published as a book — Currie, 1968), as well as from the unity conversations in Britain in the 1950s and 1960s between Anglicans and Presbyterians and between Anglicans and Methodists.

Like Wilson, Currie (1968: 109) held that in industrial societies ecumenism arises as a response to the decline of religion, especially as this decline is reflected in membership statistics. He argued that the processes of division within Methodism arose largely from lay protests; by contrast, the movement for reunion was predominantly a ministerial activity. In his view, ecumenism has been essentially an attempt to substitute 'lateral' growth through amalgamation for the 'frontal' growth which has eluded the churches in recent times. But he found little evidence from the history of British Methodism that church amalgamations arrested the rate of decline, much less that they resulted in a religious revival. He concluded that ecumenism not only arises out of decline and secularisation but also that it leads to further decline, an opinion which was shared by Wilson (1966: 176).

Various critiques have been made of the Wilson/Currie thesis. Pinder (1971) argued that historically there has been much more *continuity* in both the structure and the culture of Methodism than Wilson and Currie recognise: that from the outset of the Methodist movement the relationship between clergy and laity has been more complex than these writers' accounts reveal; that, in at least some cases, ecumenical concern has been associated with movements for decentralisation and greater lay responsibility rather than centralisation and greater ministerial power; and that to interpret ecumenism primarily as a form of defensive accommodation by religious professionals to the processes of decline and secularisation is to oversimplify the character both of ecumenism and of secularisation.

The last of these points has been amplified by several other writers. Till (1972: 20-31) argued that church leaders are generally neither as cynical nor as aware of their situation as the Wilson/Currie thesis suggests. He admitted that throughout the nineteenth century the Western churches had been steadily losing their previous influence over various power structures and social institutions such as the educational system; but he argued that the early leaders of the ecumenical movement, such as those who convened the first World Missionary Conference at Edinburgh in 1910, scarcely felt that the churches were in a desperate position. Till (1972: 30) concluded that 'Wilson has diagnosed *one* of the motives of some of the leaders of the present-day [ecumenical] movement. But it still remains necessary to look for a more satisfactory explanation of the rise and persistence of ecumenism'.

Likewise, Towler (1974: 165) was critical of Currie's tendency to overgeneralise from his study of British Methodism. Towler raised also the question of causality: even if it could be shown that all and only those churches which are declining in numerical strength are interested in reunion it would not follow that such ecumenism is necessarily caused by the numerical decline. It could be that both ecumenism and numerical decline are brought about more-or-less independently by some third factor or group of factors. Towler saw modern technology as one such factor: rapid modes of transportation and communication have broken down the social and cultural isolation in which separate religious traditions formerly flourished. The resultant awareness of the *diversity* of traditional beliefs and practices has prompted questions about the credibility of any particular religious system. The greater mobility and affluence produced by modern technology have also made it easier for some people to 'do without' the ministrations of religious organisations. In this way, technological developments have contributed to church decline. At the same time, modern means of communication have helped to produce what Mehl (1970: 196) has called a 'world civilisation' with a great deal of uniformity in prevailing beliefs and life-styles, and religion has not been exempt from this process. Thus, modern technology has helped to produce both church decline and ecumenism, but neither of the latter two phenomena is necessarily a cause of the other.

In any case, as Turner (1972: 236-7) pointed out, various church mergers took place in the USA between 1905 and 1960, when religion appeared to be booming in that country. If, in reply, it is said that during that period America showed evidence of 'secularisation' even if not of decline in membership among the churches, how then are we to account for the failure of the Consultantion on Church Union to produce organic union of American churches in the period since 1962? Furthermore, if the circumstances of the churches in Britain were as Wilson and Currie described them, why did the fairly recent British plan for union between Anglicans and

Methodists not succeed? (See Till, 1972: 367–80; Turner, 1972: 243–4; Gill, 1974: 8–10.) And why in 1978 did the Methodists in Scotland reject a plan for union with the Church of Scotland?

Although I would not want to reject the Wilson/Currie thesis entirely, it is clear that their thesis is incomplete as an explanation of ecumenism and that it is unable to predict the outcomes of particular church union negotiations. In an effort to throw more light on these phenomena, other writers have examined the personal and social correlates of attitudes to ecumenism in general and to church union schemes in particular. One of the earliest writers to do so was Hans Mol (1969), whose data were drawn from his larger study of religion in Australia (Mol, 1971). Mol asked a random sample of Australian adults 'Would you like to see your own denomination (if you belong to one) merge, or join together with any other denomination?' Of the 1825 respondents, 15 per cent had no opinion or said that they did not belong to any denomination. A further 21 per cent stated that they did not want their denomination to merge with another. The remaining 64 per cent were in favour of such a merger. Respondents in this last category were then asked whether there were any denominations with which they would not like their denomination to unite. In answer to this, 37 per cent of the sample made no exceptions, 12 per cent wished to exclude Catholics, 8 per cent wished to exclude one or more of the so-called 'sects' such as Jehovah's Witnesses, Mormons and so on, and a further 6 per cent gave several or other replies (Mol, 1969: 25).

Mol found that differences of opionion on the above questions were not significantly related to the age of the respondents nor, keeping denominational affiliation constant, to the frequency of church attendance. There was quite a strong association between orthodoxy of belief in God and whether respondents cared about the issue of church mergers; but, among those who did care about the issue, orthodoxy of belief in God was not significantly related to whether one was *for* or *against* such mergers. Nor were differences of attitude on the merger question significantly related to other differences of religious belief or experience, such as whether one regarded the church as God-given and sacred, the frequency of one's practice of prayer, or whether one had experienced 'a sense of having been saved in Christ'. On the other hand, Mol's data suggested to him that anti-merger sentiments were often closely associated with what various writers have termed an 'authoritarian personality' or a 'closed mind'. He based this conclusion on (a) whether respondents agreed with the statement that 'the most important thing for a child to learn is to obey rather than to think for himself', (b) whether they thought it all right if a person treats people differently according to how important they are, and (c) whether they had the majority of their five closest friends in the local church.

Like Mol, Kaill (1971) found that attitudes of lay members of the Anglican Church of Canada and of the United Church of Canada to a proposed union of their churches were not significantly related to degree of theological conservatism or liberalism, as reflected in respondents' answers to questionnaire items on the doctrine of the Trinity, the divinity of Christ, mystical experiences, individual conversion, and hopes of heaven. Nor, despite the Wilson/Currie thesis, were respondents' attitudes to merger very strongly linked with their perceptions of whether the church was facing difficulties. Of the variables tested by Kaill, the one most strongly influencing lay attitudes to merger was their perception of their local clergymen's attitudes on this matter; and, as a matter of fact, most respondents doubted whether their clergyman was in favour of such a merger. If these respondents' perceptions were accurate, they cast doubt on Wilson's (1966: 125) contention that 'there has been something of a mass conversion of the clergy to ecumenism', which has now become 'a new faith — something to believe in'. It is possible, of course, that some respondents mistook their clergy's view on this matter or projected their own views on to the clergy.

Kaill also found that pro-church-union sentiment was negatively correlated with what he called 'economic liberalism' and positively correlated with what he called 'civil liberalism', and that these relationships persisted when variables such as age and socioeconomic status were controlled. He measured economic liberalism on the basis of the extent to which respondents agreed with the propositions that 'the free enterprise system favours the rich and discriminates against the poor' and that 'the government should control and operate all vital industries such as mining, railways and airlines'. As indicators of civil liberalism (or belief in freedom of expression) he used the extent to which respondents disagreed with the propositions that 'any university professor who talks like a Communist should be fired' and that 'the government should not permit so many obscene movies to be shown'. In so far as civil liberalism is the antithesis of authoritarianism, Kaill's findings on the significance of this variable parallel those of Mol, a fact noted by both writers (Kaill, 1971: 161; Mol, 1976: 86). Yinger (1970: 249) has put forward a similar hypothesis, arguing that 'the insecure person, the possessor of a "closed mind", and the individual with authoritarian tendencies are all less likely to accept loss of group identity in favour of some larger pattern' than are those who are secure, open-minded and non-authoritarian.

Although terms such as 'authoritarian', 'closed mind' and 'open mind' describe certain psychological characteristics, they tend also to be somewhat value-laden. What to one person is evidence of a 'closed mind' is to another person a case of 'adherence to principle'. Conversely, what one applauds as 'open-mindedness' another might despise as 'vacillation'. Likewise, what one sees as 'freedom of expression' another might regard as 'moral subversion' or 'unbridled licence'. The use of such labels reveals to some extent the labeller's own value hierarchy. This is not to say that the terms used by the writers cited in the previous paragraph lack significant empirical content; rather, that they also have evaluative overtones. It should be noted here too that a correlation between two variables does not necessarily mean that there is a causal relationship between them. It could be that there is some more basic factor which governs attitudes both to church mergers and to other social issues.

In a study of Episcopalians in North Carolina, Roof (1978) found that there was a fairly weak negative correlation between ecumenism and theological conservatism ('literal orthodoxy') and a stronger negative correlation between ecumenism and localism. By 'localism' he was referring to the tendency to regard one's residential locality as the usual boundary of one's interest and involvement. The contrasting tendency, called 'cosmopolitanism', regards interest and involvement in the larger society as at least equally important as participation in local affairs. Roof found that the weak negative relationship between ecumenism and theological conservatism disappeared when he controlled statistically on the local-cosmopolitan dimension, whereas the somewhat stronger negative correlation between localism and ecumenism remained significant even when he controlled statistically for theological orientation. In so far as the local-cosmopolitan scale measures what Roof (1978: 175) terms 'breadth of perspective', this conclusion is broadly consistent with the findings of Mol and Kaill.

Have any other studies identified alternative factors which are more powerful determinants of attitudes to ecumenism? In Table 7.1 the main findings of survey research on this issue, including the results already discussed, are summarised. Two general comments may be made on these results. First, most of these studies were made independently of one another; there has been relatively little continuity in research design. Secondly, where similar variables have been measured, the results have not always been consistent. For example, whereas Mol (1969) in Australia, Kaill (1971) in Canada and Hay (1979) in England found no significant relationship between lay persons' ages and their attitudes to ecumenism, Hill and Wakeford (1969) and Turner (1969) found that older Methodist laity in England were less likely to be in favour of an Anglican-Methodist

Table 7.1 *Studies of correlates of ecumenism*

Author:	Mol	Kaill	Kelly	Ro
Year of publication:	1969	1971	1971	197
Country of study:	Australia	Canada	USA	US
Location of sample:	Dispersed	Western Ontario	Lexington, Mass.	Nor Caro
Denominational composition:	Various	Anglican & United	Various	Episco
Persons in sample:	1825 laypersons	408 laypersons	854 laypersons	486 layp
Measure of ecumenism:	Favour merger with another denomination?	Favour Anglican-United merger?	Five-item general	Favour in gen
Age	0	0	(0)	(0
Male gender	(0)	(0)	(0)	(0
Educational level completed	+	0	(0)	(0
Socioeconomic status (occupation)	(0)	0	(0)	(0
Income			(0)	(0
Degree of church involvement	0		+ Cath 0 Prot	(0)
Majority of closest friends belong to local church	—			(0
Localism rather than cosmopolitanism in orientation				—
Parent(s) belonged to same denomination as respondent		0		
Parent(s) belonged to denomination with which merger is proposed				
Degree of cognitive interest in religion			+	

Continued on pages 96 and 97

Hill & Wakeford		Turner	Bryman *et al.*	Hay
1969		1969	1974	1979
England		England	England West Midlands	England
London		Yorkshire		Nottingham
Methodist		Methodist	Anglican	Roman Catholic
328 laypersons avour unity general?	(b) Favour Anglican-Methodist merger?	600 lay, 36 clergy Favour Anglican-Methodist merger?	228 laypersons Favour merger with particular denoms?	638 laypersons Favour unity in general?
—?	—	—	—?	0
0	+?	+	0	0
0	+?			+
0	+?		0	
			0	
—	—			0
—?	—?			

Table 7.1 *Studies of correlates of ecumenism* (Continued)

Author:	Mol	Kaill	Kelly	Ro
Year of publication:	1969	1971	1971	197
Country of study:	Australia	Canada	USA	US
Location of sample:	Dispersed	Western Ontario	Lexington, Mass.	Nor Caro
Denominational composition:	Various	Anglican & United	Various	Episco
Persons in sample:	1825 laypersons	408 laypersons	854 laypersons	486 layp
Measure of ecumenism:	Favour merger with another denomination?	Favour Anglican-United merger?	Five-item general	Favour in gen
Theological liberalism	0	0	– Cath 0 Prot	+*
Supports greater secular involvement of church			+	
Approves liturgical innovations		0		
Pessimistic over church's future		0	0	
Reports that local clergyman supports church union		+		
Civil liberalism	See next item	+		
Authoritarianism	—	See previous item		
Economic liberalism		—		

Key   + = positive correlation
0 = no correlation
– = negative correlation
* = relationship disappears when one controls statistically for localism
? = relationship slight or debateable
(0) = presumed no correlation, as data collected but not reported as significant

merger than were the young (on this, see also Hill and Turner, 1969). In another study conducted in England, Bryman *et al.* (1974) discovered that among lay members of Anglican deanery synods, a larger proportion of those under the age of 40 than of those aged 40 or over were in favour of union between the Church of England and the Presbyterian Church but age differences were not statistically significant when the same respondents were asked about other forms

Hill & Wakeford		Turner	Bryman *et al.*	Hay
1969		1969	1974	1979
England		England	England West	England
London		Yorkshire	Midlands	Nottingham
Methodist		Methodist	Anglican	Roman Catholic
328 laypersons		600 lay, 36 clergy	228 laypersons	638 laypersons
vour unity general?	(b) Favour Anglican- Methodist merger?	Favour Anglican- Methodist merger?	Favour merger with particular denoms?	Favour unity in general?
			Depends on particular denomination	+

of ecumenical co-operation and about union between the Church of England and other, individually named, major denominations. Ranson *et al.* (1977) found that among Anglican clergy in England there was no significant correlation between age and attitudes to ecumenism, whereas among Roman Catholic priests and Methodist ministers in that country the young were, on average, more ecumenically minded that the old. In short, openness to ecumenism has been found to be partly related to age only in studies conducted in England, and then not always so. Where age is related in this way, the old tend to be less ecumenical than the young.

The only studies which have revealed significant differences between the sexes in attitudes to ecumenism are those of Turner (1969) and, to a lesser extent, Hill and Wakeford (1969). Their finding that females tend to be less ecumenical in outlook than males was not paralleled in the other studies mentioned in the previous paragraph even though most of those studies gathered data on this factor. Likewise a positive relationship between educational level and support for ecumenism has been reported only by Hay (1979) and, on one measure of ecumenicity, by Hill and Wakeford (1969). Elsewhere, respondents' educational level was either found or presumed to be unimportant as an explanatory factor. Nor, except possibly in one study (Hill and Wakeford, 1969), does socioeconomic status appear to be a significant determinant of variations in attitude to church union. Details of other variables which have been measured are given in Table 7.1

It is possible that some of the apparent differences in findings between various studies spring in part not only from differences in the independent variables considered but also from differences in the measurement of the dependent variable, support for ecumenism. Thus, whereas Kelly (1971a, 1971b) used a five-item general index of support for ecumenism, Turner (1969) asked members of a particular denomination (the Methodist Church) about a proposed merger with another particular church (the Church of England). Hill and Wakeford (1969) asked questions both about unity in general and about the proposed Anglican-Methodist union; age appeared to be related in a similar fashion to responses to both questions, but sex, educational level and socioeconomic status appeared to be related to responses to the second question somewhat differently than to the first. It would be wrong, however, to exaggerate these differences, for they were seldom very striking.

It should be clear by now that a mono-causal explanation of movements towards or against church union is unlikely to be adequate. One possible way of combining various elements into an explanatory scheme is by using some sort of political model, recognising that political processes are the result of an interplay between various factors. Warwick (1974) has suggested that the following five assumptions are basic to an understanding of the politics of ecumenism:

1 Most people are basically conservative about organisational change of any kind and doubly so when the changes touch the deepest levels of their belief.

2 The larger the organisational apparatus in a church, the greater the resistance to change from incumbents of official positions (hereafter called bureaucrats, in the non-pejorative sense)...

3 Church bureaucrats, particularly those holding full-time positions, are no less inclined that other bureaucrats to protect their own positions and political interests...

4 The greater the extent of internal conflict, tension, or friction within a denomination, the more remote the prospects of organisational union with other churches...

5 As groups expand from small, face-to-face units into multi-level bureaucracies, communication takes more time and becomes more difficult, decision making grows more complicated, and control becomes more diffuse. In this respect there is social psychological substance to the fears sometimes voiced by free churches that their autonomy would be overwhelmed by the organisational superstructure emerging from ecumenical mergers...

There is undoubtedly some validity in each of Warwick's axioms. If, however, axioms (2) and (3) are taken to imply that enthusiastic support for proposed church mergers does not generally come from denominational officials, this does not fit with the observations made in various cases (e.g. Silcox, 1933; Sjölinder, 1962; Currie, 1968; Newman, 1970; Till, 1972; Smith, 1977), nor does it apply to the formation of the Uniting Church in Australia.

Another study which used a political model to analyse both support for and opposition to church union was that of Bullock (1975). Starting from the premise that within each of the major Protestant denominational in America there are two broad ideological groupings — liberal and conservative — Bullock hypothesised that the outcome of church union negotiations will in part be determined by the perceived and actual balance of power between these two factions within the negotiating churches. Resistance to union will come from those groupings which perceive that the balance of power within the proposed united church will be against them. Support for union will come from the parties whose power is likely to be preserved or enlarged in the proposed united church. Bullock also contended that the types of arguments advanced by each wing either to support or to oppose a proposed merger are directly related to the particular position occupied by that wing in the negotiating configuration rather than to its liberal or conservative stance *per se*. Bullock illustrated his hypothesis with evidence drawn from various negotiations for union among Presbyterian and Reformed churches in the USA between 1937 and 1969.

Bullock's general conclusions may help to reconcile some apparently contradictory findings in prevous studies. Mol (1969), Kaill (1971) and Kelly (1971a; 1971b) found that at least among mainline Protestants theological liberalism or conservatism was not significantly related to attitudes to ecumenism. Roof (1978) discovered that among Episcopalians in North Carolina a weak negative relationship between theological conservatism and ecumenism disappeared when he controlled for localism. On the other hand, Bryman *et al.* (1974) observed that forms of churchmanship (which are partly related to theological orientations) differentially affected the attitudes of Anglicans in Britain to possible mergers with various denominations; for example, Evangelicals tended to be more sympathetic to union between the Church of England and the Baptists than to union between the Church of England and the Roman Catholic Church, whereas among Anglo-Catholics the reverse order of preferences tended to apply. Thus, although theological orientation may not determine attitudes to ecumenism in general, it might influence attitudes to particular church union schemes.

The Uniting Church in Australia

How applicable are the above theories in the case of the formation of the Uniting Church in Australia? As the study of this phenomenon is only just beginning, it is not possible to provide a definitive answer to that question at this stage. It is clear, however, that a satisfactory explanation of this merger must take account of the following facts:

1 Negotiations for union among Congregationalists, Methodists and Presbyterians began in the first decade of the present century, shortly after the formation of the Commonwealth of Australia and the establishment of united, national assemblies within each of the three denominations.
2 Although the Methodists and Congregationalists generally approved of the basis, a proposed basis of union was eventually allowed to lapse in 1924 after the Presbyterians had failed to gain sufficient support for the plan in their various state assemblies.
3 In the 1940s, a sharp division of opinion among Presbyterians over the merits of a suggested scheme of federation among those three churches led to the abandonment of this proposal.
4 The negotiations which finally brought the Uniting Church into being began in 1957, the reopening of negotiations having being approved in 1955 by a 75 per cent majority in a plebiscite of communicant members of the Presbyterian Church.
5 The final decision to form the Uniting Church was taken by the national assemblies of the three denominations after individual

members of the churches had voted on the issue. Among members who voted in the latter poll, the majority in favour of the proposed union was 85 per cent for Methodists and 83 per cent for Congregationalists. These results were similar to those which had been recorded in favour of union by members of these denominations in the 1920s, when the percentages were 86 and 84 respectively.

6 Whereas the structure of Methodism enabled its General Conference, on the basis of the above vote, to carry all Methodist congregations and property into the Uniting Church, Congregational polity was such that a congregation of that denomination did not become part of the Uniting Church unless more than two-thirds of the members who voted were in favour of the union. Very few Congregational churches in Victoria, Queensland, and South Australia failed to become part of the Uniting Church. Although about a quarter of the Congregational churches in Western Australia, Tasmania and New South Wales remained out of the Uniting Church, the number of Congregational churches in the former two states was quite small. Consequently, most of the continuing Congregational churches were in New South Wales. Taking Australia as a whole, about 85 per cent of the Congregational churches became part of the Uniting Church.

7 Communicant members of the Presbyterian Church were asked to vote on two questions:

   a Do you desire this congregation to become a congregation of the church which may result from the proposed union?

   b Should the required majority vote for union be obtained in presbyteries, state general assemblies and the general assembly of Australia do you desire to remain in membership of any Presbyterian Church of Australia continuing to function on the present basis?

In the first poll, taken in 1972, 75 per cent of those who voted said 'yes' to question (a), but only 61 per cent said 'no' to question (b). Because of the apparent discrepancy in the pattern of voting on these two questions, it was decided to take a second poll in the following year. On this occasion 72 per cent of voters gave an affirmative reply to question (a) and 69 per cent gave a negative reply to question (b). Only if more than two-thirds of the voting members of a given congregation said 'no' to question (b) would that congregation and its property becomes part of the Uniting Church. On this basis 916 former Presbyterian congregations jointed the Uniting Church, leaving 521 congregations in the continuing Presbyterian Church.

8 Continuing Presbyterian congregations were not randomly distributed geographically. Whereas such congregations in New

South Wales constituted 54 per cent of the undivided Presbyterian Church in that state, the corresponding proportion in Victoria was only 24 per cent. The proportions for the other states were as follows: Queensland, 46 per cent; Tasmania, 34 per cent; South Australia, 26 per cent; Western Australia, 13 per cent.

In a protest to a General Assembly of Australia, one group of Presbyterian ministers and elders gave the following as reasons why they opposed the union:

1. That this church, in entering into such a union on the Basis of Union approved by this Assembly,
    (a) is denying the doctrinal standards of the Presbyterian Church of Australia which each of its ministers has pledged to maintain and defend, namely, its Supreme Standard, the Word of God, as contained in the Old and New Testament to be the only rule of Faith and Practice,
    (b) as a church of Word and Sacrament, is forsaking its subordinate Standard of the Westminster Confession of Faith and specifically in relation to the Sacrament of Baptism, it is denying the convenantal relationship of this Sacrament.
2. The office of the ruling elder in the tradition of the reformed churches will no longer be given its pre-eminent place in the government of the church which will result from the said union.
    (*Minutes and Proceedings of the 35th General Assembly of the Presbyterian Church of Australia*, May 1974, p. 24).

Whether or not these reasons were soundly based, they clearly had to do with theology and church government. As the sociologist W. I. Thomas once wrote, 'If men define situations as real, they are real in their consequences'. But it is doubtful whether such reasons do justice to the variety of motives which prompted opposition to the union.

Speaking in the New South Wales Parliament on the legislation which enabled the Uniting Church to receive its share of the properties held by the three separate denominations, J. A. Cameron, himself a continuing Presbyterian, said:

So far as continuing Presbyterians are concerned, the attitudes that predominate among clergy are basically conscientiously held attitudes that are doctrinal in nature, whereas the attidues that prevail among lay Presbyterians are somewhat more pragmatic...I think that the ordinary man in the pews in the Presbyterian church who has elected not to go into union, simply feels that the church he knows is just too precious to him to be voluntarily laid aside. There is a special problem. All Scottish Presbyterians who see embodied in the Presbyterian church much of the Scottish tradition, feel that would be lost if merged in a new church without a predominantly Scottish character.

(*New South Wales Parliamentary Debates*, 29 March 1977, pp. 5890–1).

Here we have the factor of ethnicity, which has also been identified as one of the bases on which some Presbyterians objected to the formation of the United Church of Canada (File, 1961; Ross, 1973). It is not easy to assess the part played by ethnicity in Australia. The ethnic factor might have been operative among those continuing Presbyterians who were born in Scotland or whose parents were born in Scotland, but self-definition in terms of overseas ethnic background does not appear to be very strong among second- or third-generation Australians. Though not ruling out this factor entirely, I would argue that it had less influence among continuing Presbyterians in Australia than it was claimed to have in Canada. In any case, it is unlikely to have been very influential among the dissenting minority of Congregationalists.

In the speech quoted above, Cameron also referred to another consideration which prevented some Presbyterians from approving the proposed merger; namely, that many Presbyterian institutions arose from benefactions given specifically for Presbyterian purposes. The implication here was that it would be a breach of trust if such institutions came under the control of a new denomination. This objection had been raised against earlier church union proposals both in Australia and in Canada. Taken to its logical conclusion, it would prevent the Presbyterian Church from ever uniting with any other, except by absorption of that denomination into the Presbyterian Church; and then, presumably, a similar objection could be raised from the other side. This objection to union had a self-fulfilling character about it: if some Presbyterians took it seriously, they would refuse to become part of the Uniting Church, and hence doubts could be raised as to whether there was proper continuity between the Presbyterian Church and the Uniting Church. It is difficult to ascertain how far this objection was deeply felt among those who opposed church union and how far it was used as a convenient buttress for objections based primarily on other considerations. That this objection was voiced much more among Presbyterians than among the other parties to the union is consonant with the somewhat greater emphasis in the Presbyterian Church upon matters of law and constitutional procedure. Depending upon one's value hierarchy, it could be interpreted as evidence either of high-minded devotion to principle or of what John Dall (1918: 270) has termed 'the overscrupulous conscience of Presbyterianism'.

Among Congregationalists opposed to union another issue was sometimes raised: should congregations surrender some of the autonomy they had hitherto exercised and accept the authority of the presbytery, the synod and the assembly within the Uniting Church? The recognition of such authority beyond the local congregation was not new for Methodists and Presbyterians but, in theory at least, it was for Congregationalists. The Hunter's Hill Congregational Church, with 32 members, voted by 12 to 8 to remain outside the Uniting Church and also decided not to join the Fellowship of Congregational Churches, a body set up by most of the other continuing Congregational churches in New South Wales for the vesting of their property and for other co-operative activities. So independent did the Hunter's Hill congregation wish to be that it requested and received a special Act of Parliament to deal with the vesting of its property. This action was, however, exceptional.

Just as it is difficult to ascertain whether points of law were primary or secondary bases of objection to union among Presbyterians, it is difficult to determine whether adherence to congregational autonomy was of primary or secondary importance among Congregationalists. What were other bases of objection? One concerned the provisions for appointment of clergy in the Uniting Church. Congregationalists and Presbyterians had a system whereby a particular congregation gave a 'call' to a minister; once called in this way, a minister could usually remain there as long as he wished. Although the Methodist Church had a system whereby a particular circuit could issue an invitation to a minister, and although such invitations were generally upheld, the final decision on all appointments was in the hands of the Methodist Conference in that state; moreover, the maximum length of time that a minister could serve in the one circuit was usually seven years. In these respects, the Methodist minister had somewhat less freedom of choice than his counterparts in the other two denominations. The system of ministerial settlements finally adopted within the Uniting Church allowed for the issuing and acceptance of calls, but in the absence of such a call the synod could make an appointment. The terms under which Presbyterian and Congregational ministers had accepted calls prior to union were to be honoured, but, for all settlements made after the date of union, the maximum period which a minister could serve in any one parish was set at ten years except in special circumstances. Although the details of this system had not been worked out at the time when the final decision to unite was made, some Congregationalists and Presbyterians feared that the new arrangements might not be to their liking.

Differences between denominations in the systems of ministerial settlement relate to another factor which can either promote or impede ecumenism, namely geographical mobility or the lack of it. Towler (1974) and Thompson (1978) noted that people who have been geographically mobile are more likely to be ecumenically mind-ed than are those who lack this experience, whether they be layper-sons or clergy. The Methodist system of itinerancy for ministers was thus more likely to produce ecumenical sentiments among clergy than was the more settled ministry which tended to prevail among Congregationalists and Presbyterians. A comparative examination of the life-histories of a sample of clergy and laity in the three denominations is needed to test the validity of this hypothesis in Australia.

Grant (1967) and Ross (1973) concluded that in Canada one of the most decisive single factors which motivated opposition among Presbyterians to church union was a fear that the United Church would espouse social policies with which they disagreed; for exam-ple, that it would favour alcoholic prohibition, the redistribution of wealth, and so on. It is possible that a similar fear existed among some Presbyterian and Congregational opponents of union in Australia. Indeed, one of the issues that had to be resolved soon after union was whether Methodist law banning the use of alcoholic beverages on church premises was to be adopted within the Uniting Church. On the other hand, some Methodist opponents of union did so partly because they feared that the Methodist stance on alcohol would not necessarily prevail within the Uniting Church. Thus in each denomination the liquor question prompted opposition to union, though the precise fears varied somewhat.

Soon after its formation, the Uniting Church was championing the cause of the aborigines at the former Presbyterian mission sta-tions at Aurukun and Mornington Island in their land rights dispute with the politically conservative Queensland government. By con-trast, the continuing Presbyterian Church withdrew from the World Council of Churches, partly because of the alleged 'grants to guerillas' in the latter body's Programme to Combat Racism. This and other evidence suggests that opponents of church union were, on the whole, more politically conservative than those who sup-ported the formation of the Uniting Church (see Blaikie, 1979: 230–3; Black, 1982).

Vipond (1974) and Ross (1973) have argued that one of the forces which helped to bring the United Church of Canada into being was a growing sense of Canadian nationalism. There the preamble to the Basis of Union stated that 'It shall be the policy of the United Church to foster the spirit of unity in the hope that this sentiment may in due time, so far as Canada is concerned, take shape in a Church which may fittingly be described as national'. It is doubtful whether nationalism had a strong influence in the formation of the Uniting Church in Australia, except in so far as there was a feeling that religious differences derived from overseas were largely irrelevant to the Australian situation. It would certainly be wrong to say that the church union movement was simply a reflection of the growing cultural unity in certain segments of Australian society. Although the latter development undoubtedly provided fertile ground for ecumenical ideas, these ideas also sprang from theological convictions which had been gaining currency throughout the world in the proceding 75 years. Even the title, 'The Uniting Church in Australia' rather than 'The United Church of Australia', was intended to convey the notion that this union was but one step in a wider movement to restore the unity of the church throughout the world. If nationalism was not a strong impulse to union, it was nevertheless invoked after the event, when one Uniting Church leader spoke of the new denomination as 'the first distinctively Australian church'.

The comments made earlier on the Wilson/Currie thesis apply in large measure in Australia. Relative to the total size of the Australian population, Methodists, Presbyterians and Congregationalists each declined in the period between 1911 and 1971, Methodists falling from 12.3 per cent of the total population to 8.6 per cent, Presbyterians from 12.5 per cent to 8.1 per cent, and Congregationalists from 1.7 per cent to 0.6 per cent. This decline was attributable in part to the increasing population of immigrants from Southern Europe, which favoured the growth of the Roman Catholic and Greek Orthodox churches, and to higher birthrates among Roman Catholics in particular. It was not until the period between 1966 and 1971 that the absolute numbers of Methodists, Presbyterians and Congregationalists recorded in official censuses began to fall. Apart from the Church of Christ, these were the only major Christian denominations to suffer such a decrease in this period. Moreover, the numbers of communicant or active members recorded in denominational reports started to fall for Methodists, Presbyterians and Congregationalists in the mid to late 1960s. It is tempting, therefore, to attribute the growth of ecumenism in these three denominations to the decline they were experiencing. But Methodist and Congregational support for church union certainly predated their membership decline, and the Wilson/Currie thesis does not explain adequately why some Presbyterian and Congregational parishes remained out of the Uniting Church. There is little evidence to suggest that support for church union was strongest in those congregations which were weakest or which had suffered the greatest decline. Nor is it correct to say that the church union movement in Australia was largely a clerical phenomenon; witness the high percentage of lay support among Methodists and Congregationalists. What we can say from the Australian data is that the opinions of clergy were highly influential in determining whether their congregations would obtain the majority needed to carry their church into union, a finding which is consistent with that of Kaill (1971). Even here there were notable exceptions such as when, despite strenuous efforts, the Rev. Gordon Powell failed to persuade more than about half the members of Scots Church, Melbourne, to vote in favour of the Basis of Union.

Further research is needed on the personal and social correlates of pro- and anti-church-union sentiments and on the networks of influence and support whereby advocacy of, or opposition to, church union developed in different parts of Australia. Only when these things are better understood will we have the beginnings of an explanation for the geographical distribution both of uniting and of non-uniting congregations.

Note

1 This paper was written while the author was on study leave from the University of New England and a Visitor to the Social and Political Sciences Committee at the University of Cambridge. The assistance of both these institutions is gratefully acknowledged.

8 Who am I in the city of Mammon? The self, doubt and certainty in a Spiritualist cult

Ralph G. Locke

> But I do not yet sufficiently understand what is this 'I' that necessarily exists. I must take care, then, that I do not rashly take something else for the 'I', and thus go wrong even in the knowledge that I am maintaining to be the most certain and evident of all. (Descartes)

Diagnoses of our times are legion, but there are some common themes amongst them which serve to characterise the state of 'post-industrial' society, for example those of anonymity, the separation of social and psychological realities, and a corresponding fragmentation of the self (Berger *et al.*, 1973; North, 1972; Roszak, 1970; Zijderveld, 1970). One vision which we are left with out of these determinations is that of a world marked by significant discontinuities in the process of sharing meanings which, in turn, seems to promote both serious confusions and a desire to change, if not the world, then the self. Transcendence and transformation of the Western legacy of 'existential doubt' and the 'oppression of Weber's iron cage' are a *leitmotif* of the counter-culture spawned in the 1960s and also of Western occult and esoteric traditions (Stone, 1976). The hope of adjustment and the instruments of personal salvation have long been fused and offered to the world by movements which see 'into' the self and 'through' the order of mundane existence.

Whether we choose some aspect of the Human Potential Movement, Rosicrucianism, Silva Mind Control, witchcraft, psychotherapy or something else for personal integration, we reach out of a world in which we are biographically installed and which largely shapes our world view. In reaching out for new meaning, there is an indirect pointing back at the constituents of the familiar world — the body, the self and our significant others — and in some sense they may be rediscovered. But it is a rare, if not unimaginable, set of beliefs and practices which would offer a completely integrated system by which this could be achieved and in such a way that ambiguity, confusion and tension within the system and the self are avoided.

For many participants in esoteric organisations, the quest for meaning and control of personal destiny is a trying one: the fundamental dialectic of self and world is 'ruptured' when the familiar reality is rejected, but then the rupture remains in a new setting with old frustrations and discontents simply transplanted or changed only superficially (Merleau-Ponty, 1967). The neophyte is often sandwiched between the abandoned world and the world anticipated in a situation of mutual indeterminacy. In this sort of setting, doubt and uncertainty may come to rule the interpretation of even the most (previously) familiar experience.

The social order of Spiritualism contains just such a 'mutual indeterminacy' as a basic feature of routine conduct, and especially where becoming a medium is concerned. I propose to analyse some of the dimensions of indeterminacy in mediumship, focusing on an urban Spiritualist cult, and against a background of persistent themes in the history of Spiritualism and other esoteric systems.

Mediumship: Divine instrument or everyman's true nature?

According to most Spiritualists, the history of Spiritualism is a history of discovery or rediscovery of special powers immanent in ordinary persons, powers which speak of the dual nature of man and the cosmos. 'Rediscovery' seems more apt a term since it has long been a tenet of Spiritualists that ancient, occult wisdom and its correlated powers have been buried in a mire of increasing materialism, individualism and science which increasingly and imperiously reigns over human consciousness. Only in recent years, in little more than a century, has the reawakening begun on this earth. For some Spiritualists, it is an expression of a cosmic transition from a Piscean to an Aquarian Age. From these points of view, Spiritualism shares significantly with Theosophy, Rosicrucianism and Liberal Catholicism — representatives of an 'established' esoteric culture (Baum, 1970). Spiritualists believe that the special powers mentioned above enable transcendence of all that is worldly in thought, act and the circumstances of conventional time and space. In thus unfettering the chains of a fleshly, material existence, the universe is unfolded to the committed Spiritualist as a unity, a universal aether which gives form to many worlds of which ours is but one.

While a horizon of infinite promise awaits as the goal of occult wisdom, of paramount concern to Spiritualists has been the expression of such wisdom and power in *this* world. While mediumship must attest to the reality and validity of spiritual and psychic abilities, questions remain about the proper stance toward acquisition of mediumistic capabilities and toward 'orthodox' religious denominations and science. These are issues which have provoked debate and schism in Spiritualism since its beginnings in 1848.[1] Even the seemingly harmless equation of 'spiritual' with 'psychic' faculties is embedded in a massive rift between some psychic researchers, non-Christian Spiritualists and Christian Spiritualists. A leading Spiritualist ideologist and medium, J. S. Morrison (1948: 1), sums up the non-Christian view: 'We regard the ideal type of Spiritualist as one who is first a scientist, then a philosopher, and then an active practitioner of...Modern Spiritualism.' In this statement, science cannot be considered as a strict, experimental undertaking; rather, it is associated with rationalism — a persistent and penetrating questioning of all that seems to inform us about the world and our place in it. As Morrison (1948: 1) puts it:

> Our main purpose is to foster the development of clear thinking on all matters which influence our secular and spiritual well-being; to evolve a sound and self-consistent philosophy based entirely on the known facts, and personal experiences; and to expound a way of life consistent with man's true nature and destiny.

Christian Spiritualists have been more concerned with the congruence between articles of Christian faith and mediumistic knowledge and practices, for example in the relationship between mediumship and the 'gifts of the spirit' which Paul describes in I Corinthians. Mediumship from this point of view is more likely to be seen as a state of grace, defining a moral and spiritual elect. In non-Christian Spiritualism, it is more likely that mediumship will be seen as a variously expressed and developed ability of all persons.

Spiritualism is basically syncretic and individualistic, and the distinction between Christian and non-Christian is blurred within this particular social matrix. Dogmatism is surrendered to 'creative originality' or a 'parallelism of spontaneities'. The potential for variety in belief and action in Spiritualism and a proclivity for fission are embodied in a loosely knit congeries of aspirants who need not abjure any previously held faith in order to 'qualify' as Spiritualists (Martin, 1965: 194).[2]

Since its beginnings, and despite its diversity of ideology, Spiritualism has systematically opposed what it calls 'religious orthodoxy'. This category usually contains the major Christian churches, especially Catholicism, which are thought to be steeped in stultifying and out-dated dogma and organisation. J.M. Peebles, an untiring Spiritualist missionary, author and apologist, formulated the enduring stance of Spiritualism on this matter when he spoke of the evils of orthodoxy in terms of its impact on what he perceived as the seed-bed of all religious movements, the children:

> Children are comparable to sensitive buds and blossoms. Their minds
> are something like sheets of white paper awaiting impression; hence it
> is morally cruel to send them to sectarian Sunday schools to be taught
> theological dogmas, or drive them into maddening whirlpools of
> insanity or atheism. (Peebles, 1910: 64)

Greeley (1971) uses the counter-culture term 'mind-blowers' to
describe the antinomian tendencies of Spiritualists and similar
movements. Within the vast proliferation of drawing-room and
parlour circles, and new churches and fellowships, nineteenth-
century Spiritualists were mind-blowers: they rejected old religious
structures, old religions, old ideas, all associated with orthodoxy,
and submitted to the 'spontaneity of the spirit' exhibited in mediumship.

By citing various biblical passages, it was a simple matter for
Christian churches to reject the power and knowledge claimed by
Spiritualists. A favourite parable cited most often by Protestant
clergy concerns the Witch of Endor.[3] Spiritualists claim that this
Old Testament story provides proof of human survival after bodily
death and of the validity of mediumship. Critics of Spiritualism, on
the other hand, adduce this biblical source when they equate esoteric
and occult beliefs with dangerous delusions and spiritual impoverishment. This and other textual rejections of Spiritualism still
have currency among traditionalists in Protestant and fundamentalist churches. As recently as 1975 the Anglican Archbishop of
Sydney reaffirmed this position when he wrote: 'The truth about the
spiritual realm is to be found in a personal relationship with Jesus
Christ. This is as authentic today as it ever was, and it discloses oc-
cultism as fake, shallow and diversionary' (Loane, 1975: 3).

However, Spiritualism has retained its appeal by staying out of
public polemics and by promoting the unique value which it accords
mediumistic ecstasy. Mediumship is primarily anchored in trance
and possession trance performances,[4] but it also involves other expressions of spiritual or psychic power: namely exceptional abilities
such as clairaudience, clairvoyance, telepathy and precognition
(collectively referred to in modern parapsychology as ESP),
and physical mediumship (psychokinesis or PK), albeit in a variety
of styles. More important than any ethical, inspirational or
phenomenal manifestations of the paranormal is the notion that the
essence of mediumship lies in the equating of ecstasy with
knowledge. Knowledge is the spark which ignites awareness of a
spirit reality over and above the transient illusion of the material
world. Moreover, it is the core of Spiritualism's esoteric tradition

and, in particular, its Gnostic view of man in the cosmos. Emma Hardinge Britten, a famous pioneer of the Spiritualist movement, used the following example to demonstrate the importance of Gnosis and its unique Spiritualist relevance:

> To one of those who had thus put his hand to the plough and turned back, the author lately queried, 'And do you still call yourself a Spiritualist?' 'In belief, I certainly am,' was the reply, 'for how can I un-know what I have once known.' And herein consists the real difference between Spiritualism and every other form of belief. Sectarian religionists believe without knowledge: Spiritualists know, and therefore believe. (Britten, 1869: 511)

This idea of a kind of knowledge which motivates a spiritual commitment involves revelation of a paranormal order which resonates in the unique experience of each individual. So what is knowledge for one may not be knowledge for another. The testimony of the spirit through spirit mediumship lies in its ideographic, ineffable and noetic qualities.

Within Spiritualism there are deep-seated strains which have shaped the development of mediumship wherever the movement has appeared in the Western world. Production and transmission of knowledge through the powers of mediumship, whether subject to rational scientific or credal scrutiny for authorisation, pose the problem of allowing for freedom and spontaneity of mediumistic expression and yet, for some, providing the security of organisational regulation and control (Nelson, 1968: 474). Moreover, the perennial issue of intergenerational transmission of the esoteric culture, once handled so effectively by the now defunct Lyceum movement, is aggravated by the emphasis placed on individual development of mediumistic abilities and the view that knowledge is intensely personal (Nelson, 1969; Thompson, 1948).

As is the case in many Gnostic belief systems, Spiritualism is embodied in the pursuit of the 'inner' man, the 'real' self and its projection on to a mystically transformed world and cosmic order in a new, more adequate form. Mediumship involves ecstatic experience which constitutes a 'looking-glass self' of social competence, ethical virtuosity and inner peace as achievable goals in this world and the next (Martin, 1965: 194).

Charisma sustains much of Spiritualism's organised activity; but it is an incomplete charisma, as Nelson (1968: 480) points out:

> It is important to remember...that a medium is not a fully charismatic leader since all members are thought to be potential mediums and a high proportion of the members of any Spiritualist

group have some level of psychic attainments, though in most cases their gifts are comparatively undeveloped.

However, Nelson paints only a partial picture: a central problem in Spiritualism is the reconciliation of ideas of unlimited psychic development open to all, the potential mediumship of all believers, with the belief that some are conferred with 'gifts' which set them apart as a spiritual and leadership cadre. This conflict is often revealed in the opposition of 'psychism', the production and investigation of paranormal phenomena (sometimes called 'phenomenalism'), and 'spiritualism', the spiritually and ethically controlled exercise of 'gifts' for the edification of all mankind. For many Spiritualists, psychic phenomena including ouija boards, psychometry and clairvoyance, for example, are 'mere material signs to arrest the attention of a material world'. All developments of spirit in man and the cosmos are believed to proceed from low powers and knowledge, psychism, to the highest, spiritualism, and many see their quest as a matter of surpassing the lower, distracting stage of psychism.

While these differences in perspective represent Spiritualism in broad strokes of the canvas, the finer detail shows the differences as frequent grounds for fission. New circles, churches, psychic research groups and lone mediums appear regularly; they flourish, mellow and die or pass into quiescence and formality which again invites the vigour of youthful and creative reconstruction.

Spiritualism and Theosophy are the popular occult old-guard in the West. The 'occult revival' of the 1960s was regarded by many Spiritualists with a mixture of relief (here is the new force which will revitalise us and carry us forward into the Golden Age) and foreboding (youthful exuberance leads to danger which can only be avoided by the wisdom derived from our experience. Will they come to us and learn?).

Claims for spiritual power, then, are unlikely to be perceived in a purified, intellectual manner; rather, they are infused with the remnants of contests in Spiritualist history and the peculiarities of the contemporary cultus of imperfect charisma. That which sets Spiritualists apart from the domains of science, 'orthodoxy' and everyday life, in the exoteric sense, is that which sets Spiritualist apart from Spiritualist: an inequality of power and the instrumentalities of authority embodied in a struggle for truth which is at once both psychological and social. In terms of social order, Spiritualism involves a counterpoint between the need for attainment of status and a perennial liminality, especially where generational differences are concerned.[5]

'Struggle' and 'counterpoint' are the essence of problems of personal adaptation and adjustment in Spiritualist cults; their resolution is the way to mediumship. Now I plan to carry these themes forward in a case discussion of a Spiritualist cult where treatment will move from a general description of the cult origins and organisation to a detailed analysis of conflict and its correlates.

The Sanctuary: A study in ambiguity

Charisma and social order

The Sanctuary was initially established in Fremantle, the port city for Perth, Western Australia, in 1954. The leader, Mrs Trudy Lucas, had emigrated from England with her third husband in 1953. For the Lucases, the setting up of the church 'in the spirit of Christian love' was the culmination of years of spiritual work in Britain and the prime indicator of their mission in life.

Trudy's development as a medium was spectacular by Spiritualist standards. Her own words are illuminating in setting out her initial contacts with the spirit world and, thereby, with her nascent mediumistic abilities:

> I was a devout Anglican for most of my early life. During the war I drove an ambulance and I had an accident in 1942. I was driving the ambulance on a slippery road with my offsider and crashed out of control into a train. My heart was bruised and my ribs and sternum were broken. I blacked out and seemed to be floating above the ground near the spot where we crashed. An ambulance came with some of my co-workers. They thought I was dead, so they covered me with a sheet. I wasn't, though, and they were ecstatic when I threw back the sheet with a supreme effort.[6]
>
> I was taken to the Freemasons' Hospital. The last thing I remembered after floating was calling out to a friend, 'I'm going! I'm going!' Then I blacked out. When I came to, there was a nursing sister sitting next to me. She said to me, 'You don't mind which way it goes, do you?' She [the nurse] then got a shove in the back [from the spirits] and a voice said, 'Get a drink, hot-water bottle, and blankets.' Well, the drink strengthened me and the hot-water bottle got some of the fever out.
>
> After that, I rallied a bit. They asked me if I'd like to see my daughter. Well, then my daughter came and I told her that I wasn't going to die. This contradicted the doctors. My daughter passed this on to the doctors. She told them, 'My mother will not die. She knows.' I had a miracle recovery. My guide [from the spirit world] did not want me to die.
>
> Two years before this [in 1940], I nearly died with kidney trouble. Really, I had died. I felt I was talking to the nursing sister from the

ceiling, and I could see my body wriggling in pain, but I couldn't feel a thing. Then I went back into my body.[7]

Anyway, when I was recovering from the accident, the sister [nurse] said, 'You'd make a lovely clairvoyant. You've got lovely eyes.' Then she said, 'You don't understand, do you?' Well, I didn't then. But the nurse told me my sister would pass over [die] on the eleventh of October. It came true.

After this, I went to a circle, seeking. The medium gave descriptions of a naval officer and his name. She also made some predictions about my two children. But I was still doubtful at this stage. Then the medium said, 'Oh, why a light?' No one else could know what that meant: those were the last words of my first husband. He died of a heart attack.

For Trudy, this was conclusive evidence of survival and, therefore, the truth of Spiritualism. After that series of profound experiences, her powers developed fully in 18 months. Not only was she capable of clairvoyance and clairaudience, usually occurring in some form of divination, but she also became a full trance medium, that is one who is possessed by a spirit in circumstances controlled by the medium, other mediums or spiritual persons, and helpers from the spirit world. Trudy worked for two years with Lord Dowding, a renowned spokesman for Spiritualism, on rescue work, which concerns bringing lost spirits, those who did not know that they had passed over and those who did not want to relinquish the earth, to spiritual light.[8] With fifteen sitters in the circle, Trudy managed five trances a night. By most Spiritualists' judgements, this was an exceptional performance.

One night at a circle, Trudy was told by spirit guides to start her own Spiritualist centre in England, and to later start one in Australia. She did not believe, at the time, that this could happen. But it came to pass. Significant proof of Trudy's destiny seemed to follow at a great rate. In England, Trudy had been a member of White Eagle Lodge, begun in 1936 by Mrs Grace Cooke. The lodge was organised at the inspiration of Mrs Cooke's guide, White Eagle, and it was primarily concerned with the philosophy and religious aspects of Spiritualism rather than with proof of survival. The tenets of the lodge were predominantly Christian. There was no concern for psychic research. Trudy was also an admirer of the Greater World Christian Spiritualist League (GWCSL) which was established in 1931 after ten years of inspirational pronouncements from Zodiac, the spirit of a teacher in the temple at the time of Jesus, who came through the medium, Winifred Moyes. These organisations served as models for Trudy's church in Australia.

The Sanctuary began in a modest way in 1954. Three and a half years later, in 1957, lack of space forced a move to premises in

Mosman Park, a suburb between Perth city and Fremantle. Trudy became the official, and by law the only, celebrant. Marriage, burial and christening ceremonies were drafted and lodged with the Commonwealth registrar. The avowed principles of the Sanctuary were Christian, with some Vedic influences.[9] Divorced people could be married in the Sanctuary, and a number of forms of pastoral counselling were provided — psychiatric, marital, parenting, amongst others — from the viewpoint of a Spiritualist psychology.[10]

Early in the life of the church Trudy engaged in a common practice in organised Spiritualism, namely serving in the capacity of spiritually inspired speaker, clairvoyant and trance medium in other churches. This is a familiar pattern throughout Australia and the United Kingdom: mediums circulate through churches on a reciprocal and invitational basis. However, as Trudy's following grew, relations with other churches in Perth became strained, and the Sanctuary's expanding activities commanded her every moment. Accordingly, Trudy ceased to serve in other churches and chose to invite only the 'most competent, clear and accurate mediums' to her platform. Her justification for this isolationism and quality control was provided and given force in a single trance in 1958 when she and her followers claimed that Christ 'came through her', elevating her above other mediums experienced by the church members.

Christ's possession of Trudy, together with consistent appearances of 'high' guides with her, greatly strengthened the appeal of the Sanctuary and magnified Trudy's charisma. Gains in attendance and commitment far outweighed the losses incurred amongst conservative Spiritualists who were outraged at the 'extravagant claims of a gifted but deluded trance medium'.[11] Trudy's devotees felt her power at every encounter, a power exemplified at its zenith in the Easter message. A close friend, confidant and fellow worker of Trudy's gave the following description of her experience of Trudy's mediumship:

> Most of the teachings come from very high guides. The power is so great when her main guide comes through that, on one occasion, when I was having Communion from Trudy, only the rail [along the front of the church altar] stopped me from levitating. I was drawn toward this light.

At the peak of Trudy's mediumship the Sanctuary was filled to capacity; up to 120 people crammed the little ex-store for Sunday services. Moreover, at this time her husband supported her in every way: with love, spiritual upliftment, tireless organising efforts and, most important, power. It is part of Trudy's belief that a man should be conductor of services while the female medium prepares for trance. Man and woman are as positive and negative in electrical current flow. Thus the symbiosis between Trudy and her husband was expressed as his providing power while she received and thereby became the vessel for spirit entities. In this way, the justification for their separate existences and their mutual dependence was made patent. The electrical analogy is typical of the way in which many Spiritualist beliefs are described within the Sanctuary and within the Spiritualist movement more generally, and especially beliefs concerning universal, spiritual 'laws'.

When Trudy's husband died in 1964, she lost her 'power station' and much of her mediumistic ability: 'I am weak now. You need a man to be a chairman.' However, Trudy was 67 at that time and her health was failing. More and more authority had to be delegated to others, and many activities which had depended upon her, such as the spiritual development classes and public seances, had to be abandoned. The role previously taken by Trudy's husband was assumed by Mrs Betty Pinnock, a pious woman whose aim was to establish 'Christianity first, Spiritualism second'. Although Mrs Pinnock (Betty) did not generate as much power as Trudy's husband (Vic), Trudy was reluctant to conduct any activity requiring her mediumship without Betty.

The manifest destiny of individuals, circles and churches in Spiritualism is largely shaped by symbolic and directive messages from the spirit world. Just as the meaning of Trudy's strange experiences in her childhood — for example, knowing that her three brothers had been wounded in World War I before official notification was received — was understood and given new meaning when the truth of spirit was revealed, so the future was projected and given substance by such revelations. Trudy and Vic were 'watched from the spirit world for three years' before they were sent a letter which was seen clairvoyantly in a seance and which told them to start a lodge within the Sanctuary.

The lodge was named the Polaire Lodge after Trudy's interpretation of the dominant symbol of the White Eagle Lodge, the six-pointed star, Polaris. Originally, there were nine members of the lodge, including Trudy and Vic, but by 1971 there were only six members. Theoretically, the lodge was open, as stated in its articles:

The Polaire Assembly

It must be understood that the Polaire Assembly is not a Masonic Lodge, but it is an Assembly of the Ancient Master Centres of Egypt, India, and Tibet, operating entirely under the direct instructions of the Masters. Masons can participate in the Polaire Assembly without any infringement of their obligations.

The Polaire Brotherhood does not confine its activity to its own members, but regards every man of every sect or creed, of every race or colour and in every station of life as its Brothers.

Polaires are not necessarily Spiritualists. They are participating in life on earth and Brotherhood towards men.

Unlimited membership is possible but is practised in a special way: the ideal brotherhood of all men is realised in the healing actions of the lodge which involve sending power, love and spiritual upliftment throughout the world from the Masters (these are high spiritual beings which include Trudy's guide), The Great Power (God) and Christ. In the social life of the Sanctuary, however, membership of the lodge is limited: a careful, spiritual screening process is continually conducted by Trudy and the other five members. Admission to the lodge comes only after extensive monitoring of an aspirant's spirituality by members who 'sense', 'feel', 'see' and are 'told about' influences about the aspirant, and by Trudy's guide, Sapheren ('this is now his name which was changed from Kepheren, the Sphinx'). In thirteen years, Trudy had not felt 'drawn to anyone'.

The lodge is highly ritualised and each member wears garments which indicate that person's stage of spiritual development. Members also wear a silver, six-pointed star on the left shoulder. Trudy is the central figure in all proceedings where she conducts activities while possessed by Sapheren. The circle formed by the membership serves to perpetuate the aims, creed and practices of the lodge, but it also serves as a development group sanctioned by Trudy and her guide.

For the lodge members, there are strong ties: a spiritual fellowship and bonds of affection extending over many years. The shortest membership time is thirteen years, while the rest have belonged for fourteen or fifteen years. Membership is totally made up of ageing females: Trudy (74 in 1971, celebrant, widow, trance medium and healer), Nancy (61, married, healer and psychometrist), Joan (45, married, trance healer), Eve (74, widow, once a healer but now with few spiritual abilities, church organist), Dorothy (50, married, a helper in spiritual healing) and Betty (50, married, clairvoyant with great power and knowledge).

This spiritual and moral elect constitutes the core of all Sanctuary activities — services, healing and counselling. Responsibility for management, logistics and control of most of this work is invested in Trudy first and Betty and Nancy second. Around this cluster, others participate in Sanctuary affairs according to spiritual power or potential and friendship relations. For example, a small number of middle-aged women make tea and set the table in the church sitting-room every Wednesday for healing and every Sunday for services.

But these women are not seen by themselves or others as having significant power or any real future as mediums. They are all close friends and do not initiate any of the church's spiritual specialisations such as healing.

For services and healing, the Sanctuary is open: anyone may attend. Spiritual healing is regularly attended by some with chronic ailments, but also by those who come for other reasons. As one said:

> I've known Trudy for eighteen years. Every week I travel the fifty-odd miles from Mandurah to Perth just to be here. Mind you, I don't have any special illness, you know. It's the rest and peace just sitting here. It's nice to know that help will be given if you need it . . . from spirit of course. I get a lot of strengthening here . . . my body and my spirit . . . If Trudy was gone, I don't know what I would do.

Some people come to the Sanctuary to 'experiment'; that is they come to see how the 'vibrations' and the 'evidence' compare with that in other churches and circles. In addition to Trudy's followers, a constant stream of people circulates through the church and other groups in Perth. There are four focal activities in the Sanctuary: healing and counselling, services, circles and 'behind the scenes' action.

1 Healing and counselling   Most healing takes place in the Sanctuary on Wednesdays in two sessions, 2–5 p.m. and 7–10 p.m. Healing opens usually with a spiritually inspired address and prayer from Trudy, or Nancy when Trudy is indisposed; this performance establishes the appropriate vibrations. Several kinds of healing are offered but not psychic surgery, which is a method of operating on the etheric body (spiritual body of a person while they are on the earth-plane) usually performed by a medium in trance. While Trudy sees herself as capable of doing psychic surgery, she tends to minimise her trance activities because of its claimed debilitating effects. Polaire Lodge members are involved in another form of healing: visiting the Claremont Psychiatric Hospital monthly, usually after a lodge meeting, and ministering to the mentally ill. The visits are not officially sanctioned; so they proceed under the guise of 'hospital visits by community bodies'. The main reason for the subterfuge lies in the fact that the Polaires hold 'unorthodox' notions about mental illness from the medical point of view. Specifically, diagnosed psychotics are believed by the Polaires to be persons who are permanently possessed by low, that is evil, spirits. Therefore, they require Spiritualist concepts in order to be understood and then healed.

Counselling is given on a wide range of matters, and especially marital and sexual problems. Financial advice is given and sometimes also a small donation which comes out of the church plate. Money is usually given only to close friends of the Polaires.

2 Services   Every Sunday at 7 p.m. a service is held, and on the last Friday of every month a Communion service is held, again at 7 p.m. Services are conducted by John Lane, Joan's husband, who gives power to the medium giving the inspirational or trance address and clairvoyance or some form of psychometry. On Sundays, Trudy usually sits at the rear of the church, welcoming and farewelling the congregation. An 'outside' medium occupies the platform with the conductor. The pattern of services, which is repeated often in Australian Spiritualist churches, is as follows: welcome by the conductor, hymn, meditation and absent healing (sending love and power to those who need it but who are not present), address by the medium, hymn, clairvoyance or psychometry for the congregation, hymn during which 'love offerings' are placed in the plate, and a closing prayer.

Occasionally, a reading from the Bible is given by Betty or one of Trudy's young and promising followers. Being 'promising' means having passed the spiritual and moral scrutiny applied by the Polaires; and, it seems, 'passing' is never complete, as I shall demonstrate in a later analysis. Alexander's hymn book is used. It is adapted for Spiritualist use with a brief history of the GWCSL in the front. Sacred texts advocated are, in order of importance, the Bible, *The Aquarian Gospel of Jesus the Christ*, an esoteric interpretation of the life of Christ in the years between his appearance in the temple at age 12 and his reappearance in Galilee at age 30, and *Onward Humanity*, a book of Spiritualist cosmology dictated to a circle in England through a trance medium. Anyone to whom Trudy feels spiritually attracted, who 'truly seeks knowledge', is given *Onward Humanity* to read. Its descriptions are complex and comprehensive of major Spiritualist beliefs and its influence is readily discerned in Trudy's ministry.

Communion is conducted only by Trudy. The service is modelled on the Anglican Communion except that Trudy is possessed by Sapheren, and the prayer of consecration is replaced by messages from the spirit world delivered to each individual in order to inspire and uplift. The sacrament is not encumbered with the theological problem of transubstantiation since it is postulated that all things are of God, in a particular way — all things share a universal, irreducible aether or vibration, and only form or appearance varies. The power of love and harmony elevates sacramental vibrations to a higher level, uplifting and cleansing the spirit and revitalising the body.

Special services are held for Easter and Christmas. These occasions, as with the Polaire Lodge, are especially important since they reinforce the connection between the Great Power and the Sanctuary as a centre of spiritual power. Trudy's charisma is reaffirmed through the association of these occasions with her possession by Christ and the continuity of his power in high guides (Masters).

3 *Circles*   Outside of formalised church activities, the circle remains the principal method of spiritual communion. Moreover, it is an opportunity for like-minded individuals to meet and experiment in friendly circumstances, usually in a member's home, and to engage personal styles of mediumship. Indeed, it is thought by many Spiritualists and observers of the movement that the circle is not only the historical foundation of Spiritualism but also its guarantee of survival in contemporary society (Britten, 1869; Thompson, 1948). It is an anchor against the tide of social change and a counter to the impersonality of increasing organisation in churches. While most Spiritualists who are involved in the management of the Sanctuary sustain a recognised cultus, they are also involved in the greater free-play of mediumistic and belief expression in home circles.

A 'free-floating' organisation of ideas and action allows for a common focus in the midst of diversity. The central belief commonality in the Sanctuary is found in the official cultus and secondarily in the fact of experimentation and innovation as a claim for each individual's personal relationship with the spirit world. At the same time, the latter social activity provides the mainsprings of rifts in the organisation.

Finally, the most important feature of circles is that they are attempts to democratise spiritual power. The nucleation of power in Sanctuary functionaries on public occasions is countered by the universality of power manifestations in circles. Circles allow a significant transformation of *spiritual* power in a circle of friends into social power in the form of a new organisation and a new leader in competition with the old.

4 *Behind the scenes*   The 'reality' of the spirit world and spiritual powers has one concrete form in the cultus of the Sanctuary and regular sittings by members in home circles. But Spiritualism as an individual quest and as a way of life has another form: that of testing and attesting to spiritual powers in casual encounters. For example, before, during and after services and healing, Trudy's friends and co-workers gather in a small, back room to engage in conversation and, more often, to discuss encounters 'with spirit' in everyday life. Occasionally, an impromptu sitting is held, perhaps a 'low power' form such as psychometry.[12] Nancy quite often gives flower

readings on Wednesdays after the first session of healing: each person present who wishes a reading (proof of survival, character analysis and predictions) plucks a flower or leaf and places it upon a tray provided, making certain that Nancy does not know to whom each item belongs. A circle is formed, with Nancy flanked by power-givers (usually Trudy and Joan), whereupon she reads for each item, sensing the unique vibrations impressed upon the leaf or flower by the person who plucked it.[13] These kinds of events are treated very seriously, since they may provide, sometimes quite unexpectedly, the key to someone's spiritual unfolding, decisive influences in the future, or health diagnostics and treatment advice. Accordingly, close attention is paid to the 'evidential quality' of the reading conditions; for example, the preservation of anonymity of item ownership, closing of the medium's eyes to reduce feedback from 'material senses' (i.e. sensory cues), and silence observed by sitters, again to reduce feedback and confusion of vibrations.[14]

Those interested in the Sanctuary and Spiritualism generally may meet in a small sitting-room and kitchen at the back of the Sanctuary where they discuss books, the latest psychic happenings, personal spiritual experiences and personal problems. For those who have received the revelatory gnosis, walking, sitting, standing, smelling, seeing, touching — the full range of human perception and action — are capable of interpretation in terms of the spiritual world at any time and in any place. Snippets of conversation at the Sanctuary give an idea of this occupancy of dual worlds and interpretive schemes.

Case 1: Gee, I just walked in here and I got pains in the head. It seems to be coming from that lady over there. She could have some trouble. I'll check that later.

Case 2: *Ivan* You don't know me. My name is Ivan.

Robert My name is Robert. How do you do?

Ivan I'm very pleased to meet you. You know, Robert, whatever you do in life will be a great success (glances over the head of Robert to see his guide and aura). Your work here will be fruitful (stares just over Robert's head). You have a wonderful light surrounding you.

Robert Thank you.

Case 3: I keep getting this feeling. Something or somebody isn't right here. I don't know whether it's me or someone else. Ahhh ... you know, I can see a man building up in the corner behind you, Jim. He's the person I saw in my dream the other night. You know what I told you. Here it is, just as I told you.

Case 4: *Les*   Who's got a bad back here?

        Fred   Me. It's an old injury that keeps coming back.

        Les   Well, this old Egyptian I can see...you know, I can see him clear as day...says to change your bed and stop eating all those acidy foods.

This is 'living Spiritualism' as a way of life. Every event retains the possibility of prophetic significance, spiritual revelation and, more important, clues to each party's standing with respect to their spiritual development in terms of the Sanctuary power structure, circles of friends and the total cosmic order. Action which is cast in these terms is an important part of sustaining one's self-image as an actual or potential bearer of power and knowledge, and the projection of this image as 'front'.

> It will be convenient to label as 'front' that part of the individual's performance which regularly functions in a general and fixed fashion to define the situation for those who observe the performance. Front, then, is the expressive equipment of a standard kind intentionally or unwittingly employed by the individual during this performance. (Goffman, 1971: 32)

Thus front at the Sanctuary is not only a matter of securing desired responses to routine performances in organised circumstances, since there is always the possibility that powers may be seen as 'situation bound' in the sense of being dependent upon the collective power and attention of others, but also a matter of demonstrating familiarity and facility with spirit in all things, and on all occasions.

Sustaining a front with the strong possibility of a favourable response as an added motivation leads to serious strains in the social life of the Sanctuary. Returning to an earlier observation, the incomplete charisma of Trudy is ensured by her own doctrine that gifts may be conferred on others. But while others search for enlightenment and power, their only access is through the single, 'official' development circle at the Sanctuary if they wish to adhere to organisational pathways. Trudy's failing health necessitates less accomplished Polaires controlling proceedings. Young aspirants seize the opportunity presented by weakened control to fulfil prophetic visions arising out of their own circles: powerful encounters with spirit soon become bases for schism.

In the eyes of Trudy and her followers, the lot of the Sanctuary is worsened by the appearance of new organisations which draw off the congregation and dilute or alter the 'truth'. An example of an organisation which drew considerable ire is the Institute of Metaphysics of Australia, a centre for occult studies and psychic research which began in Perth and expanded to other states. It was perceived by the Polaires as a stronghold of egoism, delusion and false claims both about the spirit world and the Sanctuary.

Attracting congregations to the Sanctuary depends upon the quality of circulating mediums used there. But Trudy and the Polaires dislike this situation since they feel that most mediums on the circuit use 'low' forms of spiritual gifts, such as psychometry, magnetic healing and weak clairvoyance. Less than optimum gifts are perceived to betray Sanctuary ideals. The charisma of Trudy has faded, however, and there is no officially appointed successor.

Consciousness and social order
While charisma fades in the old as a consequence of its imperfection and of attrition, it arises anew in the young. The ascent of neophytes to the status of medium, however, is not simply a matter of mechanical replacement of lost spiritual power in an organisation; rather, it is a complex social process involving an accentuation of the uncertainty and liminality ubiquitous in the maintenance of front. Specifically, transitional status in the Sanctuary involves a heightening of social and psychological indeterminacies which emerges out of stress and the ways in which both stress and status are understood. The result is that the neophyte is quite often caught in a dilemma revolving about reciprocal recognition of status, authority and the meaning of actions. The following case illustration exemplifies this dilemma, first in general, descriptive terms, and then in terms of the dimensions of meaning sharing which are central to the dilemma.

Consider this scene: healing has been scheduled for 7 p.m. Trudy is ill and incapable of conducting proceedings. After a brief consultation amongst those present, excluding patients, Les has been chosen to lead. Les is an ambitious, young (35), aspiring medium who is supported by several others in his age group. He says a brief prayer of welcome to the patients, spirit guides and Sanctuary workers and then goes quietly into trance. He remains in this state, guiding healing, for some 30 minutes. Suddenly, he is overcome by violent, clonic jerks as well as choking and staggering. His helpers quickly identify his condition as the result of an attempted possession by an unknown spirit. As this took place, Joan entered. The following interaction ensued, after Les had recovered from the 'symptoms'.

Jan (Les's wife)   How do you feel?

Les	All right. But there was something different there. He doesn't always come through that way. It's only on certain people. He comes through very strong on Anne [a patient] always. I don't know who he is yet. I haven't discovered it yet. But he...different people, where the healing power is necessary, he comes through strongly. He comes through not as strongly on you, Jan.
Jan	That worries me. I get a shakeup at times. The only way you could stop...Les could go on the ground [fall down], I think.
Joan	Well, that shouldn't happen.
Jan	I asked the spirit guides and they said if I didn't shake, then you wouldn't believe it...what's happening. But I feel he shouldn't go so long. He shouldn't be so distressed.
Joan	Did you see who it was [i.e. the possessing spirit]?
Jan	Some saw a light. But I can't see the face. They don't have any clothes...just the outline, the light.
Les	There's just this one guide who does it, and I don't know who he is or what he is. I know when I get this one, that I get a terrific amount of power, and, um, he's bigger than I am.
Joan	Well, this is where you see the advantages of being in a circle. That is, a circle run by experienced mediums...someone like Trudy. You sit nearly every week and they [the spirits] get used to your body before they come. They shouldn't come in like this.
Jim (Jan's brother)	I really don't agree with this. In my experience, I think you can over-control the guides. I think this has been the case. A little bit too much emphasis has been placed on rigid control which has stifled the development of some young mediums.
Joan	This is not exactly what I said. It's not a case, exactly, of controlling your guides; it's a case of your guide getting used to coming into your body, gently. It shouldn't use your body like that. He should come in more gently. And the

more often they do this in a circle where you have an experienced medium...she can tell them how to behave whilst you're going into trance and she can see them coming in. She can tell them how to treat you. You see, if you're small, for instance, and you've got a huge guide...I had this experience once when I was in a circle: I was being stretched up and up. With an experienced medium, they know how to handle the situation until they get used to you...gently, which is what they should do...because otherwise, um, you get a newcomer, you could get a mob of demons. You need a good circle, you see.

Jan   But there's no use telling anyone you want to go [to the circle run by Trudy]. You virtually have to be invited to them.

Joan   Oh, yes. It's a case of keep pressing. If they think that you're keen, you know.

Jan   Les was told [by spirits] to hold a meeting on Saturday night. And Les's guides are coming together and developing through him. That one is just the healer. The other ones just come through. Sometimes they tell us who they are. Sometimes we tell them.

There are some interesting features to this exchange which bear directly upon the exploration of the neophyte's dilemma. In the first place, there is a representation from the upper echelon of the Sanctuary in confrontation with a group which comprises a spiritual fellowship, but which is not officially sanctioned. There is no doubt in Joan's mind, or Trudy's (I later confirmed), that Les has power: he attracts and uses it. And all present are possessed of the fundamental gnosis which makes them into seekers of wisdom. Yet, the differences between perspectives are equally apparent and important. Joan, in her attachment to Trudy, speaks with an authority invested by lengthy spiritual development guided by a charismatic light. She perceives Les to have power, but in an uncontrolled form. It is uncontrolled in the sense that it is not manifested as a function of Les's free will, and it therefore violates his body and psyche. Equally, it is uncontrolled because it is not identified; its potential for good or evil is not established. So, from her point of view, Les's knowledge is rudimentary: it is not the master of his power. For Joan, knowledge is control of the self and the spirit. It is therefore equal to spiritual development. But knowledge is also the result of both active seeking and conferral by spirits. Older, more experienced mediums are required to pass on knowledge which is at once practical (i.e. how to go about spiritual activities) and moral (i.e. how to ensure one's enlightenment and safety). In pursuing a course of separate experimentation, an independent quest for knowledge, Les and his circle court danger as the Polaires see the situation.

For Les and his fellow seekers, a glimpse of the spirit world has brought its own imperatives. Limited access to the inner sanctum of development has generated a need for spiritual unfolding in a situation which brings new spiritual horizons for the whole circle, and especially Les. In the exchange with Joan, Jim felt that young mediums had been suppressed through an unwarranted emphasis on control (i.e. 'control' in the spiritual sense becomes a political device). Jan's position can be summed up in the following statements which counter Joan's, and thereby Trudy's, authority:

A   While we are denied access to the leader's circle, we develop unaided by her and her spirit guides.
B   What is more, such meetings are authorised by spirits themselves, not by us or the leader.
C   While we experience spiritual phenomena of varied kinds, and so develop, spirits also come to us for knowledge and development.
D   The validity of Les's mediumship is ensured, anyway, by the fact that his taking over the healing occasioned by the leader's absence was foretold that morning by Les's guide.

Certainly, the assertions made by Jan did not meet the standards demanded by many Spiritualists for verification of mediumistic abilities, and certainly not where researchers are concerned. However, the statements served a purpose other than the business of establishing the evidentiality of Les's mediumship; they were aimed at demonstrating the consequences of closing off opportunities for spiritual development within the Sanctuary. Les's mediumship had become the line of demarcation between separate fields of social interaction and correlated spiritual horizons, between the Sanctuary 'old guard' and the renegade circle.

The stuff of the interaction surrounding Les's possession, although brief, is sufficient to demonstrate some important differences in meaning attached to a single event in a Spiritualist church where there is a sustained and dynamic tension between order and spontaneity in mediumship. The discontinuity in meanings assigned to the episode in question within the Sanctuary expresses a divergence in the rationality of action of the two competing groups, centred on generational differences. At the same time, the conflict shows the relative, and necessary, opacity of each group's gnosis to the other. But for Les and his circle, the incident was the tip of a pyramid whose ever-broadening base consisted in successively illuminating encounters with their spirit helpers so that spirit communications achieved an authority and force of their own, underscored by the bonds of common travail and moral siege mounted by the Polaires.

Despite the enumerated differences between the two groups, they certainly also shared various beliefs: the notion of Spiritualism as a way of life, the centrality of mediumship in communications with the spirit world, ideas about spiritual development, and so on. But such sharing poses a problem in a religion which sets itself against orthodoxy: the tension between collective ideals and individualism, and between ritualism and creative worship, becomes institutionalised. In Spiritualism, co-operation and sharing actions and ideas comprise a tenuous union, for in the midst of apparent commonality, the very assumed core of discourse expressed in terms like 'spiritual', 'material', 'evidence' and 'development' is but a loosely floating set of markers for widely disparate experiences, motivations and interpretive schemes. The social structure floats in another sense which is closely related to the first, and that is in the fact that mediums are perennially liminal — in a position of inferiority or dominance as context dictates, while 'context' has to be constantly determined with ambiguous criteria. Perhaps one may argue successfully that all of social life is like this, and I would offer little by way of contradiction except to say that for the Spiritualist who wishes to become and remain a medium, it is 'more so'; that is, the conflicts and indeterminacies of meaning endemic to the social world are accentuated. A closer look at this is in order.

In Spiritualism, the ideas about mediumship and spiritual powers are tied to a developmental world view. All things in this world and the next are believed to be in a constant state of movement to a higher or lower state of spiritual attainment. Stasis is rarely mentioned, except where it is applied, indirectly, to great spiritual Masters at the top of the spiritual pyramid in the spirit world. It is a moral imperative for Spiritualists to seek out their state of development — that is to have it clearly measured — in order, then, to transcend it. Having special abilities means being able to see one's state of development earlier than others and also more clearly. Transcendence should also follow sooner and easier than in others who are less fortunate. But both the 'fact' of special abilities and correlated discernment of developmental status are negotiated in the 'floating' social structure of Spiritualism.

For Les and his associates, the larger 'game' of Sanctuary life excludes a satisfactory settlement of their claims to spiritual knowledge. Separate development, in the social sense initially, with all of its risks seems the only course to take. At least, that is the way they see it. The risks are those of permanent exclusion from the Sanctuary and, more seriously, the possibility that their knowlege is really delusional (i.e. the lurking fear that Trudy is right about them). Les faces the threat, in addition, that his steadily accumulated, though marginal, status may dissipate in the democratisation of spiritual powers within his circle. The dilemma remains.

So far, I have presented mediumistic liminality in terms of power, authority and meanings. It also concerns consciousness; or, rather, the other dimensions of liminality are void without an address to the changes which occur in individual and shared consciousness within Spiritualist groups. The world of intentional objects, the meaningful constitution of consciousness, is transformed through the mediumistic commitment: the 'halos' or 'fringes' of the exoteric order become the substance of the esoteric and new (Schutz, 1944). This change applies to perceptions of the body, the self, others, the psyche and all fundamental frameworks for knowing and being in the everyday world. One way in which to capture the dilemmas of being and becoming a medium is to focus on liminality and change within the experience of a neophyte. The major, typical elements of this matrix can be expressed in a particular 'as if' way, namely as an act of reflective consciousness in which a neophyte engages after a crucial and potentially revealing encounter with other mediums. Here we can gather some of the flavour of problems associated with the destruction of the 'unspiritual' world, an exoteric one, and its replacement with a new, spiritual order.

The primary focus is upon the meaningfulness of perceptions in terms of self-other relations for a particular subject (the neophyte). I shall *idealise* the constructions in three ways: (a) idealisation of verbal objectification where objects of consciousness are reduced to linguistic artifacts and conventions; (b) idealisation of reflexive consciousness where the subject is fully conscious of the phenomenal content of his consciousness; (c) idealisation of uniform epistemic level of subjectivity which establishes a cultural, linguistic and intellectual competence which stands as the grounds of all judgements relevant to mediumship. Two comprehensive constructions are proposed. They are the idealisations of experiential location or relative liminality (IE) and the idealisation of assumed normality or universal liminality (IN).

IE I, the being formulating this statement, am human. I have taken as my paramount reality to date the material world of everyday life made up for me in the evidence of my senses, my feelings, my bodily appetites, and my thinking. In so far as I recognise the existence of another, ultimate reality of spirit, I also recognise that my being is dual in the sense that there are not only material and spiritual states within the cosmos, but also that there are identical states within my self. Recognising the spiritual side of my being allows me a glimpse of reality which is the foundation of my knowledge and further development, if only I can control my material or physical self and assert my spiritual self. In this, I depend upon you, there, physically and spiritually not of me . . . a human agent who has superior knowledge and powers to help me discern the reality and truth of what I see, think, and do. This dependence may continue or be supplanted or supplemented by the knowledge and powers of spiritual beings of a high order. But, until that time, I am uncertain of the relative strengths of my material and spiritual selves, and correspondingly I cannot accurately discern the truth of your actions. For example, in our first sitting [seance] together, I felt heat and prickling in my body. I saw a bright light in front of me and a voice seemed to say, 'Go toward the light, my son, and you will see and speak the truth.' I seemed to go forward. I stood up and said, 'Thank you, friend. Amen'. My questions are: Who is the 'you' you addressed? Is it me, my material body, or my spiritual body, or another spirit within me or influencing me? How am I to tell? You say that the sensations, the light and the voice are all signs of psychic power and development; but these are things which could all be in my mind's eye . . . which could be produced by my physical circumstances [sitting for a long time with a straight back, hands palm upwards on my knees, breathing deeply, and all in the dark]. When you replied to my prayer, I could hear you. Am I experiencing this materially and spiritually directly or is this 'hearing' authored, owned by some other agent — a spirit, or you — whose experience is impressed upon me according to some purpose which is as yet unknown to me? I must know who the 'you' is in your address. And that question can only be answered by knowledge of who I am now formulating these questions, and how much of your claimed knowledge and powers are real. But in the final analysis, an answer to the first question must depend partly upon me and my powers since they, jointly, constitute you as an object for me.

IN   I assume a minimum standard of development for the production of evidence of mediumship, and that this same standard is held by me and you of me and of you. I assume this to be so for all practical purposes when we speak of 'evidence' and 'quality mediumship' in terms of what is right and acceptable. If I fail to satisfy you with respect to my development and consequent evidence and mediumship, then this may arise from the non-congruence of what I assumed you assumed of yourself and of me concerning appropriate action. It may be that my assumed reciprocity of perspectives on development was in error in that your development may be greater or less than mine. In so far as these assessments constitute counter evidence for you or me at any time, then the reality of the situation lies in the pronouncements of other mediums whom I assume to be of greater development than I, and whose judgements I trust to produce knowledge for me of my powers and development. It may be that such superior judgements can only come from me, in that others like me, whom I assume are not deluded, regard my development as high and my mediumship as satisfactory to them, in conditions which satisfy me.

The first construction expresses the anxiety which results from the transitional state of the neophyte when there is a re-ordering of world view to incorporate previously occult influences on the body and mind. In this, the 'I' could refer to Les or one of his associates, for example. In the second construction, the dilemmas and ambiguities of IE are related to the problem of establishing co-ordinated action with other mediums or aspiring mediums. It is essentially a statement of social *conventions*.

Conclusion

Spiritualism has often cast itself as a spark in the darkness of a materialistic world. Yet its very history, its internal struggles and its relationships with the wider society reflect the foibles of the world which is seeks to transcend, albeit in a quietistic and not a revolutionary fashion. This is hardly surprising: even the loftiest interpretation of paranormal abilities must recognise that whatever sense is made out of mediumship socially, it is subject to ordinary human judgements as well. The difficulties of managing a 'purified' organisational front are, then, not much different from those of negotiating a personal, spiritual front within Spiritualism. Both are subject to serious social and psychological ambiguities which arise out of social liminality.

Liminality has particular relevance to the analysis of Spiritualism in the following areas: (a) the legitimacy of the movement from a social point of view in terms of how its evidence for paranormal abilities compares with the requirements of modern parapsychology and the scientific establishment; (b) the imperfect charisma of mediumship which qualifies the claims of mediums in relation to both science and religion and the spectrum of competing mediums; (c) problems of order, authority and organisational continuity in relation to the appeal of spontaneous expressions, ecstasies and the democratisation of spiritual and, hence, social powers; (d) the way in which these factors are introjected into the structure of social perception and action as dilemmas of experiential validity and social co-ordination. Maintaining both front and personal stability seems to be dependent upon the ways in which these issues are addressed and resolved; or should I say, what kind of adaptation is made to these circumstances, since they are perennial.

Notes

1　Modern Spiritualism, as opposed to examples of mediumship which are claimed to have appeared in antiquity, is usually traced to the activities of the Fox sisters in Rochester, New York. They heard rappings which were later asserted to be from a deceased former occupant of their house. Communication had been established with the 'spirit' and with that the mediumistic potential of two of the girls began to be realised and, later, publicly recognised.

2　Raymond Firth (1960) states that a kind of 'floating belief system' often grows up around mediumistic practices in many cultures. There are several consequences of this but not the least is an emphasis on the creative and aesthetic abilities of mediums.

3　I Samuel 28 and I Chronicles 10. An enumeration of biblical references and correlated arguments against Spiritualism is given by Pink (1920).

4　The distinction between trance and possession trance is a common one in anthropology. While they are not homogeneous categories, they serve to set out the spectrum of altered states associated with mediumship. Trance covers a range of states, from hallucinatory conditions to physiological collapse, fugue, toxic deleria and so on, while the addition of 'possession' concerns an explanation of a given trance state in terms of a folk belief about the behaviour being caused by an invading entity.

5　Liminality refers to the state of being between statuses, where one is nascent. It is often discussed in relation to *rites de passage* (see Turner, 1969).

6　In modern parapsychology, Trudy experienced a classical Near Death Experience, which often involves a sense of floating and awareness of the surrounds.

7　Part of the Near Death Experience is autoscopy: seeing oneself from some distance. Hospital patients sometimes report seeing their bodies from near the ceiling while they are on the operating table or in bed. They may also hear a doctor pronounce them dead, as Trudy did.

8 Lord Dowding was concerned to contact dead servicemen during World War II. His activities brought him into some disrepute in political and military circles since he was for a time Marshall of the Royal Air Force.

9 For example, the notion of Karma is translated in Spiritualism into the universal Law of Compensation.

10 Spiritualist psychology is not a highly developed discipline. What I am describing here is a range of procedures which mediums use to locate sources of destructive interference in the physical and spiritual bodies and to eradicate them, for example by spiritual healing.

11 Many Spiritualists believe that one may be possessed by spirits lower than Christ, Buddha and other exalted spirits. To claim possession by Christ from this point of view is to be grossly egotistical, at the least, and seriously deluded, at the worst.

12 Spiritualists regularly make distinctions between low powers which involve very little spirituality, and high powers such as possession trance which involve advanced spiritual adeptship.

13 Sensory leakage is a serious problem in parapsychological investigation; that is, where one wants to convincingly rule out transmission of information by ordinary means in order to offer evidence in support of, say, an ESP hypothesis.

14 The situation would not satisfy a serious parapsychologist as one which could yield good evidence of paranormal ability.

9 A case study of the 'Hare Krishna' movement

Leslie N. O'Brien

The growth and the maturation of industrial capitalism have been regarded by some as producing an increase in conflict and in human misery. For Marx, capitalist relations of production have a devastating effect on those subject to them, on their physical and mental states and on the social processes of which they are a part (see Ollman, 1977). Weber (1968) saw the rationality of modern capitalism, especially when applied to the organisation of human behaviour, as leading to the creation of a society in which members are trapped in an 'iron cage' of reason. Nevertheless, in the capitalist countries of the West, the 1960s and early 1970s were a period of boom and expansion. The spectre of mass impoverishment, which Marx had predicted would emerge with the maturation of capitalism, had not occurred there.

Despite the relative economic prosperity of the era, the late 1960s to mid-1970s were turbulent years. During this period there were various manifestations of dissatisfaction with industrial capitalism, perceived technological determinism, bourgeois ideology and the foreign policies of the Western capitalist nations. Dislocation between the promises of the system and the experiences of everyday life; the war in Indochina; continued racism in the home countries; the lack of opportunity for mass participation in supposedly participatory democracies — such experiences generated a variety of riots, rebellions, 'revolutions', retreats and a generalised questioning of social roles. This was the era of what Hole and Levine (1971) termed 'the rebirth of feminism'. Student revolt erupted on the campuses and in the streets of the United States, France, West Germany, Britain and Australia. There was a proliferation of urban and rural 'communes' which aimed at economic self-sufficiency, socio-political self-determination and cultural satisfaction. At this time, too, a variety of so-called 'counter-cultural' religious movements, sects and cults emerged (Mandic, 1970; Rowley, 1971; O'Brien, 1972; Judah, 1974; Daner, 1975; Zaretsky and Leone, 1975).

It has been argued by some (Gouldner, 1971; Buckner, 1971) that the 'affluent society' itself, via such processes as the spread of higher education, the mass media and freedom from material want, generated such social movements, whose members sought to establish greater 'congruency' between their 'subjective' expectations and interpretations of reality and their 'objective' experiences in the world. Certainly it was a time when dissatisfaction was everywhere obvious, although its expression assumed a variety of forms. In so far as the protagonists were not necessarily from the most disadvantaged sectors of society, there was some evidence for the thesis that unrest was related to affluence. As Altman (1970: 130) remarked: 'Studies in the United States have shown that student radicals are drawn largely from upper-middle class professional families... The same is true of hippies; to drop-out implies that one has something to forsake.'

This paper will examine one group of disaffected people, a group who adopted a religious response to the difficulties they encountered in the dominant institutional order — the International Society for Krishna Consciousness (ISKCON or the 'Hare Krishna' movement) Melbourne centre.[1] The questions of why they sought to adopt an alternative lifestyle and different belief system will be addressed, as well as the types of problems they met in doing so. Data are based on research undertaken in 1972, with such updates of information as are relevant. Research methods included participant observation, an analysis of literature produced by the group, and a series of structured and unstructured interviews with Krishna devotees.

Structure and beliefs

ISKCON was founded in New York in 1966 by an Indian national, A. C. Bhaktivedanta Swami Prabhupada, one year after his arrival in the United States.[2] Arriving at a time when societal unrest was widespread, Prabhupada's philosophy of non-violence and anti-materialism was well received. The movement grew, spread throughout the United States to Canada, Mexico, Britain and, in the early 1970s, Australia. There are now 108 centres throughout the world, including eighteen in India (one with an attached five-star hotel which does not serve alcohol)[3] and six in Australia.

Until his death in 1977, Prabhupada was the *acarya* or 'spiritual master' and temporal leader of the movement. Regarded as 'God's (i.e. Krishna's) representative on earth', his authority was based upon his claim to be a 'pure devotee' of the Lord Caitanya, via an unbroken chain of spiritual masters. Caitanya, a fifteenth-century Bengali mystic, founded the original Krishna sect, and is hailed by his devotees as an *avatara* or incarnation of the Hindu deity Krishna. As the Hare Krishna movement spread, a highly structured bureaucratic machine was developed, exemplifying what Weber (1968) called the 'routinisation of charisma'. Centred in the United States with Prabhupada at its apex, this organisation served to disseminate philosophical information and administer the various centres throughout the world. Prabhupada spent most of his later years travelling from one centre to another, an activity which served to heighten the potential of administrative control of the group, drawing the physically dispersed devotees into a close spiritual circuit. Today, the fusion of sacred and secular leadership continues, with a chain of command from top spiritual leaders-cum-upper-echelon bureaucrats through to the rank and file, in a caste-like patriarchal hierarchy.[4] Since the death of Prabhupada, the movement has been managed by eleven disciple-like 'successors', each located in one of the eleven administrative 'zones' of the ISKCON empire.

ISKCON is also big business. Initially financed by public donations and funds brought to the movement by members, ISKCON now owns property all around the world. Moreover, given that the mass of devotees are unpaid workers, the movement can also be seen as a major 'owner' and controller of labour. Commodities such as incense, scented oils, soap, candles, health food and clothing are produced by devotee labour and sold in a number of ISKCON-owned retail outlets, under the trade name 'Spiritual Sky'. Restaurants, art galleries, hotels and food-producing farms are owned by ISKCON and operated by Krishna followers. According to one recent report (*Australian*, 7 October 1981), ISKCON owns $1.5 million worth of rural property in Australia alone, including an 800-hectare farm at Murwillumbah in northern New South Wales, a 720-hectare farm on the banks of the Murray River near Renmark and a 100-hectare property on the Colo River. In addition, property ownership in Australia includes schools, vegetarian restaurants in Sydney and Adelaide, as well as the six city 'temples' and the land upon which they stand. Economic activities provide for the subsistence needs of the various temples. The surplus is used for the publication of movement literature and other forms of proselytisation and, beyond that, the acquisition of property.

A principal tenet of Krishna philosophy (as with other Hindu belief systems) is belief in the idea of reincarnation, which encompasses the notion that the body is transient, unimportant, an illusion which covers the 'real' transcendental self. Further to this is the idea that man is trapped in sense gratification, which prevents the realisation of true essence of being. Moreover, as the consequences of our actions are seen to determine our fate in the next life, man should act in such a manner as to overcome the temptations of worldly existence. The *Bhakti* solution of the Krishna movement is devotion: the only way for an individual to transcend the urge towards physical indulgence, overcome past *karma* (consequences of actions)[5] and avoid being reborn in some lowly form (e.g. as a dog) is to love and serve Krishna and to chant the *mahamantra* (lit. great religious song). 'Hare Krishna, Hare Krishna, Krishna Krishna, Hare Hare, Hare Rama, Hare Rama, Rama Rama, Hare Hare', which exalts Krishna[6] (Prabhupada, 1968 and 1970). Devotees are constrained by a most elaborate and detailed set of prescriptions and prohibitions governing everyday life. Such norms of behaviour are meant to control the senses and guide the devotee towards a more spiritual plane of existence. These rules of behaviour will not be reproduced here, as there are many hundreds of them, but they cover sacred and secular activities in fine detail: aspects of existence such as diet (vegetarianism and the avoidance of drugs of any description, including tea, coffee and alcohol); dress; birth, death and marriage; how and when to pray; how to feel; behaviour *vis-à-vis* the 'outside' world and other devotees. The Krishna belief system describes, explains and integrates physical, mental and spiritual existence and represents what Berger (1967) has termed an all-encompassing 'sacred canopy'.

Membership — Who joins, why, and some methodological difficulties

Participant observation is the accepted anthropological method of data gathering and participation in the day-to-day routines of devotees, as well as attendance at all important ceremonies, aided understanding of the movement's philosophy and activities. Many of the issues under examination did not lend themselves to quantification, nor was enumeration always desirable. Some measurements were taken, however, to test hypotheses regarding membership and to convey something of the dimensions of the movement. Towards this latter end, a formal questionnaire was constructed to obtain biographical and comparative attitudinal data, not always possible in the course of unstructured interviews, as devotees were strongly resistant to questioning about their pre-Krishna lives. Most believed their pre-'conversion' existence to have been characterised by ignorance, and few were sympathetic, let alone proud, of their earlier 'selves'. This posed a number of methodological difficulties, for in attempting to obtain attitudinal, even 'objective', biographical data, the methodological problem was encountered of informants/respondents having psychologically reorganised their pasts to fit in with their present attitudes, beliefs and existence. This tendency to redefine past experiences is not necessarily a deliberate or intentional distortion The individual may unintentionally 'reshuffle' the past within his/her present cognitive experience in order to integrate biography.

No formal records of membership were kept by the Melbourne group at the time of research. From interviews undertaken and 'head counts' at major ceremonies, it is estimated that there were 30 devotees attached to the centre in 1972. Of these, 24 were resident in the temple whilst six lived outside. The male–female ratio was approximately 2 : 1 and most devotees were in their late teens or early twenties. The Hare Krishna movement proper, in Melbourne at least, was very much a youth phenomenon. In addition to devotees, however, a floating population of between six to ten 'interested others' — some of middle age — attended significant ceremonies on a fairly regular basis.

Most devotees were willing informants and prepared to participate in unstructured interviews, although responses to questions often consisted of lengthy quotations of Krishna philosophy, particularly when asked about anything considered by the devotee to relate to aspects of 'material existence'. In an attempt to overcome the resistance to these types of questions encountered in face-to-face interviews, the 'impersonal' questionnaire was constructed and distributed to devotees through the temple leader. Only thirteen devotees (43 per cent) completed the questionnaire, although four others (13 per cent) made a variety of comments about the instruments itself. This is a fairly high response rate, given that Krishna philosophy holds that knowledge cannot be obtained by intellectual processes. This belief is expressed in the words of one of the four devotees who returned an uncompleted questionnaire:

> I cannot see what the purpose of this questionnaire is, as all questions are of a very basic material nature, and have no bearing on spiritual life. You cannot statistically work out who is going to be attracted to Krishna consciousness, as one must have performed pious activities to incur the grace of the spiritual master. These activities may have been done many lives previously so we cannot speculate as to who will join K. C. Krishna says in *Bhagavat Gita* that anyone, even a dog eater, can come to the perfection of life by accepting a spiritual master.

Another 'non-respondent' provided lengthy quotations from the movement's most sacred book, the *Bhagavat Gita*, and closed with the words 'Chant Hare Krsna (and you won't need to do this stuff)'. The thirteen devotees who did complete the questionnaire are most likely respresentative of the group as a whole. Unstructured interviews with other devotees on some of the issues raised in the questionnaire did not reveal any apparent differences between respondents and non-respondents other than that the respondents appeared more willing to 'humour' the researcher in her 'misguided' scholarly activities; none the less, information obtained is best regarded as illustrative rather than definitive. As regards those who did respond: an analysis of the thirteen questionnaires confirmed the impression regarding devotees' ages. The youngest respondent was 16 years old; the oldest was 26; the mean age was 22.

Devotees were asked questions about the educational levels, occupation and income of their parents or guardians. In addition, and in anticipation of the likelihood of respondents' providing non-comparable information on the subject, they were asked to indicate the socioeconomic background of their family of orientation on a fixed-choice scale. None of these questions reveals much about social relations, but given that devotees were so reluctant to discuss any details of their past lives outside the framework of their present belief system, the researcher was hesitant to risk goodwill for detailed information. Questionnaire data allowed for the following breakdown of the socioeconomic status of the family of orientation of the thirteen respondents: upper middle/upper, four; middle, two; lower middle, one; working, four; no response, one; other, one. Follow-up questioning revealed the non-respondent to this question to be the son of a medical doctor. The 'other' response was 'landed gentry', and as this devotee was of mixed Polish and English ancestry this may well be so, though whether 'landed' in Poland, England or Australia is not known.

The majority of the respondents, particularly the males, had been educated to a level at or above the national average. Two were university graduates, seven had begun a degree or diploma course but had not completed it, another had obtained the Higher School Certificate, and three had not completed secondary education. As in the population as a whole, male devotees had higher levels of education than female devotees, and all three high-school 'drop outs' were women. Amongst non-respondents, two of the male devotees had university degrees and at least three had left university prior to completing their course. None of the female devotees had commenced or completed tertiary ecuation. As regards the relevance of their education, most devotees seemed to regard the whole experience as having been a waste of time. The following comments are typical of those made: 'robot manufacturers staffed by industrial puppets'; 'totally useless as far as informing one what life really is'; 'concentrated solely on material gains'.

It was suggested earlier that a partial explanation for the emergence of 'youth protest' in the late 1960s and early 1970s may lie with the fact that industrial capitalism was not living up to its promises, that there were many gaps between the 'ideal' and the 'actual'. At the level of the individual, this may have been experienced as a discrepancy between 'subjective' beliefs acquired in the process of socialisation, and that person's experience of 'objective' reality (Berger and Luckmann, 1966). When there is such a disparity, a 'reality flaw' (Buckner, 1971) may be generated. The discrepancy may be one of material deprivation, that is a gap between socialised expectations and existing opportunities (Merton, 1965), or it may be moral, that is a disparity between an individual's value system and experiences of society in everyday life. Material want is no guarantee of deviant behaviour, and beliefs generally differ to some degree from experience. Many will be unaware of logical inconsistencies, and others able to tolerate greater or lesser discrepancies most of the time, perhaps until some situation arises in which the 'ideal' and the 'actual' confront each other (Toch, 1965). Even if a crisis situation occurs, individuals will react in different ways. Some may deny the existence of the incongruency and continue to hold their beliefs and values as before. Others may adopt one of several problem-solving perspectives, such as a 'psychiatric' solution, apportioning the blame to themselves. Some may adopt a 'political' solution, laying the blame on the social structure. Others may adopt a 'religious' interpretation of the situation, seeing the source of the difficulty and its solution as a metaphysical problem (Lofland and Stark, 1965). These are of course 'ideal type' solutions; there is no guarantee that those who experience a 'reality flaw' will respond in a positive or organised manner, or find some acceptable 'solution'.

Devotees of Krishna, by their very membership of ISKCON, were expressing dissatisfaction with some aspect of their previous lives. At the time the research was conducted, as compared to the situation that pertains now, there was no 'second generation' of members. All those who belonged to the movement had made an active choice in this regard. Data on family background and education (hence 'marketability', particularly in the context of employment opportunities available in Melbourne in 1972) of devotees, suggest that the problem was not one of material necessity, although the possibility of material wants cannot be discounted. As will be shown, devotees had no apparent difficulties in obtaining work when they wanted it, and their own statements reveal that their dissatisfactions were predominantly of a non-material nature.

Devotees were asked to detail any jobs they had held, activities and interests engaged in, after they had left school/college/university and before they had joined the Krishna movement. Responses included details of a variety of work roles undertaken by the various individuals, but mainly consisted of answers in which past activities were expressed in terms of the present value attached to them. In general, there was a debunking and devaluation of earlier behaviour. For example: 'Odd jobs. Sense gratification'; 'Drugs and sex'; So many material activities I couldn't list them. For a few years I made jewellery. For a few years I experimented with drugs. I followed astrology, occult, always looking for satisfaction. This satisfaction of complete knowledge is Krishna Consciousness. Not that I have fully realised it yet.'

Although one respondent had trained and worked for a time as a psychiatric nurse, most had worked only on a casual or part-time basis in non-career occupations, if they had worked at all. Two of the non-respondents were known to have started work in occupations with established career-development paths prior to joining the movement, and ISKCON literature mentions the high occupational status of devotees in North America in their pre-Krishna conscious days. This appears to have been the exception rather than the rule in Melbourne. The general pattern amongst devotees seems to have been for some degree of dissatisfaction with the world to have developed during the educational process, such that the capitalist work ethic was rejected prior to involvement in any nine-to-five routine. Respondents and non-respondents alike tended to have worked for a while after finishing with formal education, often drifting in and out of employment. In between jobs, some experimented with communal living and/or drug taking, worked again for a time, generally to earn sufficient money for a further period of drifting, rather than as a way of life.

All respondents and those 'non-respondents' prepared to discuss the matter seemed to have followed a fairly distinctive sequential pattern which began with a questioning and eventual rejection of family and dominant institutional (including orthodox religious) beliefs, values and practices as 'meaningless'. This dissatisfaction was, in most instances, generalised, although in some cases it was linked with a specific not simply 'moral-issue' experience (e.g. parental divorce; reaction to pregnancy). The next 'stage' was a period of 'drifting around', trying to find a more satisfying, meaningful existence. It was during this time that nearly all devotees had experimented with drugs and other 'alternative' lifestyles, both religious and non-religious (e.g. communal living; other sectarian movements such as Meher Baba, Divine Light), some more, some less structured. Some devotees had 'drifted' right throughout this period, others had actively sought a more structured and satisfying alternative lifestyle but failed to find one. The process 'ended', so far as this research project was concerned, with the formerly dissatisfied 'seeker' joining the Hare Krishna movement, which advertises itself as 'The Positive Alternative' and which according to all devotees was *the* solution for them. The following example typifies the process and the experiences of other members of the movement:

> Apprentice fitter; mechanic; labourer; chainman; fitter's mate; trades assistant etc. hash, grass, LSD — speculating about everything. I was trying to find out who I was, why I was here and what life really was. Srila Prabhupada answered all my questions and told me so much more by injecting me with Krsna Katha.

Sociological studies carried out in the United States confirm the above findings on socioeconomic backgrounds of members of other counter-cultural religious movements, motives for joining and the 'path' to satisfaction (see Adams and Fox (1972) on 'Jesus Freaks'; Robbins and Anthony (1972) on Meher Baba; Judah (1974), Daner (1975) and Zaretsky and Leone (1975) on the Hare Krishna movement). As with the Melbourne study, the latter researchers found a high proportion of members of the Krishna movement to be ex-hippies who had been dependent on the psychedelic experience for expressions of inner cognitive urges and perceived ultimate concerns and who, moreover, appear to have discovered that drugs produce a temporary state of transcendence whilst living in *Vrindavan* (close communion) with Krishna is a permanent 'high'.

Maintaining internal cohesion

At the time of the research, all devotees expressed deep satisfaction with their membership of the movement. It appeared to meet the diverse needs of the individuals concerned for experiential congruence, meaning and the warmth, friendship and security of communal living. At least some of those earlier devotees are known to be in the movement today, most having married other devotees and produced children. The attrition rate, if such exists, is not known, and no longitudinal component to allow for the study of eventual disenchantment was built into the research programme. What was studied, however, was the related issue of how such 'alternative' realities as the Hare Krishna movement maintain their viability against the danger of internal dissolution and the ever-present threat of external nihilation by the dominant institutional order. This first aspect was studied by way of an examination of the process of socialisation into the norms, beliefs and values of the Krishna movement, and evaluating how effective that process is.

When someone acknowledges the existence of a 'reality flaw', that person's beliefs and values are called into question and may be weakened. Disillusionment is a slow process, and between disaffiliation from one set of beliefs and the eventual (if ever) acceptance of an entirely different set, there is usually — as was the case with Krishna devotees — a period of 'shopping around'. Some people may experience a mystical conversion and suddenly 'see the light'. Most, however, seek alternatives in both familiar and unfamiliar patterns of interaction. For most people, the closest they come to conversion is the discovery of what Toch (1965: 122) has termed an 'attractive item on the ideological counter'.

Once a person has made contract with an alternate reality, two analytically distinct processes begin. The first is the process of socialisation into the norms of behaviour, beliefs and values of the particular group. The second is the process by which the new member comes to accept the group's ideology as part of his or her own subjective reality and definition of 'self'. These processes occur concurrently, one reinforcing the other. As the novitiate becomes more familiar and at ease with the new social milieu, the particular beliefs and values of the group may seem increasingly attractive, although the reverse can, of course, occur and assimilation cease. If beliefs and values are incorporated into the new member's subjective reality, then the norms of behaviour of the group will more readily be accepted as the 'right' and 'proper' way to act. The extent to which the two processes coincide represents the degree of congruity or 'fit' established between subjective and objective reality.[7]

Devotees may have rejected the beliefs and practices of industrial capitalism or experienced difficulty in finding a place within the system and actively sought an alternative lifestyle. This does not mean, however, that they do not need to be 'resocialised' into the specific ISKCON world view. Broom and Selznick (1963) have suggested that there are certain conditions which facilitate resocialisation. The process of acquiring a 'Krishna' identity and the potential for maintaining such an alternative 'self' in face of the nihilations of the wider society will be examined within the framework developed by those theorists.

Total control over the individual

Before an individual can become a devotee of Krishna, there are certain preliminaries which must be observed. The aspirant member must be accepted by a recognised 'spiritual master', who is followed, obeyed and respected as a means of venerating Krishna. The 'spiritual master' is the devotee's guide into Krishna consciousness and interpreter of the sacred and secular edicts of the group. Although a would-be devotee need not live in one of the communal-residence spiritual centres or 'temples', such a move probably aids transition from one lifestyle to another. It is clearly more difficult to obtain and maintain an alternative set of beliefs, values and practices in isolation or amidst non-believers than amongst like-minded individuals whose words and actions continually reaffirm one's own developing reality. Communal living is not enforced but in those instances where it is adopted it serves to enhance ISKCON control over members, as well as exposing devotees to the continual 'relational control' (Buckner, 1971) of peers.

All devotees are expected to give up their material possessions upon entering the movement. Even if a 'spiritual master' decides a devotee can or should continue with his/her outside occupation as a particular form of devotion, any income earned must be dedicated to Krishna (i.e. is appropriated by ISKCON). This seeming contradiction as regards devotees' behaviour can be explained within the framework of the movement's philosophy. The accumulation of wealth, per se, is not condemned, although its privatisation is. Krishna followers perform those acts we might term 'economic' as a devotional act to their deity, such devotion also being a means towards the end of their own spiritual betterment. The motivation behind these economic acts is in direct contrast to the ethic of capitalist accumulation, as is the entire lifestyle of devotees.[8]

The rank and file operate within a 'moral economy' (Weber, 1968), although ISKCON is, amongst other things, a capitalist enterprise. As regards the potential for total control over the individual: the implication of these practices for the individual devotee is that in the here-and-now he or she is totally economically dependent, and must look to the movement for the satisfaction of all material wants and needs. The movement is not a prison, and there is considerable evidence to suggest that one can always leave. If ongoing membership is chosen, then the element of economic dependency greatly increases the degree of organisation control of the individual.

Suppression of past statuses
Alternate realities face the problem of providing members with a plausible identity. This means that former statuses from which the participant gained approval must be ignored (Broom and Selznick, 1963). When a new member joins the Krishna movement, that person is treated as if his or her past did not exist; a new identity is

bestowed upon the novitiate by the movement and, depending upon the success or otherwise of the resocialisation process, this 'persona' will be absorbed into subjective reality as that person's Krishna 'self'. The transition from pre- to post-membership identity is fairly radical and involves the adoption of a new name, (usually) a new address, a distinctive style of clothing and personal adornment,[9] a new 'occupation' and an all-consuming Krishna-centred lifestyle in which the day begins around 3.30 a.m., with the chanting of prayers, and rarely ends before 11 p.m.

Although the movement downplays material existence for matters metaphysical, there is both differentiation and stratification of members within the movement by gender and by what can best be described as 'perceived degree of spiritual advancement'. All members classify themselves as 'Brahman', the priestly or learned class in the' Indian caste system. The first six to twelve months of membership of the movement constitute a 'student' period, during which time devotees are closely supervised by their 'spiritual master'. The ideal devotee of Krishna does not indulge in any form of sense gratification or egoism. To reduce the urge towards these impulses, the student studies the sacred texts of the movement and adopts a number of practices designed to overcome the weight of the physical and mental planes which detract from the attainment of the spiritual. In addition to practices already mentioned such as vegetarianism, celibacy and avoidance of all drugs and intoxicants, devotees also engage in a process termed 'self-noughting'. They are advised to regard themselves objectively, as if in the third person, so as to overcome ego urges.

The 'student' period continues until the devotee feels so attached to Krishna that he 'executes devotional service out of natural love' (Prabhupada, 1970: 21), that is until fully resocialised. At the end of student life, the devotee is formally initiated into the movement, and acquires the status of mature member or 'householder'. Householders are permitted to marry but many prefer not to, as they consider it detracts from spiritual development. If marriage is desired, it is arranged with another 'suitable' member. Sexual activity, even between married members, is discouraged as sense gratification and, ideally, is to be engaged in only for the purpose of procreation. Even after marriage, 'householder' devotees stay in the appropriate male or female quarters of the temple. If cohabitation is desired, an outside household must be established. In later life, householders — especially male — are encouraged to renounce such meagre comforts as they have enjoyed, including marriage, and become *sannyasa*. The *sannyasin* does not seclude himself in mystical isolation but demonstrates his control of the senses by living in the world. As was the case with Prabhupada in his later years, a *sannyasin* travels continually, chanting, praying and spreading the word of Krishna, eating little, sleeping less, and demonstrating transcendence of all gross physical impulses.

Denial of the moral worth of the old self

Not only must past statuses be ignored but successful resocialisation involves a denial of the moral worth of the old self. The ISKCON philosophy is ideal in this regard, for the time prior to membership is regarded as a time of unenlightenment, when the now-devotee was trapped in material existence and involved in sense-gratification to the detriment of spiritual advancement. This attitude was reflected directly or indirectly in responses to questions asked in the course of unstructured interviews and in the answers given in the formal questionnaire. As regards former occupations and undertakings, and as noted above, respondents detailed activities which now contravene their code of ethics, for example 'drugs and sex'. When asked to comment whether they considered their parents or guardians to be/have been religious people, more than half the respondents made remarks which were openly condemnatory, for example 'They occupy their time with social drinking, gambling, meat eating, illicit sex and useless conversation'; They are gross materialists'.

Statements such as these and supplementary data obtained in the course of interviews revealed a generalised pattern of denial of the moral worth of the old 'self' and all associated with it. Of course the possibility that devotees held themselves in low esteem prior to their involvement in the movement needs to be considered, rather than regarding 'self-devaluation' as a simple function of reinterpretation of the past in terms of present values. The 'self-noughting' practised by devotees might eventually overcome any difficulties in this direction experienced by the individuals concerned, for ideally it should be destructive of both self-esteem and self-hatred. Commenting on this, Thouless (1971: 62) notes: 'If one regards oneself as an instrument for the carrying out of divine will, self esteem and self hatred are equally irrelevant, and the energy behind these sentiments may be liberated for love of others.'

Participation of the individual in his own resocialisation

This is, according to Broom and Selznick, another factor which contributes to successful resocialisation. Self-criticism is encouraged in the Krishna movement. By engaging in self-analysis and self-criticism, devotees are actively involved in their own resocialisation. Although there is no institutionalised pattern of 'confession', the researcher noted a number of occasions on which devotees discussed their weaknesses and failings with those other devotees with whom they had established a close relationship. Another way in which devotees participate in their own resocialisation is by preaching ISKCON doctrine to others. Members of the movement do not live in isolation from the wider community but continually interact with the public in seeking proselytes to Krishna philosophy. In the course of such interchanges, devotees are constantly in a position where they must defend their atypical patterns of behaviour and belief. In making such defences, the recruiter may become more confirmed in his or her belief (Buckner, 1971: 187–8).

Sanctions
Another element which often features prominently in the process of resocialisation is the use of extreme sanctions. In the Krishna movement there is no extreme sanction such as physical cruelty or social isolation. Few negative sanctions are employed at all. If a devotee was to contravene any of the regulative principles as prohibited by the movement's doctrine, for example meat eating, intoxicants, gambling, illicit sex, and so on, no 'official' action would be taken against the offender, although other devotees might comment that the deviant had 'slipped back into material existence'.

Successful resocialisation depends upon the use of subtlety, not force. Resocialisation agencies rarely rely upon formal social control (Broom and Selznick, 1963; Buckner, 1971). Like other 'counter-cultural' or 'alternate' realities, the Krishna movement lacks access to such formal agencies of control as the law to enforce its norms. Legally the movement could invoke such control measures as ostracism or 'excommunication'. ISKCON is many things but its manifest aim is to awaken the Krishna consciousness said to be latent within all of us. ISKCON literature and all devotees interviewed lay stress upon the importance of the metaphysical rather than material. When questioned about movement control of 'deviant' members, devotees stated that a person must come to and stay in Krishna consciousness because he or she wanted to, and that ISKCON 'did not want to police anyone'. Within the movement there are two sets of rules in operation: one ethical, the other instrumental. If a devotee fails to adhere to one of the instrumental norms (e.g. by leaving wet clothes in the bathroom, or by failing to wash the dishes when it is his or her turn), peers criticise. In some ways, day-to-day life in the temple is much like life in a non-religious commune, and interpersonal co-operation is expected. Matters of dogma, however, are (theoretically) the concern of no one but the individual devotee. In principle, one is answerable only to Krishna as regards deviation from or conformity to the philosophical tenets of the movement. During the course of the research, a few minor transgressions of doctrine occurred, and the response of other devotees was one of tolerance or disinterest. Given some major deviation from doctrine, particularly by someone living in the temple, a different response might have been elicited, especially if such action was perceived to be a threat to the group's integrity.

Intensification of peer group support
Intensification of peer group pressure and support are very important elements in the resocialisation of devotees, and hence of significance as regards the potential for the internal cohesion of the group. Factors such as the idiosyncratic language used by Krishna followers, distinctive style of dress and shared experiences, both sacred and profane, do more to develop a sense of belonging to the group than the threat of negative sanctions. The chanting, singing and dancing often induce a trance-like state (O'Brien, 1972), and those with whom one has shared such an experience are part of the memory. In addition, as will be elaborated below, the movement has been subject to considerable external opposition. This outside challenge, in combination with the development of internal solidarity, goes a long way towards crystallising the feeling of attachment to the group.

The success or otherwise of the resocialisation process and the issue of the potential of internal dissolution relate not only to the mechanisms employed by the movement to transfer ideology to new members but also to the particular reason any individual sought to join ISKCON. Toch (1965) identifies two types of members. The first is the 'instrumental believer', who joins a social movement to obtain security or social support, material rewards or other fringe benefits. Such membership is precarious because conception of the ideology is self-centred, and loyalty to the movement is conditional upon needs being satisfied. The other type of member is what Toch terms the 'pure devotee', who is fully committed and dedicated. Such a person joins the movement because he agrees with what the movement stands for. The pure devotee is 'belief centred', and likely to withstand ideological or physical attacks upon these beliefs until such time as some event precipitates disillusionment, in much the same manner as an earlier disillusionment or 'reality flaw' led him to reject the system of meaning acquired during primary and subsequent socialisation. Adams and Fox (1972) confirmed the Toch hypothesis and identified amongst their informants 'teeny boppers' who became 'Jesus Freaks' in an attempt to gain peer group approval, and 'more mature individuals' who had dropped out of the drug scene and into the Jesus movement as their 'new high'. Some Krishna devotees in Melbourne had had pre-membership experiences of the type which suggest they might have joined the movement for instrumental reasons, but most members appeared to be more belief-centred, that is 'pure' devotees. The data gathered during the Krishna research suggest that the instrumental/pure categories developed by Toch are best regarded as 'ideal types', and that in reality elements of both may be found in any one member. In those instances where membership was initiated primarily for instrumental reasons *and* to the extent that the resocialisation process has not overcome any hesitancy or opposition to elements of the Krishna system, then that devotee may be susceptible to disaffiliation. In those instances where membership was more related to a belief in the Krishna ideology *and* the resocialisation process was largely successful, then we might expect that devotee to remain within the movement unless troubled by some highly significant incongruity.

The threat of external nihilation

The legitimations of alternate realities are generally difficult to maintain, for they are legitimations of isolated institutions of behaviour. They are neither integrated within nor supported by those legitimations which would give them a place in the dominant institutional order (Buckner, 1971: 26). Alternate realities not only fall outside the symbolic universe which legitimates capitalism, in many instances the beliefs of the alternative movement are 'counter' to those of the dominant culture. Ideas alone do not change the world, and it is not suggested that the Krishna movement represents a threat to the structure of industrial capitalism. ISKCON philosophy is, however, expressed as a fundamental challenge to bourgeois materialism. The dominant institutional order appears to have accorded the movement 'nuisance value', and for this reason (perhaps also in combination with a distrust of that which is different) has not evidenced a great deal of tolerance. Indeed the threat of external nihilation has been fairly constant and is perceived by devotees to be evidence of religious persecution in a society which ostensibly upholds the ideal of freedom of thought and worship.

At the time of the research, the most manifest sign of repression was the discretionary invocation of the law against devotees. When the movement began its activities in Melbourne in the early 1970s, the behaviour of the 'Hare Krishnas' was considered to be extraordinary, even given the presence of hippies on the streets at that time. The saffron robes, shaven heads of the males, chanting, dancing, banging of drums and clashing of cymbals attracted attention. Furthermore, whilst street preaching, devotees distribute leaflets, brochures, magazines, books and incense, for which they sometimes ask, and always expect, a donation. Such activities are at once a source of income and a means of spreading Krishna consciousness. There was no precedent for this in the Melbourne Central Business District (CBD). Other religious groups such as the Salvation Army also engaged in street preaching but generally outside the CBD, not in the early afternoon and not six days a week. Further, these groups were recognised by the establishment, whereas ISKCON was not granted 'official religion' status until 1974, and *de jure* approval is no guarantee of acceptance.

The shopkeepers of the CBD considered the activities of the Krishna movement bad for business. They claimed the noise drove customers away. There was also some public opposition, expressed in 'Letters to the Editor', to the manner in which devotees distributed their incense and literature. The Melbourne City Council acting 'in the public interest' (and business ones) issued writs against devotees for transgressions of Local Government By-Laws. The first charge was laid against the group in October 1971 under By-Law 418, which has two clauses, one to prevent the soliciting of alms, the other to prevent the collecting of money without the written permission of Council. The case was heard in January 1972. The Council was unable to prove the first charge but devotees were fined under the second clause. Between late January and mid-September 1972, 222 cases were brought before the courts under By-law 418. In addition, at that date, 37 further charges under By-law 418 were listed for hearing, 80 summonses were waiting to be served and 40 were in various stages of preparation. In each case of successful prosecution by the Melbourne City Council, fines and costs were imposed; fines ranged from three to twenty dollars and costs from two to four dollars.

Besides the above charges, devotees were summonsed under several other By-laws. There were three successful charges of 'failing to state name and place of abode', one successful charge of 'threatening an officer of the Melbourne City Council', one charge of 'assault' (which was held over for twelve months) and a successful charge against a devotee for 'failing to walk on the left-hand side of the footpath'. Another By-law which has been invoked also has two clauses, one concerning the making of noise above a specified decibel level, the other concerning disturbances of the peace. The latter is most difficult to prove, for someone's comfort is an arbitrary evaluation. Although several storekeepers complained about the group's disturbing their peace and quiet, the devotees have only been charged under the first clause. A final illustration of establishment reaction to the movement is Melbourne City Council By-law 489, drawn up early in 1972, which has 37 of clauses. Of these, 34 are long-standing rules regarding behaviour in public places; the other three are new and appear to have been aimed at curtailing the activities of the Krishna group in the CBD. These particular clauses are:

4(f)   No person using or being upon or in any place of public resort shall play or operate any musical instrument, radio, or television set in such a manner as to materially interfere with the resonable comfort and convenience of any other person (but nothing in this paragraph shall operate to prevent the playing of any musical or noisy instrument in the place of public resort where the consent of the Council has been given . . .)

5(e)   No person using or being upon or in any place of public resort shall, without the consent in writing of the Council, solicit or collect gifts of money or subscriptions; or

(f)   declaim, deliver any address, harangue, preach, speak to any assembly of other persons, or play on any musical or noisy instrument.

Interviews with members of the central business community and Melbourne City Councillors revealed that the main objection to devotees took the form of opposition to the consequences of ISKCON beliefs (i.e. behaviour). The establishment stated it was not interested in suppressing the movement on ideological grounds. The basic source of contention between devotees and the dominant institutional order, however, stems from a conflict of values. To a devotee, daily public preaching (or *sankirtan*) is a prescribed duty and a basic tenet of belief. *Bhakti* yoga involves devoting all actions to Krishna, and chanting the *mahamantra* to the world as an overt declaration of submission is most important. By contrast the Council see their prime function as maintaining the smooth, quiet, efficient running of the city of Melbourne; they consider the Krishna movement a threat to that peace, a nuisance, therefore it is 'their duty to repress them on any possible technicality'. Similar attitudes have been expressed and tactics adopted by other authorities in other cities in Australia and elsewhere throughout the world. To devotees, this continual 'harassment' is seen as more of an irritation than a threat to existence. Such obstacles as encountered, however, seem to heighten group solidarity rather than weaken it.

Conclusion

Viable alternate realities present a challenge to established interpretations of reality, to the legitimations of the dominant institutional order. This is evidenced in the nature and extent of the reaction of mainstream authorities to such peripheral phenomena as
counter-cultural religious movements. Organised opposition to the
International Society for Krishna Consciousness has been almost
constant since its inception, and seems to have increased with time.
No 'normalisation' process appears to be taking place, by which is
meant some degree of incorporation of ISKCON into the orthodox
religious world, even though the involvement has been recognised as
an official religion since 1974. Local government authorities in
Melbourne and elsewhere in Australia continue to exercise discretionary invocation of the law against devotees. A number of parents
of those who have 'defected' to organisations such as ISKCON have
themselves joined together in a concerted effort to 'win' their
children back from their alternative beliefs and behaviour patterns.
'Deprogramming' centres have been established to deal with those
willing to leave their new lifestyles and re-adopt the old. Parents,
other family members and orthodox religion authorities act together
to counter the content of alternative religion ideologies acquired in
the process of resocialisation such as detailed above. When the co-
operation of the recalcitrant young has not been forthcoming, 'persuasion' tactics have been adopted.

Conflict, both ideational and physical, has been fairly constant.
There have been several instances of devotees being abducted from
the movement by their families. One Victorian member so objected
to such an event that she brought an (unsuccessful) charge of kid-
napping against her mother, step-father, brother and a Roman
Catholic priest (*Herald*, 27 April 1977). In March 1977 a young
female devotee died after she had poured kerosene on herself and set
herself alight. This tragic death was an isolated incident and in no
way related to ISKCON philosophy. Subsequent investigations
revealed that the suicide was linked to an unhappy secular relationship. The movement received considerable adverse publicity because
of this death, and suggestions were made that the group practised
human sacrifice, an idea totally at variance with ISKCON beliefs. In
June 1977 a Member of Parliament in Victoria called for a probe into the methods of operation of such religions as the Hare Krishna
movement, Moonies, Children of God, 'and other similar cults...
placing many young people under serious threat' (*Age*, 11 June
1977). In other places even more serious challenges have issued from
the dominant institutional order. In West Germany, for instance,

authorities raided a Krishna temple early one morning, found two or three hand guns on the premises and arrested all present. Members of the movement have been charged with treason. According to an ISKCON spokesperson, this event evidences both an attempt to nihilate the movement and seek monetary advantage. On the latter point, authorities have confiscated more than one million dollars of the movement's funds held in West German banks. On the former, ISKCON claims that private arms ownership is as common in West Germany as it is in the United States. The charge of treason is, according to the movement, an 'example of capitalism wanting to stamp out anything that teaches anti-materialism'.

Notes

1 ISKCON is here treated as a 'counter-cultural' religious movement because of the expressed opposition of its philosophy to the materialist ethic and fetishism of commodities of the dominant capitalist society.
2 *Bhakti* or 'devotional' yoga has as its base the Vedic texts of ancient India, thus 'Bhaktivedanta' Swami Prabhupada: 'devotee'. For a more detailed discussion of the linkage between ISKCON and Hinduism, see O'Brien, 1972: 91–104.
3 Devotees attach considerable importance to the establishment of the movement's activities in India. They say there is an ancient prophecy that the true practice of devotion to Krishna would be debased, re-established in its pure form outside India and then reintroduced there from the West.
4 For bureaucratic organisation, see Weber, 1968.
5 For further discussion of the *Karma-samsara* complex, see Berger, 1967, Ch. 3.
6 Devotees contend that we all have a Krishna consciousness latent within us. This can be reached and activated on a transcendental level through the chanting of the *mahamantra*, either by ourselves or others. This explains the importance devotees attach to their street preaching or *sankirtan*. It is a world-saving activity and demonstration of devotion. This particular tenet of belief aided the research project. From its inception, informants were aware of the identity of the researcher and the purpose of the study. Provision was made that the researcher should outwardly assimilate to the group, thus enabling participant observation. Devotees were unfailingly patient as regards my spiritual 'underdevelopment' and informed me that the frequent exposure to the good vibrations of the *mahamantra* would eventually contribute to my enlightenment.
7 For further discussion of the socialisation process, acquisition of conception of 'self', and their relationship to social control, see Mead, 1934; Berger and Luckmann, 1966; Buckner, 1971.
8 For the distinction between 'wealth' and 'capital', see Marx, 1976.
9 In fact a Krishna 'uniform'. For discussion of the importance of this manifestation of distinctiveness for internal solidarity, see Joseph and Alex, 1972.

10 Organised irreligion: The New South Wales Humanist Society

Alan W. Black

Relatively little attention has been given by sociologists to humanist organisations, especially in Australia. Campbell (1965, 1969 and 1971) studied aspects of the British Humanist Association and made some steps towards formulating a 'sociology of irreligion'. Budd (1967 and 1977) examined 'varieties of unbelief' in Britain, looking at the various organisational forms associated with such unbelief in the period from 1850 to 1967. Between 1967 and 1971, chiefly through the work of Fairbanks, the *Australian Humanist* published the results of three surveys of Humanist Society members in Australia. The third survey, which was more comprehensive in form and based on a more satisfactory sample than the first two, will be discussed later in this chapter. Glasner (1974) reviewed some of the then available literature and made an analysis of the content of resolutions passed by the Council of Australian Humanist Societies between 1966 and 1972.

The present paper goes beyond these studies by looking in some detail at the New South Wales Humanist Society from the time of its inception until the present.

Origins and objectives

The Rationalist Press Association, which was one of the original sponsors of the British Humanist Association, was also one of the influences which helped to bring the New South Wales Humanist Society into being. The immediate event which triggered the forma-tion of the latter society was the visit to Australia in 1959 of the American evangelist, Billy Graham. Bill and Daphne Weeks, two Sydney school teachers who were members of the Rationalist Press Association, felt a need for an organisation to promote humanism in Australia. Even prior to the Graham visit, they and others of similar persuasion had been writing to the *ABC Weekly* urging the

Australian Broadcasting Commission to include humanist views in its programmes.

Using a notice in the *Humanist* — a Rationalist Press Association journal — Mr and Mrs Weeks managed to locate six other persons who were interested in forming a humanist group in Sydney. After several house meetings, they inserted an advertisement in the amusements columns of the *Sydney Morning Herald* on 16 July 1960. The response to this enabled the group to call its first city meeting a month later. Attended by approximately 60 people, this meeting resolved to form the Sydney Humanist Group. Shortly afterwards it was renamed the New South Wales Humanist Society. As stated in its constitution, the aims of the society were

> To encourage a rational approach to human problems, to promote the fullest possible use of science for human welfare, to defend freedom of expression and to provide a constructive alternative to theological and dogmatic creeds.

Except that they made no reference to publishing, these aims were similar in wording to those of the Rationalist Press Association (see Budd, 1967: 387). Although the first clause spoke of encouraging 'a rational approach', the founders of the Humanist Society had in mind a type of activity rather different from that conducted by the Rationalist Association of New South Wales. They regarded the latter as having a largely negative, anti-religious stance with little concern for practical action in other spheres. By contrast, the humanists wished to use human intelligence and scientific inquiry to seek solutions, even though provisional ones, to human problems, and thus to promote human welfare. While not expecting a future utopia, the humanists looked forward to 'the evolution of a society based not only on reason but also on concern for other human beings' ('The Humanist View', reproduced in New South Wales Humanist Society *Viewpoints*, September 1970: 71). They saw this concern as implying a respect for the individual and affording the maximum possible individual freedom consistent with the rights of others. They recognised that in any society there must be some restriction of personal liberty but maintained that one freedom should be unassailable: freedom of expression, and in particular the right to dissent. The humanists felt no need for the supernatural as a guiding force in human affairs. They regarded superstition and dogmatic religious beliefs as barriers to human progress and unity. Rather than simply tearing religion down, the humanists sought to put forward a constructive alternative.[1]

Relationships with other humanist societies

Humanist societies were formed in Victoria in 1961, South Australia in 1962, and Canberra in 1964, modelling their objectives on those of the New South Wales Humanist Society. In 1965 representatives of each of these societies formed the Council of Australian Humanist Societies (CAHS), to co-ordinate activities and to present the humanist viewpoint at the national level, to promote research, conferences and publications on matters of interest to humanists, and to assist in the development of further humanist societies. In 1966 CAHS organised a national convention, an event which has been held annually at Easter since then. In the same year CAHS commenced publication of the *Australian Humanist*, a quarterly journal which continued until 1975. Most of the state societies also published their own newsletters. In 1967 the Queensland Rationalist Society, which had been in existence for over 50 years, and which had already broadened the range of its interests beyond those of classical rationalism, became affiliated with CAHS and was soon renamed the Queensland Humanist Society. In 1968 the Western Australian Humanist Society, which had been formed in 1965, also became affiliated with CAHS.

By far the largest and most active of the humanist societies has been that in New South Wales. From a membership of about 100 at the end of its first year, the New South Wales society grew steadily to about 900 in 1970, a plateau maintained until 1974. Thereafter, it fell sharply so that by 1977 there were only about 400 members. Since then it has hovered in the 400–500 range. By contrast, the membership in Victoria has never been much above 400 and, at the time of writing, stood at about 160. This difference between the states in not adequately explained by differences in population, for New South Wales is only about 30 per cent more populous than Victoria. The theological and social temper of the major religious denominations, especially the Anglican Church, has for many years been more conservative — humanists would perhaps say 'more reactionary' or 'more backward' — in Sydney than in Melbourne. This might have spurred the New South Wales humanists to greater efforts than their Victorian counterparts. Moreover, the Unitarian Church, to which some humanists belonged, has for a long time been much stronger and more vocal in Melbourne than in Sydney. Consequently, the need for a new organisation was less keenly felt in Victoria than in New South Wales. Also important in explaining the difference between these states was the long period of continuous and virtually full-time service, from 1960 to 1974, given by Daphne

Weeks as honorary secretary of the New South Wales society, and by Bill Weeks as a committee member. Their organisational skills and commitment to the humanist cause were reflected in the growth and influence of the society during that period. Other leaders such as Ian Edwards and Bridget Gilling also contributed much to the public image and achievements of the society at that time.

Membership

In 1970 Fairbanks undertook a survey of the society's members. Out of 911 questionnaires despatched, 709 were returned, giving a response rate of 78 per cent. Although Fairbanks did not make an exhaustive analysis of the data thus obtained, some results have been published (Fairbanks, 1971). Where appropriate, these will be compared with those obtained in Campbell's (1965) study of the British Humanist Association, in Mol's (1971) study of churchgoing population in Australia, and in the 1971 Census of New South Wales.

Of Fairbanks's respondents, 58 per cent were males. This preponderance of males was similar to, though not so marked as, that in the British Humanist Association. It contrasts with the situation in most churches, where males form a minority of the membership though not of the designated leadership. Assuming a predominantly instrumental rather than expressive orientation in the Humanist Society, these results were fairly consistent with the then-prevailing definitions of sex roles in our society (see Mol, 1971: 30–31).

Only 17 per cent of Fairbanks's respondents were aged 30 or under, 23 per cent were 31–40, 34 per cent were 41–50. 18 per cent were 51–65, and 8 per cent were over 65. This age structure was less similar to that of the adult population of New South Wales than was the age structure of Campbell's sample similar to that of the adult population of Britain. Thus, persons aged 18–30, who constituted 31 per cent of the adult population in the 1971 Census of New South Wales, were markedly under-represented in the Humanist Society. The age category most over-represented was 41–50 years: 34 per cent of members fell into this category, compared with 19 per cent for the adult population at large. In short, the Humanist Society was predominantly made up of persons in middle adulthood. Sixty-nine per cent of its members were married, the same proportion as in the adult population of New South Wales. It would be wrong, therefore, to think of the society as being made up mainly of the young and unattached.

Thirty-five per cent of society members were university graduates, and a further 13 per cent had completed some other tertiary course. The occupations of 44 per cent were classified as 'professional'. Without necessarily approving of class distinctions, 20 per cent described themselves as upper middle class, and a further 43 per cent as middle class. Fairbanks's results thus indicate a membership which had a higher than average level of education and of occupational and social status. In these respects, the New South Wales Humanist Society was very similar to the British Humanist Association. This is probably partly explained as another instance of the widely observed phenomenon whereby it is persons of this socioeconomic status who tend to be the main joiners of instrumentally oriented voluntary associations other than trade unions (Tomeh, 1973). The emphasis in the Humanist Society's aims on rationality and on the use of science for human welfare is also likely to attract persons whose educational level and occupation provide skills and scope for such activities.

Activities, Achievements and Problems

At the time when the survey was made, the society held monthly public meetings in Sydney, with speakers on topics such as 'Pre-school Education: A Vital Need', 'Evolution, Pollution and Revolution', 'Power and Resources in Australia: What of Our Future?', 'Aspects of Law and Order', 'The Women's Liberation Movement in Australia', 'Homosexuality and the Law', and 'What is Saigon's Future?' Such meetings had commenced in 1961 and continued on a regular basis until 1971. They served the function of consciousness-raising both for members of the society and, through reporting in the media, for members of the public at large. In addition, there were nine suburban groups in various parts of Sydney, and branches at Newcastle, Wollongong and Armidale. These groups and branches also generally held monthly meetings, with a speaker followed by discussion, and social events from time to time. Furthermore, in Sydney the society had three youth groups for those aged 8-11, 11-12, and 13-15 respectively.

There were thus many Humanist Society activities in which members could participate. Although over 90 per cent of members lived in the Sydney metropolitan area or in one of the other centres where there were branches, only 3 per cent of Fairbanks's respondents described themselves as 'very active' members, 13 per cent as 'active', and 12 per cent as 'attending meetings fairly often'. This left 27 per cent who attended meetings occasionally, and a further 45 per cent who did not attend at all. Of course, some meetings were attended by persons who had an interest in the particular topic even though they were not members. From time to time, there were comments in the society's newsletter, *Viewpoints*, about some members' apathy. Under the heading 'Moribund or Merely Tired?', the Editorial Committee wrote in February 1972:

> Sadly, a once-vigorous and leading body has become listless and dull. The membership is static, suburban groups and country branches are slipping and the General Committee spends its time examining minutes and correspondence minutely for signs of meaning and, finding none, gratefully sinks back into somnolence.

In the correspondence stimulated by these comments, there were differences of opinion as to whether the society was suffering from malaise and, if so, why. On behalf of the General Committee, one member reviewed achievements and argued that the society was still as actively concerned with important social issues as in earlier years. As well as growing in membership to about 900 and acquiring a headquarters 'humming with activity' on a valuable city block, the society had produced offshoots, such as the Council for Civil Liberties, the Secular Education Society and the Abortion Law Reform Association, which had been allowed to develop autonomously, 'thus ensuring the selection of further talent from a broader non-humanist range'. In 1969 the society had published two books: *Sex for Modern Teenagers* and *A Humanist View*. It had produced reports on Religious Education in New South Wales State Primary Schools (1961), Humanist Education of Children (1962), Termination of Pregnancy (1962), Sterilisation (1963), Contraception (1964), Venereal Diseases (1966) and Marriage and Divorce (1970).[2] The *Australian Humanist* was on public sale throughout the nation. The society had backed the Vietnam Moratorium movement, and had recently sought to have conditions improved at a Children's Shelter in Sydney. There were now known humanists in Parliament, Senator Lionel Murphy had asked the General Committee to submit proposals on law reform, and the Committee continued to make recommendations to various government authorities on matters of humanist concern (*Viewpoints*, July 1972: 53–4).

Despite only limited success on some issues, these were certainly significant achievements, and more were to follow after the Australian Labor Party came to power in Canberra in December 1972. In 1973 the Federal Attorney-General, Senator Murphy, appointed various persons, including Humanist Society nominees, as civil marriage celebrants. This was a fulfilment of representations made for more than ten years by the Humanist Society, and was later claimed by some members of the society to have contributed significantly to a decline in the number of church adherents (see *Viewpoints*, September 1977: 92). Also in 1973 the society issued a report on euthanasia, with the result that a Voluntary Euthanasia Society was formed. In the same year, the New South Wales Parliament passed the Evidence and Oaths (Amendment) Act, so that it was possible for a person to become a Justice of the Peace without taking an oath on the Bible. This, too, was a change which the society had been seeking for many years.

Nevertheless, within the society, there were signs that things were slipping. By early 1973, the number of suburban groups had fallen to five, and only one youth group remained. Due to the lack of adult help, the latter group ceased functioning in 1974. Although a Humanist Telephone Referral Service, staffed by volunteers from 6 p.m. to 10 p.m. each week night, was started in September 1973, it lasted only a few months. A proposal to establish a humanist retirement village came to nothing. In short, the society failed to sustain social service programmes similar to those conducted by some overseas humanist societies, such as that in Holland. Plagued with financial problems, the *Australian Humanist* ceased publication in 1975. Furthermore, between 1974 and 1977, membership of the society fell from 937 to 401.

Several factors contributed to this decline. At the end of 1974, Mr and Mrs Weeks resigned from the General Committee after that body had resolved by a narrow majority to write to the Foreign Minister condemning the Australian government's *de jure* recognition of Russia's 30-year-old annexation of the Baltic states. The Weeks considered this resolution hasty and irrational, but failed in their attempt to have it rescinded. Their resignations set off a chain of events. First, the work which Daphne Weeks had done freely for the previous 14 years was so extensive that the committee considered it necessary to offer renumeration of up to $50 per week to her successor as secretary. This, coupled with sharp rises in postage rates, led to a doubling in the annual membership fee between 1974 and 1976: from $6 to $12. With such an increase, those persons who had any criticisms of the society's activities were tempted not to renew their membership.

One source of such criticism related to the role of the Humanist Society in politics. By the late 1960s it was clear that the vast majority of members were opposed to Australia's military involvement in Vietnam (see, for example, survey results in *Australian Humanist*, Spring 1967: 39; Fairbanks, 1971: 16). By and large, they supported the society's call for an immediate withdrawal of Australian and all foreign troops from Vietnam. Although at least two members protested publicly at the society's adoption of such a stand (*Viewpoints*, June 1970:51-2), the society managed to weather this storm without too much dissension or loss of membership. By contrast, there was much more dispute over the resolution on the Baltic states. There was further controversy after the society wrote to Sir John Kerr in December 1975, protesting at his dismissal of the Whitlam government, and calling for his resignation from the office of Governor-General. Differences of opinion on issues such as these inevitably took their toll on society membership.

Membership numbers probably also suffered as a result of the formation of other, more specialised, organisations such as the Abortion Law Reform Association, the Council for Civil Liberties, the Secular Education Society, the Campaign Against Moral Persecution, the Council for the Defence of Government Schools, and so on. Though their objectives were not generally in conflict with those of the Humanist Society, such organisations had the potential to draw away persons whose main interests were less extensive than those embraced by that society. If, moreover, some of the objectives sought by members were achieved — as indeed happened during the 1970s — those persons for whom such objectives were uppermost felt less incentive to join or to continue their society membership.

Relationship to religion

One of the aims of the society is to 'provide a constructive alternative to theological and dogmatic creeds'. One might ask to what extent humanism is itself a religion, or how far it is a 'functional equivalent' of religion. In the 1957 edition of *Religion Without Revelation*, Sir Julian Huxley, who later became the first President of the British Humanist Association, argued that evolutionary humanism provides the basis for a new religion. In the course of his exposition, he wrote:

> Earlier religions and belief-systems were largely adaptions to cope with man's ignorance and fears, with the result that they came to concern themselves primarily with stability of attitude. But the need today is for a belief-system adapted to cope with his knowledge and his creative possibilities; and this implies the capacity to meet, inspire and guide change. (Huxley, 1957: 211)

Most humanists would probably agree with these words. They would also accept the notions of biological and social evolution as fundamental to their thinking. But very few would regard humanism as a new religion. Nevertheless, from time to time this issue has arisen within the Humanist Society.

In 1970 the Annual General Meeting agreed to 'appoint a special committee to research the desirability and feasibility of the Humanist Society claiming to be a religious organisation and trying to win official recognition of this claim, with all its attendant privileges' (*Viewpoints*, August 1970: 61). This idea, which was presumably intended to embarrass the accepted religious organisations, did not secure much support within the suburban branches, and nothing came of it. In 1974 Victor Bien, who had just served two terms as President of the Council of Australian Humanist Societies, expressed the view that 'In a sense *humanism seeks to be a kind of "religion"* — in the sense of providing some valid framework for individual identity and a basis for social relationship' (*Australian Humanist*, Winter 1974: 15; italics in original). Like Huxley, Bien saw organised humanism as capable of fulfilling important social functions served by traditional religion: providing meaning, purpose and a bond of fellowship with others.

Huxley went even further. He was willing to contemplate the possibility that the new religion of evolutionary humanism might practise rituals or ceremonies, develop a professional body or priesthood, erect buildings and adopt symbols (Huxley, 1975: 236). Steps in each of these directions were taken within the Humanist Society. One of the civil marriage celebrants nominated by the society devised ceremonies not only for marriages but also for funerals and for name giving (*Viewpoints*, August 1977: supplement). Marriage celebrants and persons willing to conduct humanist funerals are regularly listed in the society's newsletter. The society has acquired its own building, where weekly meetings and some humanist weddings are held, and has adopted as its symbol a stylised 'happy person' in the form of a figure H. However, in 1978 the Annual General Meeting resolved to oppose the establishment of a humanist church in any form.

What is the society's attitude to existing religious organisations? The 1970 edition of the society's brochure, 'The Humanist View', stated that 'Humanists find themselves opposed to orthodox religious organisations on many issues but anti-religion is not the basic purpose of Humanism. Humanists will support religious organisations in those areas of agreement where enlightened attitudes prevail' (*Viewpoints*, September 1970: 71). In keeping with this, when a branch was formed in Armidale in 1969, it resolved to advise the churches in that city of its readiness to co-operate with them in social betterment action where there was common ground (*Viewpoints*, August 1969: 58). Likewise, in 1970 members of the society spent a weekend with the Wahroonga Society of Friends (Quakers), comparing the philosophical bases and modes of operation of the two organisations, and exploring the possibilities for combined action on various social issues (*Viewpoints*, November 1970: 84–5). The 1979 version of the 'The Humanist View' no longer stated that 'anti-religion is not the basic purpose of Humanism', but it declared that 'Although humanists are intrinsically opposed to religion, they will co-operate with religious organisations on matters of common concern' (*Viewpoints*, January 1979: 1).

From time to time there were complaints from some of the Humanist Society's members that it was failing actively to oppose organised religion. In similar vein, the President of the Rationalist Association of New South Wales claimed in 1972 that his association was the only militant anti-clerical association in New South Wales and possibly Australia (*Viewpoints*, November 1972: 85). The leaders of the Humanist Society nevertheless resisted attempts to change their organisation into a copy of the Rationalist Association. In 1975 the Annual General Meeting rejected a proposal that the aims and objects of the society be amended as follows:

> While continuing debate on a wide variety of subjects within the society, or with other like minded groups, any public stance or public policy decisions should be restricted to furthering the cause of secularism and to counteracting the church and transcendentalism in politics and social traditions. (*Viewpoints*, July 1975: 51; see also May 1975: 39–40)

Likewise, in 1980 the retiring secretary stated that in her five years' occupancy of that position she had resisted all efforts to turn the society into a pseudo rationalist society. In response to those past and present members who wished to see the society doing more church-baiting, she declared that 'there are many ways to kill a cat' and that the society's efforts in pressing for the appointment of civil marriage celebrants had done more to win people away from the churches than had all the pamphlets and letters to the editor. Moreover, she considered that most churches were increasingly showing signs of becoming humanised (*Viewpoints*, July 1980: 68).

Other issues

The society's resistance of attempts to narrow its aims left it open to the danger that it would become like a horse trying to gallop off in several directions at once or that in its efforts to deal with every conceivable social issue it would end up as little more than a society of dilettantes. To some extent this problem was overcome by appointing sub-committees to prepare reports on particular issues or by helping to initiate new organisations with more specialised aims. The sub-committees appointed during the first fifteen years of the society's life generally dealt with matters relating either to sex or to education — issues on which there was a fairly general consensus within the society. More recently, sub-committees have dealt with issues such as uranium, family violence, female genital mutilation, and alternative cancer therapies. On some of these issues, especially the last, there have been sharp differences of opinion within the society. There have also been conflicts over whether the society should endorse the activities and publications of the Humanist School of Philosophy, a study group established by some society members in 1976 and still continuing.

By 1980 complaints were beginning to be voiced about the emphasis of articles appearing in *Viewpoints*. Various members alleged that certain topics, such as feminist issues and alternative cancer therapies, were being given excessive space; that the treatment of these topics was unbalanced, for example that the writers were overwhelmingly critical of orthodox treatments of cancer and too ready to give credence to unorthodox practices; and that a left-wing political bias was present. A tart comment by the co-ordinator of the Humanist School of Philosophy (HSOP) provides an example of one of these criticisms: 'New South Wales Humanists have been preoccupied for some time with the mutilation of female genitals. The HSOP is concerned about the mutilation of minds. . .' (*Viewpoints*, September/October 1981: 84). At a special General Meeting called towards the end of 1981, the General Committee defended both itself and the editor against such criticisms, arguing that the Editorial Committee had given fair consideration to all material submitted for publication and that if members wished to change the balance it was up to them to submit material on topics they felt strongly about.

Early in 1982 the editor for the previous five years resigned. Material on issues which had recently caused dissension was thereafter not wholly absent from *Viewpoints* but was less prominent. A correspondent was informed that although humanists were generally less reactionary than non-humanists on political and economic questions, it was not the policy of the society to take sides in party politics. The only sub-committee included in the list of the society's activities was one which had been dealing with ways out of unemployment. Two new sub-committees were, however, proposed: one to 'promote humanist views and counter reactionary pressure groups', the other on humanist education. With reference to some of the more militant opponents of abortion, the convenor of the first of these sub-committees wrote: 'The political push of the anti-humanists is going to get stronger and even more unscrupulous. The Humanist Society has to be in the vanguard of those who fight back' (*Viewpoints*, January/February 1982: 2). It remains to be seen whether this scenario proves to be correct.

Summary and conclusion

Like the British Humanist Association, the New South Wales Humanist Society had its period of greatest growth in the 1960s, which was an era of relative affluence, little unemployment, and the emergence of various counter-cultural movements. Despite Australian involvement in the Vietnam War, this was a period of growing confidence in the possibility of social progress. In the early 1970s, when the New South Wales Humanist Society reached its zenith, some of the changes it had sought were achieved, partly as a result of the Labor Party's coming to power in Canberra for the first time in over twenty years. On other fronts the society lost ground, for example in its fight against the granting of government aid to denominational schools. The withdrawal of Australian troops from Vietnam, the economic downturn triggered by rapidly rising oil prices, the swing of the political pendulum in a more conservative direction — these changes preceded and accompanied a halving of Humanist Society membership between 1974 and 1977 to a plateau which has remained ever since. In society at large, the social optimism of the earlier period had collapsed.[3]

When surveys were made in the early 1970s, the members both of the British Humanist Association and of the New South Wales Humanist Society were predominantly middle class and middle aged. Given the society's style of activity, it is unlikely that its socioeconomic composition has changed substantially since than. Further research is needed on its present age structure. Possibly some of those who attended its youth groups in the mid to late 1960s and the early 1970s have now become society members. But the lack of any youth groups since 1974 suggests either an ageing membership or a loss of conviction about the value of such groups. Suburban groups and country branches have also declined in number since then. In being predominantly middle class and in attracting relatively few young adults, the Humanist Society is similar to most of the churches.

There are also other respects in which the problems faced by the

Humanist Society are similar to those faced by many churches. The goals of each type of organisation are fairly diffuse. This allows for changing emphases over time but can also lead to differences of opinion on priorities and methods. In both types of organisation there is a fundamentalist element which seeks to pursue a narrower and more militant set of objectives. Likewise, there are differences of opinion in both as to how far and in what way their organisations should become involved in political issues. Both types of organisation have to contend with a large measure of apathy among members of the public whom they wish to draw into their activities. Even among those who are enrolled as members of these organisations, a substantial proportion is relatively inactive. And in both types of organisation there are recurrent financial problems.

These similarities between humanist organisations and religious organisations do not necessarily enable us to conclude that humanism is a form of religion. As was noted earlier, organised humanism might perform some of the same functions as traditional religion: providing a framework within which to view one's place in the universe, establishing a bond of fellowship among members, and even making provision for rites of passage at various life-stages. If one defines religion simply in terms of the social functions it performs, such evidence might be used to draw the conclusion that organised humanism is a religion. If, however, one adopts a substantive definition of religion, one is obliged to look more closely at the *content* of humanist practice and belief before one can decide whether humanism is a religion or not. Here one is confronted by the society's claim that 'Humanism is a view of life which is based on the belief that human problems are solved by people themselves and not by reliance on some supernatural force' ('The Humanist View', reproduced in *Viewpoints*, January 1979: 1). Thus, if belief in the supernatural is an essential element of religion, it is clear that humanism falls outside the latter category. These conclusions are based on the premise that the sociologist should take seriously the meanings and intentions of social actors, not necessarily as the last word but at least as a starting point. This principle is as important in the study of religion as it is in the study of irreligion.

Notes

1 For a fuller outline of the views of Australian humanists, see Edwards, 1969.
2 In subsequent years, reports were produced on Euthanasia (1973), Marihuana (1974) and Prostitution (1977).
3 For a critique of humanist optimism, see Ehrenfeld, 1978.

11 The study of Australian folk religion: Some theoretical and practical problems[1]

Peter E. Glasner

This paper is concerned with an analysis of the variety of empirical manifestations which can be subsumed under the general heading of folk religion in Australian society. It is based on the premise that *a priori* there is no reason to assume that the processes of secularisation in contemporary society necessitate the total demise of religion. Hence there is an attempt to specify some theoretical approaches which may help articulate the reasons for this assumption within a sociological framework.

I have summarised elsewhere the evidence suggesting that secularisation is indeed occurring in our society (Glasner, 1975). This evidence is not without its limitations, which may be briefly summarised thus: secularisation has become something of a *social myth* for sociologists who have used (or in some cases misused) specific studies and concepts developed in a variety of empirical and theoretical settings and applied them to contemporary societies for ideological reasons (Glasner, 1977). In most cases, these reasons are implicit (and doubtless also unrecognised) in their work, and usually take the form of some notion of what Robertson (1970: 240) has called 'presentism' or 'that posture which tends to claim the uniqueness of the modern period, clouds our judgement as to the long-drawn-out historical unfolding of changes we diagnose in the modern world, and also persuades us that the changes we see are inevitably coming to some early point of termination or fruition'.

However, in spite of this, changes in the nature of religion in modern society are occurring, and these are often not wholly welcomed by those whom we may label here as 'traditionally religious'. They would see religion as an ailing institution, a mere reflection of its glorious past. Whatever our own views, this position has its advantages, as Demerath (1974: 1) has noted, for it allows the sociologists to legitimately don the garb of the physician who learn more by studying *illness* than he does by investigating *health*.

Two further points need to be made before the 'illness' can be diagnosed. The first concerns the commonplace that the decline of religion should not be identified with its demise. Institutions in society may come and go for various reasons, but these have to be very carefully specified before one can assume that religion has been banished forever. Secondly, religion and religiosity must not always be identified with their *institutional* manifestations. There is a conceit, as Martin (1969: 36) has rightly noted in his now classic attack on the concept of secularisation, that assumes an 'historical baseline (eleventh to thirteenth centuries?) when men were "really religious"'. Studies are now becoming available which suggest that religion in feudal society had nowhere near the hold over the people that history of institutional religion may suggest. In *Religion and the Decline of Magic*, Thomas (1971) has gone so far as to suggest that we do not know enough about feudal society to make any judgements concerning the decline of religious institutions in modern society. In his judgement, the distinction between religion and magic was not one made by the common people of the sixteenth and seventeenth centuries, let alone any earlier. He concludes (Thomas, 1971: 516) that such people not only held both sets of beliefs together, making no distinction between them, but also would have been indignant if anyone had suggested they were anything other than devout citizens.

These two points bring us to the heart of the matter at hand; if religion is alive and well and living in Australia, would we do best to look for it among the 'common people' and not the religious institutions? In addition, should we be surprised to find that the religion of the 'common people' (and I clearly use this term to designate you and me) is more than a little tainted with traditionally non-religious beliefs? For example, I am reminded of a parish minister interviewed on television during the Whitlam administration who had, along with his congregation, prayed to God that Jim Cairns be sacked. The parallels with this instrumental approach to the manipulation of this-wordly means and ends and those of magic need not be elaborated on further.

However, we may certainly agree with Luckmann (1967: 91) who notes in *The Invisible Religion* that:

> One thing we may assert with confidence: The norms of traditional religious institutions — as congealed in an 'official' or formerly 'official' model of religion cannot serve as a yardstick for assessing religion in contemporary society.

Official religion, that is institutional religion, may include the religion of the common people, but this is not to suggest more than an empirical correlation.

The concept of folk religion

The concept of folk religion, as originally suggested by Mensching (1964), makes a fairly common distinction between communal and associational forms of sociation and is contrasted with universal religion. Bock (1966) extends the discussion by substituting 'official' religion for universal religion, thus bringing it in line with later analyses. He suggests, following Mensching, that

> The folk religions have persisted because people are not completely differentiated from primary group relations but maintain relationships in communities through which...folk beliefs are transmitted. Individuals are reluctant to relinquish these folk beliefs because they are symbols of group membership and because, as Mensching suggests, the holy or sacred items of universal religion are too remote for the daily lives of the believers. (Bock, 1966: 205)

Martin (1967: 74) has labelled this series of interconnected attitudes and beliefs 'subterranean theologies'. Towler (1974: 149) has drawn attention to the complex of often disparate beliefs which lie behind a religious institutional framework in his conceptualisation of 'popular' or 'common' religion. Robert Bellah, talking specifically about American society, has isolated a phenomenon existing alongside, although differentiated from, institutional forms of religion, which he labels 'civil religion' following Rousseau.

This embarrassment of terms constitutes more of a hindrance to the sociologist than a help. It is not entirely clear from the discussion how much similarity of meaning at a theoretical level is involved, and the overall impression is one of empirical sleight of hand. Most definitions of folk religion, whatever it may be called, appear to be negative ones, which delimit it in terms of what it is not, namely official, church or institutional religion. This leaves the field wide open for the sociological entrepreneur to develop a new sub-area, and give it a new name.

One interesting example of this is based upon the 'third term' in the church–sect controversy: mysticism (Troeltsch, 1931). It is generally accepted (see, for example, the discussion by Wallis, 1974) that mysticism forms the basis of religious movements called 'cults' in modern society. By virtue of their emphasis upon the role of charismatic authority in their development and organisation they are usually transitory in nature. However, they develop in what Campbell has described as 'the cultic milieu' which sounds suspiciously like some of the elements which give rise to folk religion and subterranean theologies.

> The cultic milieu can be regarded as the cultural underground of soci-

ety. Much broader, deeper and historically based than the contemporary movement known as *the* underground, it includes all deviant belief-systems and their associated practices. Unorthodox science, alien and heretical religion, deviant medicine, all comprise elements of such an underground. In addition, it includes collectivities, institutions, individuals and media of communication associated with these beliefs. Substantively it includes the worlds of the occult and the magical, of spiritualism and psychic phenomena, of mysticism and new thought, of alien intelligences and lost civilisation, of faith healing and nature cure.(Campbell, 1972: 122)

In a similar vein, Lemert (1975) attempts to define 'non-church religion' with reference to three main variables: its ethos, or social base, which corresponds closely to Campbell's 'cultic milieu'; reification, by which the ethos is transformed from human activity into objective facticity; and cosmisation, or the rooting of the ethos in something transcendent. He then concludes that non-church religion exists simply 'where persons take it for granted that their own ethos corresponds to the meaning of the cosmos' (Lemert, 1975: 192). However it is unclear just how the three elements which make it up can be operationalised in the way that Lemert himself considers necessary. Such broad conceptions can be applied to a variety of non-religious as well as non-church phenomena which poses an unsurmountable problem for Lemert's methodology.

We may conclude, therefore, that the exact meaning of such concepts as folk religion, common religion, subterranean theology and civil religion remains essentially unclear. This appears to be the case because they are often inclusively defined in a negative way. Sociologists seem clear about what they are *not*, but a little less clear about what exactly they *are*. The next part of this discussion will look at some more substantive examples of folk religion (or perhaps, more specifically, folk beliefs), in order to clarify the concept more rigorously.

It has been suggested that the study of folk religion is still in its sociological infancy. Most sociologists have concentrated upon more orthodox interpretations of religious phenomena, which have the advantage of being theologically as well as sociologically circumscribed, and present the investigator with coherence and structure. This leaves aside discussion of the point made by Towler (1974: 153) concerning those traditional sociologies of religion which fall into what Worsley has labelled the 'natural disease of academics': over-systematisation. The serious student of subterranean theologies, however, is faced with a diversity that almost beggars the imagination. His plight is furthered by the semi-structured or unstructured nature of the objects of his research, as well as their apparent internal incoherence. Some of the richness and variety can be illustrated by reference to the following cases.

The Hare Krishna movement

It is probably a good idea to use a fairly well-developed cultic movement as the first example of the kind of social formation under discussion. Cults, as noted earlier, have become objects of interest only recently, and mainly because of the growth of new, exotic and esoteric religions in Western society which, according to Wallis (1974: 299) reached their peak in the late 1960s. Characteristically, cults are based upon the charismatic appeal of the leader, who propounds a deviant ideology and practice as defined by normal societal conventions.

These factors are probably most clearly seen in the case of the Hare Krishna movement, which was formed in 1966 by 'His Divine Grace A. C. Bhaktivedanta Swami Prabhupada' who claims to be in a line of succession to the Lord Sri Krishna who first spoke the *Bhagavat Gita*. Initially two centres were established in Australia, one in Sydney which had some 45 devotees in 1972, and one in Melbourne which had 30 (Breckwoldt, 1973: 70). Krishna consciousness teaches that there is no reality other than Krishna, rejects any form of rational planning, and backs this up with a powerful ritual, the chanting of the Krishna Mantra 2000 times per day. As Breckwoldt (1973: 71) notes, this has the manifest function of cleansing the spirit and communicating with Krishna. It also has the latent function of keeping the devotee fully occupied, and thus unlikely to succumb to the temptations that were the cause of his joining the movement in the first instance. The deviant nature of the group is well illustrated by their distinctive clothing, shaven heads, and public performance of San Kirtana — chanting in the street. The group is clearly a part of capitalist society, running a flourishing business in the manufacture and sale of incense, Indian clothing and literature. Its members are also opposed to 'official religion', often as the result of disillusionment. Breckwoldt (1972: 7) quotes one relatively senior member of the Sydney group:

> Christianity tells you what not to do but not what to do or how to do it. Here everything is combined and our life is one... In the outside world everyone is concerned with 'who am I, am I the great businessman? Am I a great footballer? Am I a great lover? Here I am one thing, a servant of God!'

Typically, Hare Krishna members are individuals who have had little or no success in the 'outside world', who have experimented with alternative lifestyles in the past, and who have frequently been addicted to drugs (Breckwoldt, 1973; O'Brien, 1973). The social organisation of the group is clearly defined and its membership closely circumscribed. It provides an alternative lifestyle and belief system to that commonly found in the existing culture.

Its emphasis on ritual behaviour and its anti-rationalist ideology indicate its close link with the subterranean theologies discussed earlier. In addition, it is one of a variety of such groups which range from the Divine Light Mission to the Church of Scientology. For the sociologist, the Hare Krishna movement and similar religious movements are relatively easy to study once access has been gained. Their belief systems may be irrational and/or incoherent, but they are clearly functional for the membership and, as with Scientology for example, very well documented. Campbell (1972: 135) summarises these concerns in regard to the cultic milieu:

> Both the culture and organisational structure of the milieu represent deviant forms of the prevailing religious and scientific orthodoxies in combination with both expressive and instrumental orientations. Two important elements within the milieu are the religious tradition of mysticism, and the personal service practices of healing and divination.

Social movements

Cultic movements are still clearly recognisable as religious movements, even though they fall well outside the sphere of 'official religions'. Social movements, however, may also be religious without apparently laying claim to be so, and in some circumstances rejecting the notion outright. Wilkinson (1971: 27) suggests that three main characteristics serve as preconditions for social movements:

1. A social movement is a deliberate collective endeavour to promote change in any direction, and by any means, not excluding violence, illegality, revolution or withdrawal into 'utopian' community...
2. A social movement must evince a minimal degree of organisation, though this may range from a loose, informal or partial level of organisation to the highly institutional and bureaucratised movement and the corporate group...
3. A social movement's commitment to change and the *raison d'être* of its organisation are founded upon the conscious volition, normative commitment to the movement's aims or beliefs, and active participation on the part of the followers or members.

One such social movement that may also quality as a folk religion is the conservation and environmentalist movement.[2] It is clearly apocalyptic in nature, and Maddox has gone so far as to label it the 'Doomsday Syndrome', describing the techniques used by its followers as similar to those of 'old preachers who would usher their listeners towards heaven with graphic accounts of what hell is like' (Maddox, 1972: 101). A 1970 issue of *Environment* includes the now classic cartoon of the bearded prophet whose tattered placard bears the immortal legend: 'Prepare to meet the recycler'. However, the environmental movement is more closely related to those deviant forms of scientific orthodoxies mentioned by Campbell above. Instead of the perfection of a world created by God, there is an ecosystem in stable equilibrium. Certainly, it is a social movement concerned with promoting radical change, but it is not so much concerned with equalising social inequality as it is with restoring the balance of nature, with its pre-Christian and Eastern mystic overtones. Its membership is active and vociferous (as in the Lake Pedder controversy) and occasionally violent, as shown recently in Western Australia.

A more introversionist off-shoot of the conservation-environmentalist movement which rarely hits the headlines is the commune or 'alternative community' (Rigby, 1974). These have always been popular in the history of Christianity either as utopian communities or millenarian movements (Cohn, 1970). In contemporary society, however, they have a broader ideological base, and often exhibit an idealistic back-to-nature syndrome also characteristic of some aspects of environmentalism.

By their very nature, such alternative communities are difficult to find and harder still to study. Cock (1974), in his article on alternative lifestyles, suggests that they vary tremendously in style and membership in Australia. Rigby and Turner, in their study of the Findhorn community in Britain, argue that a reorientation of the sociology of religion can start at this level. The community is a religious one, but not in any official way. This is made clear in Rigby and Turner's (1972: 75) quotation from a statement about the history of Findhorn:

> The community of Findhorn consists of a group of people pioneering a new way of living. There are no blue prints... my wife Eileen hears the still small voice within and receives detailed guidance which we have followed with astonishing results... We are living a way of life which is undenominational and therefore cannot be labelled... Our aim is to bring down the Kingdom of Heaven on Earth AND THEREFORE EVERYTHING MUST BE AS NEAR AS PERFECT AS POSSIBLE...

Although the community is sited on a sandy and wind-swept part of the Scottish coast, it produces sufficient vegetables on two acres of ground to be virtually self-sufficient. This is seen as the working of divine laws demonstrated specifically so that others, who are willing to learn, can see and recognise. The authors conclude that it is difficult to label Findhorn as just another sect: 'While Findhorn draws on the mystical Christian theme, it also combines adventism (the Age of Aquarius), dualism (the light and darkness), animism (the elementals) and aspects of the drug culture (Rigby and Turner, 1972: 84).

This last point, of course, opens the way to analysing a very broad range of phenomena in this way. They may be loosely characterised by the term counter-culture, as used for example by Theodore Roszak (1970) or the anti-science movement (as discussed by Cotgrove, 1976). However, the extent to which, for example, the politics of ecstacy can be classified as a folk religion is open to some reservation. Although the noted Catholic sociologist Andrew Greeley, in his article on 'Superstition, Ecstacy and Tribal Consciousness' (1970), describes it as one of new religions which is also certainly very old, and concludes that: 'the tribal gods are being worshipped once again, in substantial part as a protest against the hyper-rationalist society'.

The occult

Another group of tribal gods 'worshipped once again' falls loosely under the heading of the occult. In terms of social organisation, the occult, which ranges from astrology to witchcraft, is much more individualistic and more clearly instrumental than either cults or religious social movements. Part of this stems from a concern with magic, and part with the disparate nature of the so-called 'occult sciences' themselves. For example, astrology, the belief that the time and place of a person's birth affects his or her personality and reaction to the world, does not require any elaborate from of social organisation for its maintenance, although it does require practitioners who, in principle, can be you or I. Recently 186 prominent American scientists publicly discredited astrology in stating that there is 'no scientific foundation for its tenets' (*National Times*, 15–20 September 1975). Defendents of astrology argue, however, that it is more than fortune-telling, and is based upon ancient and pre-scientific conceptions about the universe and man's position in it.

Undoubtedly astrology, or at least its representation in news-papers and magazines in the form of horoscopes, is popular in Australia. Hans Mol, in his Religion in Australia survey in the late 1960s asked adult respondents whether they ever acted upon the ad-vice of their stars. Although 85 per cent said they never did, 13 per cent, a significant proportion, said they did often or sometimes. In fact, Mol was forced to conclude that for 'some of these people the horoscope takes the place of Christianity...' (Mol, 1971: 3). It should also be noted that astrologers are not limited only to stargazers, but include such groups as palmists, graphologists, numerologists and tea readers. Abercrombie *et al.* (1970) have ex-plained some of their appeal in terms of 'gods of the gaps'.

Practitioners of astrology in Australia have formed a federation, which clearly acts as some form of professional association. Thus it reacted strongly to the 1975 Anglican Church report on the occult, calling it a 'classic example of cheap sensationalism' and suggesting that the members of the Anglican Church should 'look within the structure of their own church to find the cause for falling atten-dances instead of blaming us and the occult sciences' (*Daily Mirror*, 18 August 1975). The Anglican report suggested that the occult is a growing force in Australian society, investigating a whole range of practices including astral projection, black magic, bone pointing, seances, white magic and witchcraft. It even suggested prohibiting the sale of Ouija boards and Tarot cards, basing the recommenda-tions on studies of the involvement of Australian school children in the occult. Further evidence for the popularity of witchcraft and satanism can be found in the rapid growth of magazines devoted specifically to it, such as *Man, Myth and Magic* and *Witch-craft Today*, and the popularity of such films as *Rosemary's Baby*.

Together these elements of the occult form a very basic return to old faiths and pagan religions which modern Christianity has in-creasingly dismissed as nonsense. Whereas early Christianity was happy to accommodate many elements of folk religion, including such symbols as the Christmas tree, holly, ivy and mistletoe, these have now become sources of tension and conflict. Bock (1966) uses the example of St Nicholas to show how Christianity institutionalis-ed folk deities and pagan gods by providing a functional alternative. The official churches now complain that Christmas has become de-Christianised, on the one hand, and that the old folk beliefs are reasserting themselves, on the other. The point was made, at the start of this whole discussion, that folk beliefs and practices may well always have been present as part of the official religion. It is of interest to the sociologist, of course, to discover whether they are now becoming increasingly autonomous.

Anzac and all that

The concept of civil religion developed by Robert Bellah (1867) has had quite a disproportionate impact upon the sociology of religion. It is based upon the fairly well-known phenomenon that as society moves from communal to associational social ties, the normative structure, once very specific, becomes generalised. Thus, in modern society

> An area of flexbility must be gained in economic, political and social life in which the specific norms may be determined in considerable part by short-term exigencies in the situation of action, as by functional requisites of the relevant social subsystem. Ultimate religious values lay down the basic principles of social action...the religious system does not attempt to regulate economic, political or social life in great detail. (Bellah, 1958)

American society, like that in Australia, is made up of people from many countries and cultures. The separation of church and state has guaranteed their religious liberty. However, suggests Bellah, there still exists a unitary religious dimension:

> Although matters of personal religious belief, worship and association are considered to be strictly private affairs, there are, at the same time, certain common elements of religious orientation that the great majority of Americans share... [They] provide a religious dimension for the whole fabric of American life... The public religious dimension is expressed in a set of beliefs, symbols and rituals that I am calling American civil religion. (Bellah, 1967)

The term and tone were set in the basically Christian elements of the Declaration of Independence and Thanksgiving Day speeches. However, it transcends Christianity by incorporating folk beliefs dear to the hearts of all Americans such as democracy, American Israelism and sacrifice — especially in just wars on foreign soil. Bellah sees civil religion as the overarching generic form of religion in American society. Clearly, the situation in Australia will be slightly different, because the specific nature of Australian religious history differs from the American case. However, elements of a *potential* Australian civil religion are readily discernible in the essentially Christian nature of many of our institutions (for example, the use of the Lord's prayer at the start of each daily session of Parliament), the whole Anzac ritual, and the myths of mateship and sacrifice associated with it. It is worth noting, in conclusion, that Thomas and Flippen (1972), in their empirical study of American civil religion, found little direct evidence that such a phenomenon existed in reality.[3]

The great Australian religion

No discussion of folk religion in our society would be complete without mention of that great Australian religion 'Aussie Rules'. Sport as religion is not a new sociological conception. Cohen, discussing America's 'great religion', baseball, makes the following points (and it is instructive to substitute football for baseball in this passage):

> To be sure, there may be people who go to a baseball game to see some particular star, just as there are people who go to church to hear a particular minister preach; but these are phenomena in the circumference of the religious life. There are also those blase persons who do not care who wins so long as they can see what they call a good game — just as there are people who go to mass because they admire the vestments or the intoning of the priest — but this only illustrates the pathology of the religious life. The truly religious devotee has his soul directed to the final outcome; and every one of the extraordinarily rich multiplicity of movements of the baseball game acquires its significance because of its bearing on that outcome. Instead of purifying only fear and pity, baseball exercises and purifies all of our emotions...(Cohen 1964: 37)

Coles (1975) has argued recently that, at the very least, football is a form of 'surrogate religiosity'. He notes that individuals rarely go to games alone, that allegiances are symbolically displayed (rosettes and car stickers), that the movement between the world of the profane and that of the sacred is facilitated by the exchange of feelings, sentiments and expectations over several drinks before the game, and that the sins of the past (the sins of the opposing team) are given symbolic absolution through the rehearsal of various possible outcomes (Coles 1975: 67). During the game itself, the feelings of the individual members of the crowd are transcended and all become one.

Two further points can be made within the Australian context. The first concerns the role of the charismatic figures on the field, like Ron Barassi, and the charismatic appeal of some clubs, like Richmond or Carlton. Clearly these provide a possible focus for religious fervour not unlike that which characterises cultic movements. The second, also with reference to cultic movements, concerns the deviant nature of the participation. This may range from the wearing of club colours in normal non-game situations such as going to work, to the quite frightening displays of aggression which are part and parcel of spectator participation at every game. Professor Ian Turner observed that at one football match 'a youngish junior-executive type removed his beer can from his lips long enough to remark to the umpire: You rotten, bloody, commo, poofter, mongrel bastard!' (*Age*, 7 October 1972).

Turner then went on to comment that this 'fine assembly of Australian political, racial and sexual prejudices' seemed to act as a satisfactory form of purgation for the barracker. Certainly the threats and violence are integral rites in the ritual of the game, and allow patterns of behaviour which, if repeated outside, would incur the wrath of the wider society, as evidenced by the reaction of the police and public to the hooliganism of English soccer fans (Harrison, 1974).

Sport generally, and Aussie Rules in particular, plays a significant role in the makeup of folk beliefs in Australian society. Along with mateship and beer, it forms the basis of Australia's cultural style. Little wonder, therefore, that a combination of all three, with a chance to release the tension of daily monotony, and the possibility of achieving, if only for a few moments, ecstatic self-transcendence, results in an experience which even non-sociologists would describe as religious.

Some theoretical considerations

Finally, it is necessary to bring together some of the diverse threads illustrated by the empirical variation of folk religion and belief in Australia. This project needs to be carried out on both micro- and macro-levels. The place of folk beliefs, or subterranean theologies, or common religion, needs to be theorised within the social formation we call the capitalist mode of production. This locates them clearly within the wider social structure, and allows us to introduce such sociological concepts as anomie and alienation, social class and social status. The fabric of social structure in industrial capitalism is a frail one, which is easily pierced. Ideology is part of the thread that holds it together. While the Protestant ethic may represent the spirit of capitalism (Weber, 1930) it is not enough to keep it alive in the present day. Most of the examples discussed above indicate a rejection, in one form or another, of the dominant Christian mode, and its replacement by a range of alternatives rooted in a bewildering variety of backgrounds ranging from

Eastern mysticism, through pre-Christian symbols, to modern science.

In addition, many of the examples quoted can be seen as a return to pre-industrial, communal forms of sociation. The impersonality of social life, the lack of individual control over individual destiny, the dependence upon secondary social relationships, and the apparent inhuman rationality all contribute strongly to this desire. Only a very few are in the position to abandon their lifestyles in order to seek new ones, and such individuals are usually already marginal in society. For the rest, such preoccupations become part-time affairs, to be indulged in at the weekends, or on holidays, or even on the occasional evening. In this way, of course, such alternative forms of religiosity in no way differ from those found in official religions, which David Martin once described as clubs for the clubbable classes. Truzzi (1972: 29), in his discussion of the occult revival in the United States, notes that for the majority 'involvement in the Occult is a leisure-time activity and a fad of popular culture, rather than serious religious involvement in the search for new sacred elements'. My contention here is to state that this viewpoint, although it has some truth, bypasses the most important element: the concept of the religious. I have explored this concept elsewhere in some detail (Glasner, 1977) and will therefore only reiterate the major points here.

I would argue that a truly theoretical account of folk religion and belief is possible at the micro-level through the posing of a distinction between religion on the one hand, and the religious on the other. The former identifies the common-sense, taken-for-granted definition of religion in our society: churches, sects and denominations. The latter bypasses these and provides a sociological account of the specific form of social interaction which allows us to isolate religion in the sorts of areas discussed above. *Religious* forms of interaction are found in essentially communal forms of sociation; they are characterised by piety, authority and mystery; and they are not necessarily present all the time. In short, religious forms of interaction are characteristics of both official religion, on the one hand, and folk religion on the other. This conceptualisation allows the sociologist to get beneath the facade of taken-for-granted reality in order to illuminate the real mechanisms of societal formation.

In conclusion, it is clear that folk beliefs or folk religion are an important element in the religious life of Australian society. It is also apparent that they lack precise formulation within the sociological literature, which treats them on the one hand as derivations of the mystically based cult, and on the other as some loose form of generalised civil religion. In between ranges the depth and breadth of the 'cultic milieu' and its various subterranean theologies. Macro-sociological theorising has not yet managed to come to terms with the phenomenon, except in general functionalist terms, and clearly a lot of work needs to be done to show just how such movements articulate with capitalist social formations. My own attempts, at the analytic level of social interaction, at least provide a key to identifying religiosity and distinguishing it from its non-religious modes, independently of the institutional manifestations commonly labelled religion.

In summary, three main points stem from this conclusion. First, it is necessary for sociologists to 'turn in' to those aspects of Australian society that are suggestive of overarching, normative structures with sacred reference at the macro-level, and the specific nature of religious social relationships at the micro-level. This will help isolate folk religion and distinguish it from the 'official' forms. Hence, secondly, the study will require a necessary historical and Australian dimension. Folk beliefs are, after all, the property of the folk who hold them. Finally, it is necessary to recognise that such a study may well reveal areas of religiosity which, by their nature, have not previously been considered 'religion'.

Notes

1 Originally published in Hayes (1977).
2 See my (1973) discussion of environmentalism as a contemporary religious movement. For a broader discussion of environmentalism, see Cotgrove (1975 and 1976). For a more general discussion, see Musgrove (1974).
3 In fact they concluded: 'Perhaps all of this indicates that a well-defined thesis of civil religion may be more the creation (and fantasy) of the liberal, political and intellectual elite than active faith among the masses' (Thomas and Flippen, 1972: 224).

12 Conclusion

Alan W. Black and Peter E. Glasner

This volume of essays has investigated several aspects of religious belief and practice in Australian society. In so doing, it has not attempted to be exhaustive but rather to supplement Mol's (1971) pioneering 'sociological map' of religion in Australia.

A conscious attempt has been made throughout to develop a sociological perspective, in the knowledge that hitherto much less research on Australian religion has been done from this perspective than from other perspectives such as that of the historian (see Bollen *et al.*, 1980; Mason and Fitzpatrick, 1982). This does not mean that the sociologist should neglect historical data and insights, but rather that he or she should try to incorporate these, where appropriate, into a sociological framework. In several of the previous chapters steps have been taken in this direction, and there is ample scope for more such work.

In speaking of a sociological perspective one does not necessarily imply uniformity in theoretical presuppositions. There are, in fact, various sociological approaches, each with strengths and limitations. Theoretical presuppositions are often implicit in the definitions used. Thus, as was pointed out in Chapter 10, if one adopts a functionalist definition of religion one's answers to certain questions are likely to be different from those one would give if one were to adopt a substantive definition. The sociologist — and his or her audience — should therefore be alert to the consequences of adopting one conceptual framework rather than another.

In recent years various writers have lamented the tendency for studies of religion in Western societies to concentrate exclusively on what has been called 'church-oriented' (Luckmann, 1967), 'official' (Towler, 1974; Blaikie, 1978; Robertson, 1978; Wilson, 1978; Vrijhof and Waardenburg, 1979; Williams, 1980), 'organised' (Hickman, 1977) or 'institutional' (Harris *et al.*, 1982) religion. A recent bibliography of social research on religion in Australia (Mason and Fitzpatrick, 1982) indicates that such research as has been done in this country often has this tendency, and this is also true of many of the contributions to the present volume. Of course, studies with this focus have a proper place in the sociology of religion, but as was argued in Chapter 11 they need to be supplemented by analyses of what has variously been termed 'common', 'popular', 'non-official', 'everyday', 'vernacular', 'extra-ecclesiastical' or 'folk' religion (see writers cited above, as well as Habel, 1980, and Clark, 1982). The interaction between 'official' and 'folk' religion, both in the past and at present, also warrants study. Some aspects of the relationship between Spiritualism and denominational Christianity were examined in Chapter 8. In parts of Campion's (1982) book, *Rockchoppers*, there are data on the interaction between 'official' and 'folk' Catholicism. The relationship between official and folk religion is obviously quite complex and in need of further investigation.

Though differences persist among sociologists concerning the definition of religion, Smart (1971: 15–25) suggests that religion typically has six aspects or dimensions. These are:

1 *The doctrinal dimension*   This refers to ideas about the supernatural, the sacred, the ultimate, and related matters. It could include not only beliefs about super-empirical entities but also such notions as those of fate, karma, omens, the meaning of life and so on.
2 *The mythological dimension*   This consists of beliefs which are cast in 'sacred story' form. Such stories may deal with the activities of God or gods, the operation of spiritual powers or forces, the career of a sacred teacher, and so on. Here the term 'myth' is used in a purely technical sense: it does not necessarily imply that the stories are false.
3 *The ethical dimension*   This refers to beliefs about moral duty, about the values one ought to live by, and so on.
4 *The ritual dimension*   As well as acts of worship and other sacred ceremonies, this includes such practices as prayer, various forms of meditation, and the like. In other words, the activity involved might not necessarily be elaborate, nor does the term 'ritual' necessarily imply meaningless repetition.
5 *The experiential dimension*   This refers to such claimed experiences as divine illumination, conversion, spirit possession, mediumship, and so on.
6 *The social dimension*   This includes not only organisational forms such as churches, sects and cults, but also various types of relationship which are important in the transmission and maintenance of the other aspects of religion. The social dimension is closely related to what Berger (1967) terms the 'plausibility structure' of religion.

Thus, the first there of Smart's dimensions have to do with what might broadly be called *beliefs*; the other three have to do with what might broadly be called *practices*. These dimensions are usually somewhat interwoven, and one of the tasks of research is to examine the extent to which there is either congruity or tension between them in any particular case.

It should be noted that these dimensions are not limited to Western, church-oriented religion. There are, of course, variations from one form of religion to another in the content of, and emphasis upon, the various dimensions. Thus, in 'official religion' as espoused in the major denominations in Australia there is a greater degree of codification of doctrine than in most forms of folk religion in this country. Likewise, the ritual dimension is generally more formalised in the former case than in the latter. Processes of codification and formalisation tend to increase as religious organisations grow in size, as full-time functionaries are appointed, as the socioeconomic status of participants rises, and as the lifespan of the organisation reaches to a second generation (see Niebuhr, 1929; Pope, 1942; O'Dea, 1966; Winter, 1977). Indeed, various writers have suggested that there is a tendency over time for 'cults' to be transformed into 'sects', and for 'sects' to become 'denominations'.

The terms 'cult' and 'sect' were discussed briefly in Chapter 1. There was further consideration of various types of sect in Chapter 4 and of cults in Chapter 11. For the purposes of the present chapter, a 'denomination' is a structured religious association which claims to maintain the essential elements of a particular religion (for example, Christianity) but which accepts similar truth claims by at least some other religious groups; it is generally less strict than a sect in membership requirements.

As cults have no firm locus of final authority beyond the individual member, they are potentially open to a wide variety of ideas, and they frequently have a fairly rapid turnover of membership. Hence, cults tend to be fragile institutions. If a cult leader or leadership group succeeds in establishing an acknowledged basis of authority (for example, by claiming a unique revelation or by formulating a codified body of doctrine), what began as a cult can be transformed into a sect. This has happened in Mormonism (O'Dea, 1957), Christian Science (Pfautz, 1955 and 1956), Scientology (Wallis, 1976) and the Jesus movement (Richardson, 1979). Although there may be rudimentary signs of this process in the Spiritualist group analysed in Chapter 8, Spiritualism has tended to remain at the cult end of the spectrum. As such, it is not sharply differentiated from the broader cultic milieu out of which its ideas and participants are drawn. More research is needed on the nature of this cultic milieu and on the way in which it is drawn upon by other religious cults in Australia.

Just as the transformation from cult to sect is possible but not inevitable, so too is the metamorphosis from sect to denomination. The pressure for the latter transformation is bound up with such considerations as the desire for broader social acceptance, the administrative problems associated with increasing size and accumulated wealth, the 'routinisation of charisma' after the death of the movement's founder, the need to make provision for the children of believers, and so on. The operation of factors such as these led Niebuhr (1929: 19) to assert that 'by its very nature the sectarian type of organisation is valid for only one generation'. Mechanisms of isolation and insulation can, however, reduce some of these pressures and may prevent or delay the process of transformation (Winter, 1977: 159–65). These mechanisms may include residential separation from the wider community, the adoption of a distinctive style of dress, and requiring a high level of commitment from members (for example, by expecting them to surrender all their possessions to the control of the religious organisation). As was shown in Chapter 9, each of these mechanisms operates within the Hare Krishna movement. Moreover, this movement builds on a Vedic rather than a specifically Christian tradition, and to that extent there is less likelihood that it will come to approximate the major denominations in Australia. It might, however, take on some of the characteristics of an 'institutionalised sect' (see Robertson, 1970: 123–8).

One would also like to know more about other smaller religious groups which have been expanding in Australia in recent years. Some of these, such as Pentecostalists, constitute variations on the prevailing Christian tradition. Others, such as Muslims, belong to a rather different tradition. The reasons for their growth — and for the fluctuating fortunes of the major denominations — vary. Careful comparisons are needed to determine the relative importance of purely demographic factors such as immigration and birth rates, and of other factors such as style of religiosity, socioeconomic status, spatial mobility, social networks, personal circumstances, and so on.

Several chapters have touched on the problems faced by clergy and on relationships between clergy and laity in the major denominations. There is no need here to reiterate the conclusions. There are, however, some issues which need further examination. Blaikie found that clergy who adopt one of the 'radical' styles of ministry tend to be younger than those who adopt one of the 'conservative' styles of ministry. Dowdy and Lupton, on the other hand, found almost no difference between younger and older clergy in views on what the most important activities of the church and of the clergy should be. How does one account for the apparent discrepancy between these two studies? It is unlikely that it arises from the fact that Blaikie's data were drawn from Protestant clergy whereas Dowdy and Lupton also included Catholics in their sample; for the latter writers failed to discover significant age differences even when denomination was kept constant. Another possibility is that there are significant differences between Victoria, where Blaikie's data were collected, and New South Wales and Queensland, where Dowdy and Lupton gathered theirs. As was noted in Chapters 7 and 10, the churches in New South Wales and Queensland tend to be more conservative in various respects than those in Victoria. This could mean that there were so few 'radicals' in the ministry in the former states that they failed to show up significantly in Dowdy and Lupton's sample. In any case, one would like to know whether any changes have taken place in the decade or so since both these surveys were made.

In Chapter 2 it was pointed out that about 11 per cent of the Australian population claims to have no religion. Chapter 10 looked at the New South Wales Humanist Society as a form of organised irreligion. As only a minute fraction of those stating that they have no religion belong to the Humanist Society or the Rationalist Association, research is needed on what might be termed 'folk' or 'common' irreligion. Using data drawn from the Australian Social Barometer, Hogan (1979) has built up a profile of Australian secularists. It would be of interest to compare and contrast the ways in which life crises, questions of social responsibility, interpersonal relationships, and so on are handled by secularists on the one hand and by religious believers on the other.

It should be borne in mind that belief and practice, whether religious or not, are not static entities; that social change is ubiquitous. Not all social change is uniform, however, and though there are indications that some aspects of religiosity in Australia have been declining (see Hickman, 1977; Wilson, 1979), one should be cautious of facile conclusions about the process of secularisation. Glasner (1977) has explored the limitations of this concept in some detail, concluding that it has some value as a generic terms which subsumes a wide range of different processes located at different points in time and space. There may be some utility in talking about an overall 'profile' or religiosity rather than just talking about religion in general. Martin (1978) sees secularisation as fundamentally related to Christianity and, as noted in Chapter 1, places Australia between Britain and America in terms of religious pluralism and participation. Clearly this needs to be explored in more detail if social change is to be mapped.

As nearly twenty years have elapsed since Mol's data were collected, the time is approaching when another major attempt should be made to chart attitudes, practices and beliefs of the Australian people. The results would provide sociologists with a broad-ranging body of comparative material to deal with for the first time. This is not to suggest that all that is required is a simple replication of Mol's 1966 survey. A comprehensive, long-term strategy for research on Australian religion needs to be developed.

The present volume gives some leads as to various elements which should be included in such a programme. Future research should take account of the different dimensions or aspects of religion, not only in their 'official' or 'organised' forms but also in their 'folk' or 'extra-ecclesiastical' forms. Clearly, several levels of analysis are involved: the interpersonal, the organisational, and the societal or cultural. These can be investigated using a variety of techniques, many of which were used in the research reported in earlier chapters. These techniques include the use of historical records, official statistics, surveys, participant observation, community study, documentary analysis, and so on. We need not go into detail here about the advantages or disadvantages of any particular technique or its appropriateness to the study of any particular phenomenon. We can however point to the value of 'triangulation' (discussed in Denzin, 1970): combining several methodologies to investigate a single phenomenon. For example, a particular denomination can be looked at in the community, or through a survey of its members, or by analysing its publications. The three together provide a fuller picture.

A research programme using the framework outlined above would provide material which could be used for comparative purposes not only from one point in time to another but also cross-culturally. In addition to those already mentioned, several research areas at different points in the matrix of possibilities can be discerned. These include: characteristics and beliefs of those who fail to answer the Census question on religion; male and female roles in religion; the charismatic movement; religion on television; current attitudes to rites of passage (cf. Inglis, 1970); 'mail order' religion; astrology; non-Christian religions in Australia; house churches; new Christian schools; religion and Australian capitalism; urban Aboriginal religion; religion in talk-back radio; and religiously based organisations which originated in Australia, such as Lifeline. This, by no means exhaustive, list needs to be supplemented within the programme framework outlined above, so that a clearer understanding of the variety of Australian religious practice and belief can be gained.

Bibliography

Government Publications

Historical Records of Australia
New South Wales Parliamentary Debates

Newspapers, etc.

Advocate (Melbourne Catholic Archdiocese)
Age
Australian
Australian Humanist
Daily Mirror (Sydney)
Herald (Melbourne)
Migration News
National Times
Viewpoints (New South Wales Humanist Society)

Other Publications

Abercrombie, N. *et al.* (1970) 'Superstition and Religion: the God of the Gaps' in D. Martin and M. Hill (eds) *A Sociological Yearbook of Religion in Britain* 3, SCM, London.

Adams, R. L. and Fox, R. J. (1972) 'Mainlining Jesus: the New Trip' *Transaction/Society* 9(4).

Altman, D. (1970) 'Students in the Electric Age' in R. Gordon (ed.) *The Australian New Left: Critical Essays and Strategy* Heinemann, Melbourne.

Anglican Information Office (1975) *The Occult: Report of an Anglican Commission of Enquiry* Sydney.

Austin, A. G. (ed.) (1963) *Select Documents in Australian Education 1788–1900* Pitman, Melbourne.

____ (1972) *Australian Education 1788–1900* 3rd edn, Pitman, Carlton.

Barrett, J. (1966) *That Better Country* Melbourne University Press, Carlton.

Baum, G. (1970) 'Does the World Remain Disenchanted?' *Social Research* 37: 153-202.

Bellah, R. N. (1958) 'Religious Aspects of Modernisation in Turkey and Japan' *American Journal of Sociology* 64: 1-5.

_____ (1967) 'Civil Religion in America' *Daedalus* 96(1): 1-21.

Berger, P. L. (1954) 'The Sociological Study of Sectarianism' *Social Research* 21: 467-85.

_____ (1963) 'A Market Model for the Analysis of Ecumenicity' *Social Research* 30: 77-93.

_____ (1967) *The Sacred Canopy* Doubleday, New York (published in Britain as Berger, 1973).

_____ (1969) *A Rumor of Angels* Doubleday, New York.

_____ (1973) *The Social Reality of Religion* Penguin, Harmondsworth.

Berger, P. L. and Luckmann, T. (1966) *The Social Construction of Reality* Doubleday, New York.

Berger, P. L. and Pullberg, S. (1965) 'Reification and the Sociological Critique of Consciousness' *History and Theory* 5: 196-211.

Berger, P. L. *et al.* (1973) *The Homeless Mind* Penguin, Harmondsworth.

Black, A. W. (1975) 'Religious Studies in Australian Public Schools: An Overview and Analysis' *Australian Education Review* 7(3).

_____ (1982) 'Church Union in Canada and Australia: a Comparative Analysis', presented at conference of Australian and New Zealand Association for Canadian Studies, Sydney (to be published in conference proceedings, ed. P. Crabb).

Blaikie, N. W. H. (1972) 'What Motivates Church Participation? Review, Replication and Theoretical Re-orientation in New Zealand' *Sociological Review* 20: 39-58.

_____ (1974) 'Altruism in the Profession: the Case of the Clergy' *Australian and New Zealand Journal of Sociology* 10: 84-9

_____ (1976) 'The Use of "Denomination" in Sociological Explanation: the Case of the Position of Clergy on Social Issues' *Journal for the Scientific Study of Religion* 15: 79-86.

_____ (1978) 'Religious Groups and World Views' in F. J. Hunt (ed.) *Socialisation in Australia* 2nd edn, Australia International Press and Publications, Melbourne.

_____ (1979) *The Plight of the Australian Clergy: To Convert, Care or Challenge?* University of Queensland Press, St Lucia.

Bock, E. W. (1966) 'Symbols in Conflict: Official Versus Folk Religion' *Journal for the Scientific Study of Religion* 5(2).

Bodycomb, J. (1978) *The Naked Clergyman* Joint Board of Christian Education of Australia and New Zealand, Melbourne.

Bollen, J. D. (1972) *Protestantism and Social Reform in New South Wales 1890-1910* Melbourne University Press, Carlton.

_____ (1973) *Religion in Australian Society: An Historian's View* Leigh College, Sydney.

Bollen, J. D. *et al.* (1980) 'Australian Religious History, 1960-80' *Journal of Religious History* 11: 8-44.

Border, R. (1962) *Church and State in Australia 1788-1872* SPCK, London.

Borrie, W. D. (1954) *Italians and Germans in Australia* Cheshire, Melbourne.

Bouma, G. D. (1982) 'The Myth of Declining Churches: the Case of Victorian Anglicans' *St Mark's Review*, forthcoming.

Breckwoldt, R. J. (1972) 'The Hare Krishna Movement in Australia: A Sociological Perspective' unpublished mimeo.

____ (1973) 'The Hare Krishna Movement in Australia' *Australian and New Zealand Journal of Sociology* 9(2): 70-1.

Britten, E. H. (1869) *Modern American Spiritualism* Burns, London.

Broom, L. and Selznick, P. (1963) *Sociology* 3rd edn, Harper and Row, New York.

Broome, R. (1980) *Treasure in Earthen Vessels: Protestant Christianity in New South Wales Society 1900-1914* University of Queensland Press, St Lucia.

Bryman, A. and Hinings, C. R. (1974) 'Participation, Reform and Ecumenism: the Views of Laity and Clergy' in M. Hill (ed.) *A Sociological Yearbook of Religion in Britain* 7, SCM, London.

Bryman, A. *et al.* (1974) 'Churchmanship and Ecumenism' *Journal of Ecumenical Studies* 11: 467-75.

Buckner, H. T. (1971) *Deviance, Reality and Change* Random House, New York.

Budd, S. (1967) 'The Loss of Faith: Reasons for Unbelief Among Members of the Secular Movement in England, 1850-1950' *Past and Present* 36: 106-25.

____ (1977) *Varieties of Unbelief* Heinemann, London.

Bullock, R. H. (1975) Case Studies in Twentieth Century American Unitive Protestantism: the Problem of Church Union in the Presbyterian-Reformed Family, PhD dissertation, Princeton University.

Cable, K. C. (1952) The Church of England in New South Wales and its Policy Towards Education Prior to 1880, MA thesis, University of Sydney.

Campbell, C. B. (1965) 'Membership Composition of the British Humanist Association' *Sociological Review* 13: 327-37.

____ (1969) 'Humanism in Britain: the Formation of a Secular Value-oriented Movement' in D. Martin (ed.) *A Sociological Yearbook of Religion in Britain* 2, SCM, London.

____ (1971) *Towards a Sociology of Irreligion* Macmillan, London.

____ (1972) 'The Cult, the Cultic Milieu, and Secularisation' in M. Hill (ed.) *A Sociological Yearbook of Religion in Britain* 5, SCM, London.

Campbell, E. and Pettigrew, T. (1959) 'Racial and Moral Crisis: the Role of Little Rock Minister' *American Journal of Sociology* 64: 509-16.

Campion, E. (1982) *Rockchoppers: Growing up Catholic in Australia* Penguin, Ringwood.

Clark, D. (1982) *Between Pulpit and Pew: Folk Religion in a North Yorkshire Fishing Village* Cambridge University Press, Cambridge.

Clark, E. T. (1951) 'Non-theological Factors in Religious Diversity' *Ecumenical Review* 3: 347-56.

Cock, P. (1974) 'Alternative Lifestyles: Theory and Practice' in D. Edgar (ed.) *Social Change in Australia* Cheshire, Melbourne.

Cohen, M. (1964) 'Baseball as a National Religion' in L. Schneider (ed.) *Religion, Culture and Society* John Wiley & Sons, New York.

Cohn, N. (1970) *The Pursuit of the Millenium* Paladin, London.

Coles, R. (1975) 'Football as a "Surrogate" Religion?' in M. Hill (ed.) *A Sociological Yearbook of Religion in Britain* 8, SCM, London.

Commission on the Church's Unity in Life and Worship (1937) *The Non-theological Factors in the Making and Unmaking of Church Union* Harper and Brothers, New York.

Cotgrove, S. (1975) 'Technology, Rationality and Domination' *Social Studies of Science* 5: 55–78.

_____ (1976) 'Environmentalism and Utopia' *Sociological Review* 24: 23–42.

Cox, D. (1974) 'Will Australia ever be a Pluralist Society?' *Migration Action* 1(1): 5–7.

Cragg, G. R. (1952) 'Disunities Created by Differing Patterns of Church Life' *Ecumenical Review* 4: 276–81.

Currie, R. (1968) *Methodism Divided: A Study in the Sociology of Ecumenicalism* Faber and Faber, London.

Dall, J. (1918) 'Presbyterianism' in J. Hastings (ed.) *Encyclopaedia of Religion and Ethics* T. & T. Clark, Edinburgh.

Daner, F. J. (1975) *The American Children of Krishna: A Study of the Hare Krishna Movement* Holt, Rinehart and Winston, New York.

Demerath, N. J. (1974) *A Tottering Transcendence: Civil Versus Cultic Aspects of the Sacred* Bobbs-Merrill, Indianapolis.

Dempsey, K. (1978) 'To Comfort or to Challenge: the Role of the Church in an Australian Country Town' *La Trobe University Sociology Papers* 1.

_____ (1981) 'The Rural Aged' in A. Howe (ed.) *Towards an Older Australia* University of Queensland Press, St Lucia.

_____ (1982) 'Successful Ageing in an Australian Context' *Australian Journal of Ageing* 1: 3–9.

_____ (forthcoming) *Conflict and Decline: Ministers and Their People in a Country Town*.

Denzin, N. K. (1970) *The Research Act* Aldine, Chicago.

Dow, G. M. (1964) *George Higinbotham: Church and State* Pitman, Melbourne.

Dowdy, E. and Lupton, G. (1976) 'The Clergy and Organised Religion' in P. Boreham *et al.* (eds) *The Professions in Australia* University of Queensland Press, St Lucia.

Dunne, E. (1923) 'The Church and the Immigrant' in C. E. McGuire (ed.) *Catholic Builders of the Nation* Continental Press, Boston.

Edwards, I. (1969) *A Humanist View* Angus & Robertson, Sydney.

Ehrenfeld, D. (1978) *The Arrogance of Humanism* Oxford University Press, New York.

Ellul, J. (1952) 'On the Cultural and Social Factors Influencing Church Division' *Ecumenical Review* 4: 269–75.

Ely, R. (1976) *Unto God and Caesar* Melbourne University Press, Carlton.

Etzioni, A. (1964) *A Comparative Analysis of Complex Organisations* Free Press, New York.

Fairbanks, G. (1971) 'The Humanist Survey — Some Results' *Australian Humanist* 20: 13-17.

File, E. (1961) A Sociological Analysis of Church Union in Canada: Non-theological Factors in Interdenominational Church Union Up to 1925, PhD dissertation, Boston University.

Firth, R. (1960) 'The Fate of the Soul' in C. Leslie (ed.) *Anthropology of Folk Religion* Random House, New York.

Garrison, W. E. (1952) 'Social and Cultural Factors in Our Divisions' *Ecumenical Review* 5: 43-51.

Gill, R. (1974) 'British Theology as a Sociological Variable' in M. Hill (ed.) *A Sociological Yearbook of Religion in Britain* 7, SCM, London.

Glasner, P. E. (1973) 'Contemporary Religious Movements: the Case of Environmentalism' in J. S. Nurser (ed.) *Living With Nature* Centre for Continuing Education, Canberra.

_____ (1974) 'Irreligion and Unbelief: A Sociological View of Australian Humanism' presented at a seminar on Religious and Antireligious Thought in Australia, Canberra.

_____ (1975) 'Religion and Divisiveness in Australia' in I. Pilowsky (ed.) *Cultures in Collision* Australian National Association for Mental Health, Adelaide.

_____ (1977) *The Sociology of Secularisation: A Critique of a Concept* Routledge and Kegan Paul, London.

Glock, C. Y. and Ringer, B. (1956) 'Church Policy and the Attitudes of Ministers and Parishioners on Social Issues' *American Sociological Review* 21: 148-56.

Glock, C. Y. and Stark, R. (1965) *Religion and Society in Tension* Rand McNally, Chicago.

Glock, C. Y. *et al.* (1967) *to Comfort and to Challenge: A Dilemma of the Contemporary Church* University of California Press, Berkeley.

Goffman, E. (1971) *The Presentation of the Self in Everyday Life* Penguin, Harmondsworth.

Gouldner, A. (1971) *The Coming Crisis in Western Sociology* Equinox Books, New York.

Grant, J. W. (1967) *The Canadian Experience of Church Union* Lutterworth Press, London.

Greeley, A. M. (1970) 'Superstition, Ecstasy and Tribal Consciousness' *Social Research* 37: 203-11.

_____ (1971) *Come Blow Your Mind With Me* Doubleday, New York.

_____ (1972) *The Denominational Society* Scott Foresman, Glenview.

Gregory, J. S. (1973) *Church and State* Cassell, North Melbourne.

Grocott, A. M. (1980) *Convicts, Clergymen and Churches* Sydney University Press, Sydney.

Habel, N. C. (1980) 'Carols by Candlelight: the Analysis of an Australian Folk Ritual' in V. C. Hayes (ed.) *Religious Experience in World Religions* Australian Association for the Study of Religions, Adelaide.

Hadden, J. K. (1969) *The Gathering Storm in the Churches: the Widening Gap Between Clergy and Laymen* Doubleday, New York.

Hansen, D. E. (1978) The Churches and Society in New South Wales 1919-1939, PhD thesis, Macquarie University.

Harris, D. *et al.* (1982) *The Shape of Belief: Christianity in Australia Today* Anzea, Homebush West.

Harrison, P. (1974) 'Soccer's Tribal Wars' *New Society* 29: 602–4.

Hay, D. (1979) 'Attitudes towards the Ecumenical Movement in an English Parish', paper prepared for British Sociological Association Sociology of Religion Study Group Conference, Guildford.

Hayes, V. C. (ed.) (1977) *Australian Essays in World Religions* Australian Association for the Study of Religions, Adelaide.

Henderson, G. (1982) *Mr. Santamaria and the Bishops* Studies in the Christian Movement, Sydney.

Hewitt, P. (1978) *Catholics Divided* Archdiocesan Research Group, Brisbane.

Hickman, D. C. (1977) 'Religion' in A. F. Davies *et al.* (eds) *Australian Society: A Sociological Introduction* 3rd edn, Longman Cheshire, Melbourne.

Hill, M. and Turner, B. (1969) 'The Laity and Church Unity' *New Christian* 93: 6–7.

Hill, M. and Wakeford, P. (1969) 'Disembodied Ecumenicalism: A Survey of the Members of Four Methodist Churches in or near London' in D. Martin (ed.) *A Sociological Yearbook of Religion in Britain* 2, SCM, London.

Hogan, M. (1978) *The Catholic Campaign for State Aid* Catholic Theological Faculty, Sydney.

—— (1979) 'Australian Secularists: the Disavowal of Denominational Allegiance' *Journal for the Scientific Study of Religion* 18: 390–404.

Hole, J. and Levine, E. (1971) *The Rebirth of Feminism* Quadrangle Books, New York.

Hromadka, J. (1952) 'Social and Cultural Factors in Our Divisions' *Ecumenical Review* 5: 52–8.

Huxley, J. (1957) *Religion Without Revelation* (new and revised edn) Max Parrish, London.

Inglis, K. S. (1970) 'Religious Behaviour' in A. F. Davies and S. Encel (eds) *Australian Society* 2nd edn, Cheshire, Melbourne.

Jeffries, V. and Tygart, C. (1974) 'The Influence of Theology, Denomination and Values Upon the Positions of Clergy on Social Issues' *Journal for the Scientific Study of Religion* 13: 309–24.

Jenkins, D. (1951) 'The Ecumenical Movement and its "Non-theological Factors"' *Ecumenical Review* 3: 339–46.

Johnson, B. (1966) 'Theology and Party Preference among Protestant Clergy' *American Sociological Review* 31: 200–8.

Johnstone, R. L. (1975) *Religion and Society in Interaction* Prentice-Hall, Englewood Cliffs.

Joseph, N. and Alex, N. (1972) 'The Uniform: A Sociological Perspective *American Journal of Sociology* 77: 719–30.

Judah, J. S. (1974) *Hare Krishna and the Counter-Culture* John Wiley and Sons, New York.

Jupp, J. (1966) *Arrivals and Departures* Cheshire, Melbourne.

Kaill, R. C. (1971) 'Ecumenism, Clergy Influence and Liberalism: an Investigation into the Sources of Lay Support for Church Union' *Canadian Review of Sociology and Anthropology* 8: 142–63.

Kelly, J. R. (1971a) 'Sources of Support for Ecumenism: A Sociological Study' *Journal of Ecumenical Studies* 8: 1–9.

_____ (1971b) 'Who Favors Ecumenism? A Study of Some of the Correlates of Support for Ecumenism' *Sociological Analysis* 32: 158–69.

Lee, R. (1960) *The Social Sources of Church Unity* Abingdon Press, New York.

Lemert, C. C. (1975) 'Defining Non-Church Religion' *Review of Religious Research* 16(3).

Lenski, G. (1963) *The Religious Factor* rev. edn, Doubleday, New York.

Lewins, F. (1978) *The Myth of the Universal Church: Catholic Migrants in Australia* Faculty of Arts, Australian National University, Canberra.

Loane, M. (1975) 'Forword' in *The Occult: Report of an Anglican Commission of Enquiry* Anglican Information Office, Sydney.

Lockwood, D. (1956) 'Some Remarks on "The Social System"' *British Journal of Sociology* 7: 134–46.

Lofland, J. and Stark, R. (1965) 'Becoming a World Saver: A Theory of Conversion to a Deviant Perspective' *American Sociological Review* 30: 862–75.

Luckmann, T. (1967) *The Invisible Religion* Macmillan, New York.

Maddox, J. (1972) *The Doomsday Syndrome* Macmillan, London.

Mandic, O. (1970) 'A Marxist Perspective on Contemporary Religious Revivals' *Social Research* 37.

Martin, D. A. (1962) 'The Denomination' *British Journal of Sociology* 13: 1–13.

_____ (1965) *Pacifism* Routledge and Kegan Paul, London.

_____ (1967) *A Sociology of English Religion* Heinemann, London.

_____ (1969) *The Religious and the Secular* Routledge and Kegan Paul, London.

_____ (1978) *A General Theory of Secularisation* Basil Blackwell, Oxford.

Martin, J. (1972a) *Community and Identity: Refugee Groups in Adelaide* Australian National University Press, Canberra.

_____ (1972b) *Migrants: Equality and Ideology* Meredith Memorial Lecture, La Trobe University, Bundoora.

Marx, K. (1976) *Capital* Penguin, Hammondsworth.

Mason, M. and Fitzpatrick, G. (1982) *Religion in Australian Life: A Bibliography of Social Research* Australian Association for the Study of Religions, Adelaide.

McKernan, M. (1980) *Australian Churches at War* Catholic Theological Faculty, Sydney.

Mead, G. H. (1934) *Mind, Self and Society* ed. C. W. Morris, Chicago University Press, Chicago.

Mehl, R. (1970) *The Sociology of Protestantism* SCM, London.

Mensching, G. (1964) 'Folk and Universal Religion' in L. Schneider (ed.) *Religion, Culture and Society* John Wiley & Sons, New York.

Merleau-Ponty, M. (1967) *The Primacy of Perception* trans. A. L. Fisher, Beacon Press, Boston.

Merton, R. K. (1965) *Social Theory and Social Structure* Free Press, New York.

Moberg, D. (1969) 'Theological Self-classification and Ascetic Moral Views of Students' *Review of Religious Research* 10(2): 100-7.

Mol, H. (1969) 'The Merger Attempts of the Australian Churches' *Ecumenical Review* 21: 21-31.

―――― (1971) *Religion in Australia* Nelson, Melbourne.

―――― (1976) *Identity and the Sacred* Basil Blackwell, Oxford.

Morrison, J. S. (1948) 'Editorial' *Psychic Forum* 24: 1-2.

Musgrove, F. (1974) *Ecstasy and Holiness: Counter Culture and the Open Society* Methuen, London.

Neal, M. (1970) 'The Relation Between Religious Belief and Structural Change in Religious Orders: Developing an Effective Measuring Instrument' *Review of Religious Research* 12: 2-16.

―――― (1971) 'Part II. The Relation Between Religious Belief and Structural Change in Religious Orders: Some Evidence' *Review of Religious Research* 12: 153-64.

Nelsen, H. *et al.* (1973) 'Ministerial Roles and Social Actionist Stance: Protestant Clergy and Protest in the Sixties' *American Sociological Review* 38: 375-86.

Nelson, G. K. (1968) 'The Analysis of a Cult: Spiritualism' *Social Compass* 15.

―――― (1969) *Spiritualism and Society* Routledge and Kegan Paul, London.

Newman, W. M. (1970) The United Church of Christ Merger: A Sociological Analysis of Ideas, Organisations and Social Change, PhD dissertation, New School For Social Research.

Niebuhr, H. R. (1929) *The Social Sources of Denominationalism* Holt, Rinehart and Winston, New York.

―――― (1951) *Christ and Culture* Harper and Row, New York.

North, M. (1972) *The Secular Priests* George Allen and Unwin, London.

O'Brien, L. N. (1972) The Social Construction of Reality and the Social Construction of Alternatives with Special Reference to the International Society for Krishna Consciousness, Melbourne, BA Hons dissertation, Monash University.

―――― (1973) 'Some Defining Characteristics of the Hare Krishna Movement' *Australia and New Zealand Journal of Sociology* 9(2): 72-3.

O'Dea, T. F. (1957) *The Mormons* Chicago University Press, Chicago.

―――― (1966) *The Sociology of Religion* Prentice-Hall, Englewood Cliffs.

O'Farrell, P. (1977) *The Catholic Church and Community in Australia: A History* Nelson, Melbourne.

O'Leary, H. (1971) 'Legislation on Migrant Care' *The Australian Catholic Record* 48(2): 127-51.

Ollman, B. (1977) *Alienation: Marx's Conception of Man in Capitalist Society* Cambridge University Press, London.

Parsons, T. (1968) *The Social System* Free Press, New.York.

Peebles, J. M. (1910) *Five Journeys Around the World* Peebles Publishing Co., Michigan.

Pfautz, H. W. (1955) 'Sociology of Secularisation: Religious Groups' *American Journal of Sociology* 61: 121-8.

_____ (1956) 'Christian Science: A Case Study of the Social Psychological Aspect of Secularisation' *Social Forces* 34: 246-51.

Phillips, D. (1970) Italians and Australians in the Ovens Valley Area: A Sociological Study of the Interaction Between Migrants and the Host Population in a Rural Area of Victoria, PhD thesis, Australian National University.

Phillips, W. (1981) *Defending 'A Christian Country': Churchmen and Society in New South Wales in the 1880s and after* University of Queensland Press, St Lucia.

Pinder, R. (1971) 'Religious Change in the Process of Secularisation' *Sociological Review* 19: 343-66.

Pink, A. W. (1920) *Spiritualism: Is It Approved of God or Is It of Satanic Origin?* The Christian Workers' Depot, Sydney.

Pope, L. (1942) *Millhands and Preachers* Yale University Press, New Haven.

Prabhupada, A. C. (1968) *The Bhagavat Gita As It Is* Collier, London.

_____ (1970) *The Nectar of Devotion* ISKCON Books, Los Angeles.

Price, C. A. (1963) 'The Integration of Religious Groups in Australia' *International Migration* 1(3): 192-202.

Quinley, H. (1974) *The Prophetic Clergy: Social Activism Among Protestant Ministers* Wiley, New York.

Raccanello, J. (n.d.) 'The Italian Community in Melbourne', unpublished paper, Melbourne.

Ranson, S. *et al* (1977) *Clergy, Ministers and Priests* Routledge and Kegan Paul, London.

Richardson, J. T. (1979) 'From Cult to Sect: Creative Eclecticism in New Religious Movements' *Pacific Sociological Review* 22: 139-66.

Rigby, A. (1974) *Alternative Realities: A Study of Communes and their Members* Routledge and Kegan Paul, London.

Rigby, A. and Turner, B. (1972) 'The Findhorn Community, Centre of Light: A Sociological Study of New Forms of Religion' in M. Hill (ed.) *A Sociological Yearbook of Religion in Britain* 5, SCM, London.

Robertson, R. (1970) *The Sociological Interpretation of Religion* Basil Blackwell, Oxford.

_____ (1978) *Meaning and Change* Basil Blackwell, Oxford.

Robbins, T. and Anthony, D. (1972) 'Getting Straight with Meher Baba' *Journal for the Scientific Study of Religion* 11: 122-40.

Roof, W. C. (1978) *Community and Commitment: Religious Plausibility in a Liberal Protestant Church* Elsevier, New York.

Ross, J. A. (1973) Regionalism, Nationalism and Social Gospel Support in the Ecumenical Movement of Canadian Presbyterianism, PhD dissertation, McMaster University.

Roszak, T. (1970) *The Making of a Counter Culture* Faber and Faber, London.

Rowley, P. (1971) *New Gods in America* David McKay and Co., New York.

Santamaria, B. A. (1961) '"The Movement": 1941-60 — An Outline' in H. Mayer (ed.) *Catholics and the Free Society* Cheshire, Melbourne.

Schutz, A. (1944) 'The Stranger' *American Journal of Sociology* 49: 499-507.

Shaughnessy, G. (1925) *Has the Immigrant Kept the Faith?* Macmillan, New York.

Siefer, G. (1973) *Sterben die Priester aus?* Hans Driewer, Essen.

Silcox, C. E. (1933) *Church Union in Canada: Its Causes and Consequences* Institute for Social and Religious Research, New York.

Sjölinder, R. (1962) *Presbyterian Reunion in Scotland 1907-1921* Almqvist and Wiksell, Stockholm.

Smart, N. (1971) *The Religious Experience of Mankind* Fontana, London.

Smith, H. J. (1977) The Formation of the United Reformed Church: A Theological and Sociological Elucidation, MPhil dissertation, New College, London.

Stark, R. *et al.* (1971) *Wayward Shepherds: Prejudice and the Protestant Clergy* Harper and Row, New York.

Stone, D. (1976) 'The Human Potential Movement' in C. Y. Glock and R. N. Bellah (eds) *The New Religious Consciousness* University of California Press, Berkeley.

Tessarolo, G. (ed.) (1962) *The Church's Magna Carta for Migrants* St Charles Seminary, New York.

Thomas, K. (1971) *Religion and the Decline of Magic* Weidenfeld and Nicolson, London.

Thomas, M. C. and Flippen, C. C. (1972) 'American Civil Religion: an Empirical Study' *Social Forces* 51: 218-25.

Thompson, D. M. (1978) 'Theological and Sociological Approaches to the Motivation of the Ecumenical Movement' in D. Baker (ed.) *Religious Motivation: Biographical and Sociological Problems for the Church Historian* Basil Blackwell, Oxford.

Thompson, E. (1948) *The History of Modern Spiritualism* Two Worlds, London.

Thouless, R. H. (1971) *An Introduction to the Psychology of Religion* Cambridge University Press, Cambridge.

Till, B. (1972) *The Churches Search for Unity* Penguin, Harmondsworth.

Toch, H. (1965) *The Social Psychology of Social Movements* Methuen, London.

Tomeh, A. K. (1973) 'Formal Voluntary Organisation: Participation, Correlates and Interrelationships' *Sociological Inquiry* 43(3-4): 89-122.

Towler, R. (1974) *Homo Religiosus: Sociological Problems in the Study of Religion* Constable, London.

Troeltsch, E. (1931) *The Social Teaching of the Christian Churches* Allen and Unwin, London.

Truzzi, M. (1972) 'The Occult Revival as Pop Culture: Some Random Observations on the Old Nouveau Witch' *Sociological Quarterly* 13(1).

Turner, B. S. (1969) 'Institutional Persistence and Ecumenicalism in Northern Methodism' in D. Martin (ed.) *A Sociological Yearbook of Religion in Britain* 2, SCM, London.

——— (1972) 'The Sociological Explanation of Ecumenicalism' in C. L.

Mitton (ed.) *The Social Sciences and the Churches* T. & T. Clark, Edinburgh.

Turner, N. (1972) *Sinews of Sectarian Warfare? State Aid in New South Wales, 1836–1862* Australian National University Press, Canberra.

Turner, V. (1969) *The Ritual Process* Penguin, Harmondsworth.

Vecoli, R. (1969) 'Prelates and Peasants: Italian Immigrants and the Catholic Church' *Journal of Social History* 2: 217–68.

Vipond, M. (1974) National Consciousness in English-speaking Canada in the 1920s: Seven Studies, PhD dissertation, University of Toronto.

Vrijhof, P. H. and Waardenburg, J. (eds) (1979) *Official and Popular Religion* Mouton, The Hague.

Wallis, R. (1974) 'Ideology, Authority, and the Development of Cultic Movements' *Social Research*, 41: 299–327.

____ (1976) *The Road to Total Freedom: A Sociological Analysis of Scientology* Heinemann, London.

Warwick, D. P. (1974) 'Organisational Politics and Ecumenism' *Journal of Ecumenical Studies* 11: 293–308.

Webb, L. (1960) 'Churches and the Australian Community' in E. L. French (ed.) *Melbourne Studies in Education 1958–1959* Melbourne University Press, Parkville.

Weber, M. (1930) *The Protestant Ethic and the Spirit of Capitalism* Allen and Unwin, London.

____ (1963) *The Sociology of Religion* Beacon Press, Boston.

____ (1968) *Economy and Society* ed. G. Roth and C. Wittich, Bedminster Press, New York.

Wilkinson, P. (1971) *Social Movements* Macmillan, London.

Williams, P. W. (1980) *Popular Religion in America* Prentice-Hall, Englewood Cliffs.

Wilson, B. (1979) 'Australian Church and Society' *Interchange* 25: 22–31.

Wilson, B. R. (1966) *Religion in Secular Society* Watts, London.

____ (1967) 'The Pentecostalist Minister: Role Conflicts and Contradictions of Status' in B. R. Wilson (ed.) *Patterns of Sectarianism* Heinemann, London.

____ (1969) 'A Typology of Sects' in R. Robertson (ed.) *Sociology of Religion* Penguin, Harmondsworth.

Wilson, J. (1978) *Religion in American Society* Prentice-Hall, Englewood Cliffs.

Winter, J. A. (1977) *Continuities in the Sociology of Religion* Harper and Row, New York.

World Council of Churches, Commission on Faith and Order (1952) 'Non-theological Factors that May Hinder or Accelerate the Church's Unity' *Ecumenical Review* 4: 174–80.

Yinger, J. M. (1946) *Religion and the Struggle for Power* Duke University Press, Durham NC.

____ (1970) *The Scientific Study of Religion* Macmillan, New York.

Zaretsky, I. I. and Leone, M. P. (eds) (1975) *Religious Movements in Contemporary America* Princeton University Press, Princeton.

Zijderveld, A. (1970) *The Abstract Society* Doubleday, New York.

Index